The Human Traditio

MW00975266

CHARLES W. CALHOUN
Series Editor
Department of History, East Carolina University

The nineteenth-century English author Thomas Carlyle once remarked that "the history of the world is but the biography of great men." This approach to the study of the human past had existed for centuries before Carlyle wrote, and it continued to hold sway among many scholars well into the twentieth century. In more recent times, however, historians have recognized and examined the impact of large, seemingly impersonal forces in the evolution of human history—social and economic developments such as industrialization and urbanization as well as political movements such as nationalism, militarism, and socialism. Yet even as modern scholars seek to explain these wider currents, they have come more and more to realize that such phenomena represent the composite result of countless actions and decisions by untold numbers of individual actors. On another occasion, Carlyle said that "history is the essence of innumerable biographies." In this conception of the past, Carlyle came closer to modern notions that see the lives of all kinds of people, high and low, powerful and weak, known and unknown, as part of the mosaic of human history, each contributing in a large or small way to the unfolding of the human tradition.

This latter idea forms the foundation for this series of books on the human tradition in America. Each volume is devoted to a particular period or topic in American history and each consists of minibiographies of persons whose lives shed light on that period or topic. Well-known figures are not altogether absent, but more often the chapters explore a variety of individuals who may be less conspicuous but whose stories, nonetheless, offer us a window on some aspect of the nation's past.

By bringing the study of history down to the level of the individual, these sketches reveal not only the diversity of the American people and the complexity of their interaction but also some of the commonalities of sentiment and experience that Americans have shared in the evolution of their culture. Our hope is that these explorations of the lives of "real people" will give readers a deeper understanding of the human tradition in America.

THE HUMAN TRADITION IN
THE OLD
SOUTH

The South

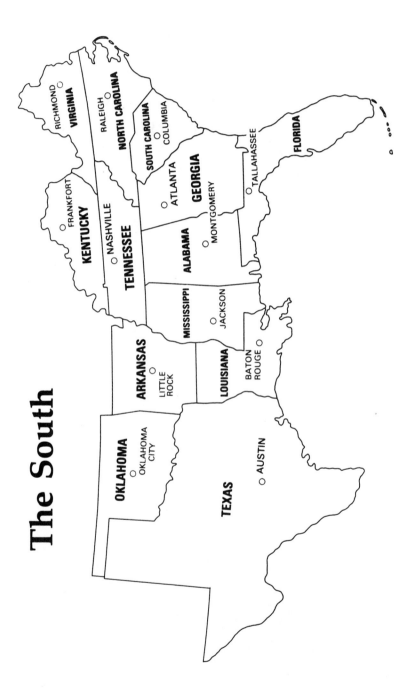

From Dewey W. Grantham, *The Life and Death of the Solid South* (Lexington: The University Press of Kentucky, 1992), 30. *Courtesy of the University Press of Kentucky*

THE HUMAN TRADITION IN
THE OLD SOUTH

No. 15
The Human Tradition in America

Edited by
James C. Klotter

A Scholarly Resources Inc. Imprint
Wilmington, Delaware

Scholarly Resources Inc.
104 Greenhill Avenue
Wilmington, DE 19805-1897
www.scholarly.com

Library of Congress Cataloging-in-Publication Data

The human tradition in the old South / edited by James C. Klotter.
    p. cm. — (The human tradition in America ; no. 15)
    Includes bibliographical references and index.
    ISBN 0-8420-2977-X (alk. paper) — ISBN 0-8420-2978-8 (pbk. :
alk. paper)
    1. Southern States—History. 2. Southern States—Biography.
I. Klotter, James C. II. Series.
F209.5.H86 2003
920.075—dc21

                         2002015782

About the Editor

JAMES C. KLOTTER is the State Historian of Kentucky and professor of history at Georgetown College. The author, coauthor, or editor of over a dozen books, he most recently wrote *Kentucky Justice, Southern Honor, and American Manhood: Understanding the Life and Death of Richard Reid* (2003). His other publications include such articles as "The Black South and White Appalachia," *Journal of American History* (1980), and he serves as co-general editor of an oral history series that has published five books to date.

Contents

Introduction—The American South

James C. Klotter*

In studying the South, questions abound. Why examine this one region? What, in fact, exactly is the South? Is there one South or several? What is its history, and how does it influence the present and the future? And, most of all, what stories can the people of this region tell to help explain the South and those who call it home? How can those human traditions help us understand this distinct place, this South?

If many questions exist, so, too, do many answers, some of them even contradictory ones. But on the matter of why the South deserves special study, the explanations generally agree. W. J. Cash, in his controversial, entertaining, and still-influential *The Mind of the South* (1941), wrote that people of all regions of America had "a profound conviction that the South is another land." With justification, said Cash, the South should be viewed as "not quite a nation within a nation, but the next thing to it." Historian Carl Degler remembered how when he grew up in the North, he considered the South "not only a different but an exotic place . . . almost a foreign country." Another student of the region's history, Charles P. Roland, similarly noted that more than any other part of the United States, the South gave expression to its sectional consciousness. The region "bore the mark of a different past reinforced by a widespread awareness and interpretation of it." Settlement patterns, culture and folkways, slavery and segregation, defeat and the Lost Cause—these and more contributed to the shaping of the particular history that created a different region, this almost-foreign place to some, this almost-nation to others.[1]

While all those observers described a distinctive South in the twentieth century, the idea of the South as a separate entity had been well developed much, much earlier, even before Charles Pinckney declared

*I wish to acknowledge the aid of John David Smith and Harold Tallant in connection with this essay.

in 1787, "When I say Southern, I mean Maryland and the states to the southward of her." Debates over slavery already had created divisions during the Revolutionary Era; sectional voting emerged more clearly by the time of the Missouri Compromise and had grown by the Compromise of 1850; discord developed into secession, full-scale war, and a separate nation by the Civil War. After what the South called the War between the States and what some northerners termed the War of the Rebellion, the former Confederacy generally became occupied territory, subject to Reconstruction, and with an emerging story not found anywhere else in America. Other chapters added to that account over the years, so that Dixie became recognized as a region different from any other in the nation. History shaped and formed a southern identity.[2]

The Region

If there is an identifiable South, with a past worthy of study, what exactly constitutes the region? Definitions vary. Most include the eleven states that formed the Confederacy as the core of the South—Virginia, North Carolina, South Carolina, Florida, Georgia, Tennessee, Alabama, Mississippi, Louisiana, Arkansas, and Texas. Most also place Kentucky in that mix; for though it was a slave state that did not leave the union, its actions before and after the war tied it closely to the South. Beyond those states, various places have and have not been included—infrequently, Delaware; occasionally, Missouri, Maryland, or West Virginia; more often, Oklahoma. Sociologists generally define a region as "an area of which the inhabitants feel themselves a part."

In asking people a series of questions, they seek to find whether the individuals consider themselves southern. As Cash said, the South might be, most of all, a state of mind. If so, the degree of "southern-ness" determines placement in the region. Using that method of preference, for example, indicates that Kentuckians consider themselves more southern than Floridians, with their large number of out-of-state retirees, or Texans, with their western traditions. Yet those and the other former Confederate states all rank high on the scale of "southern-ness." Combining, then, history and preference, the South, as defined in this work, consists of the eleven original Confederate states that left the Union, plus Kentucky and Oklahoma—the definition also used by national polling organizations. Still, as John Shelton Reed notes, "some are born southern, some achieve it, and some have it thrust upon them."[3]

The Enduring South

What has created that South, however defined? What has formed this region, this enduring South? First, as others have noted, many Souths exist in memory and mind, not just one. Various images make up the national—and the southern—view of the area. For example, there is the Romantic South of "moonlight, magnolias, and mint juleps," where Rhett Butler—or Colonel Sanders—and Scarlett O'Hara sit on the porches of their white-columned mansions, sipping drinks—perhaps iced tea—watching thoroughbreds romp or cotton grow, while dutiful black servants in white coats stand nearby. On the other hand, another image focuses on the Defensive South, one that supports first an indefensible slave system and then, later, segregation. This South, under attack from without, resulted in what Jim Cobb terms "the siege mentality that prevailed among white southerners."

Similarly, another stereotype addresses the Fundamentalist South. Baltimore satirist H. L. Mencken in the 1920s contemptuously snarled about the "degraded nonsense which country preachers are ramming into yokel skulls" and the "Baptist and Methodist barbarism" of a region 90 percent Protestant. That portrayal of wild-eyed, religiously intolerant evangelist preachers has not disappeared over the years. Conversely, however, a newer image of the Sunbelt South has pictured it as a place of promise, more so than the so-called Rustbelt North.

As the nation has faced its own identity crisis and self-doubt over Vietnam and Watergate and has had to deal with poverty and racism, the South has been viewed more favorably. Balancing that, however, the Bubba South continues as strong a portrayal of the region, one featuring "hillbillies" and "rednecks," with Klan sheets in the back of their pickups and whiskey on the seat. And there remains the Tragic South, where every battlefield and every grave is a reminder of the deaths and defeats of long ago, still alive in the memories, the statues, the symbols. Such different images have formed—and continue to form—various aspects of both the region's view of itself, and the nation's. Some might explain the past and the people of the present; others may simply cloud and confuse with their exaggerations. Like an early morning fog, the various myths and realities of the region make it difficult to see clearly the heart and soul of the South.[4]

Moreover, any look at the region should remind us to ask, as Paul Conkin does, "But which South?" For many heartbeats run through the

land, and it has many faces, many souls. In Conkin's youth, the majority of
the South stood Confederate in sympathy and Democratic in politics,
with African Americans all around. Yet his Tennessee mountain area
was a white, Republican, Union, non-grits South. When we speak of the
South, then, are we talking about the plantation South, or the later South
of textile mill workers, mountain miners, and poverty-stricken share-
croppers, or the New South of skyscrapers and steel? Is it the region of poor
education and one-room schools, or the literary South that produced
writers such as Thomas Wolfe, William Faulkner, Robert Penn Warren,
Eudora Welty, and Richard Wright, among others? Is this the South of
slavery, then segregation, white supremacy, lynchings, church burnings,
fire hoses, and police dogs, or the place that produces courageous leaders on race such as a Judge Frank M. Johnson Jr., a President Lyndon B.
Johnson, a Rev. Martin Luther King Jr., or a Fannie Lou Hamer?[5]

When the South is discussed, is it the black and white Protestant
place; or the Cajun, Catholic South; or the Native American one; or the
Hispanic South? Is it the lowland, coastal region, or the Piedmont, or
the Appalachian, or the Western Plains South? Does it have an urban or
suburban locus, or a rural, agricultural one? Is it the deeply moral and
religious South that would support Prohibition, or the cavalier, hedo-
nistic South that can reconcile religion, horseracing, and red-eye whiskey? Is it a region of bluegrass and country music, or of jazz and the
blues, or of Elvis Presley and rock 'n' roll, or of big city symphonies? Is
it a political place of demagogic speakers making racial and class ap-
peals, or the place of presidents and New South leaders? Is this a South
of farms or factories, of furrows or fax machines, of forests or forges?

Obviously, the South is all these things and even more. Just as there
are many Souths, so, too, does each of them have various faces, all part
of the region's overall makeup. At the same time, such differences should
not obscure the underlying unity of a section that goes beyond the divisions within it and considers itself distinct and special. As one author
concluded, "If it can be said that there are many Souths, the fact remains that there is also one South," a place with "a fairly definite mental pattern, associated with a fairly definite social pattern." And all of
that has emerged through the region's history.[6]

History and the South

Historian C. Vann Woodward stressed that a central theme of the
region may be southern history itself. Another author has suggested that

the two sections did differ historically, but turns the argument around and asks if the South with its rural and traditional society was not more the norm: "Perhaps it was the North that was 'different,' the North that departed from the mainstream of historical development, and perhaps therefore we should speak not of southern exceptionalism but of northern exceptionalism." In any case, understanding sectional distinctiveness must begin—not end—with studying the area's heritage and history. Doing that makes it plain, also, that the buildings, the battlefields, the oral traditions, the stored memories all combine to form a special past, a "history with a southern accent." As one author concisely noted about the differences in the history of the South versus the history of the United States overall: "The South retained slavery while the rest of the nation abandoned it; the South ruptured the national union; the South stayed agricultural while the nation industrialized; the South expanded legal segregation as the nation relinquished it; the South remained rural as the nation became urban; the South remained poor while the nation grew rich; in a nation of immigrants, southerners were overwhelmingly natives."[7]

However, the South has more recently gone beyond that history. Slavery and segregation have died and race relations have changed. The region has industrialized as well; by 1980 only a little more than 3 percent of southerners farmed. Currently, the area's per capita income nears national averages and, given the lower cost of living, may in reality exceed it, though poverty remains a problem. Finally, people from outside the region—migrants or immigrants—dot the landscape. But in change, the ghosts of the past still ride, still influencing the present, still shaping the future of the region.

On the whole the South's history is an interesting and important one. Much of it can never be recaptured, for the American Indian story before contact with white settlers can only be recreated through archaeological digs, or a few long-distant oral traditions. Nor has the South done justice to non-English aspects of its early European settlement. Places such as St. Augustine in Spanish Florida had settlers forty years or more before Jamestown's founding by the English in 1607. French explorers traveled the region as well.

Nonetheless, the emerging South soon spoke with a predominantly English, or Scots-Irish, accent, although other voices could be heard. By 1619, when the first records speak of slaves, the racial mix of the region began to change. John Blassingame has called this process "the Americanization of the Slave and the Africanization of the South." For some historians, the resulting quest by whites to maintain racial supremacy soon became a central theme in the region's history. To them, although the South might speak of state rights, or of a fear of centralization of power, or of tariff discrimination as causes of the eventual Civil War, at the core of all the debates, behind most arguments, lay the greater issue of racial controls. Fear of a world without slavery troubled white thoughts; hopes for a place without the "peculiar institution" dominated black ones.[8]

By the eve of the war, slave states had almost four million blacks in servitude. One man, in 1850, owned 1,843 other human beings. While only one-fourth of white southern families had direct involvement in slavery, many others sought to join their ranks, and even more wanted the system to endure, to keep their place secure in the racial pyramid.

One of the many ironies of southern history is that the region played such an important role in shaping the new nation and in formulating its documents of ideals and governance, ones that did recognize slavery but that also spoke of the inalienable rights of "life, liberty, and the pursuit of happiness," in a world where "all men are created equal." Yet women, blacks, and others did not share those rights or that equality. Much of the military and civil leadership of the early nation came from the South—George Washington, Thomas Jefferson, James Madison, James Monroe, Chief Justice John Marshall, and many others—but these often enlightened and certainly learned men could still never apply or even reconcile those ideals to the curse of slavery. Over the years, millions cried out for justice for the enslaved and freedom for those held in life-long servitude. Yet that would come only at the cost of hundreds of thousands of lives.

Various and often contrasting themes made up the threads in the tapestry of that antebellum world based on slavery. For instance, four slaveholders took different approaches to the issues. Presidents Andrew Jackson and Zachary Taylor both spoke out forcibly against southern threats to federal power; Senator Henry Clay helped forge compromises to keep the nation united, and John C. Calhoun sought, first and foremost, the protection of southern interests. Similarly, the Great Revival of 1801 brought forth a religious renewal and more diversity in churches, and from that some churches challenged the slave system. But, over time, the debate over the issue grew so strident and the South so defensive that discussion became increasingly difficult, action almost impossible. The seeds of separatism, present at the birth of the nation, grew and grew over the years, fed by the waters of sectional anger. And then the war came.

In the eyes of the white South, they had sought to preserve the liberties and rights of an earlier age but, under increasing attack, could no longer do so under the aegis of the existing government. They saw the fight as a second American Revolution. They were the true Americans, inheritors of the traditions of an earlier time; the North had changed. Others feared that the new administration of Abraham Lincoln would not only restrict slavery but also attack it where it existed and thus make war on property rights—and resultant racial controls— they considered protected by the Constitution. Still others fought for less philosophical and more personal reasons. For whatever cause, soldiers went off to war while family members struggled at home, waiting for the next letter, to find out if a loved one had lived or died. The North, with a white population four times that of the South and one later boosted by the enlistments of black soldiers, would win the war in the end, but the secessionists' fight, their Lost Cause, their legendary leaders such as Robert E. Lee and Stonewall Jackson, would mean that defeat would be transformed into a special history, almost a civil religion. The human losses of many of the best and brightest of that generation; the destruction of property and the loss of money invested in slaves, now free; the scars left on the psyche of the white population of the South all meant that to understand the South since 1865 requires understanding the long influence the war had on southerners, in fact and memory.

Southern Stories

To tell the story of the Old South in the few pages of this book is a daunting task. It would take many more chapters and a much longer work to make this volume even come close to being fully representative of the myriad sides of this place called the South. But people's lives help us see through the mists of history and aid us in understanding the many Souths, the different individuals, the varied stories. Often looking at the human condition at an elemental level reveals larger truths and greater insights. After all, history is often presented as a story of individuals, and this book thus seeks to tell some of those same stories and, by so doing, to explain the region. Seven of the essays are original to this volume, the rest being taken from other volumes in Scholarly Resources' Human Tradition in America series.

In the chapters the authors tell of people from the Upper South to the Deep South to the Southwest; they tell of men and women from varied backgrounds and eras. Since the Old South was not some monolithic place, some of these accounts portray those who viewed the land from different perspectives—such as of a slave or an Indian or a humorist or a nonconformist politician or even a traveler from the North. Yet there existed also the more traditional South—one of fundamentalism, of conventional marriage, of fighting for the Confederacy. Those accounts appear here as well. Many stories, many places, many themes remain untold. But in their totality, the lives recounted here tell us of various worlds of the past while speaking to us still about our own world and about our future.

Notes

1. W. J. Cash, *The Mind of the South* (New York: Vintage Books, 1941), vii, viii; Carl N. Degler, "Thesis, Antithesis, Synthesis: The South, the North, and the Nation," *Journal of Southern History* (hereafter *JSH*) 53 (1987): 3; Charles P. Roland, *The Improbable Era: The South since World War II* (Lexington: University Press of Kentucky, 1975), 1.

2. Quotes from Monroe Lee Billington, *The American South* (New York: Charles Scribner's Sons, 1971), 35.

3. John Shelton Reed, *The Enduring South* (Chapel Hill: University of North Carolina Press, 1986), 13, 12.

4. Roland, *Improbable Era*, 2, 191–92, 189; James C. Cobb, "An Epitaph for the North: Reflections on the Politics of Regional and National Identity at the Millennium," *JSH* 66 (2000): 4, 8, 6–7, 16; Dewey W. Grantham, *The South in Modern America* (New York: HarperCollins, 1994), 112.

5. Paul K. Conkin, "Hot, Humid, and Sad," *JSH* 64 (1998): 3.

6. Cash, *Mind of the South*, viii.

7. C. Vann Woodward, *The Burden of Southern History* (Baton Rouge: Louisiana State University Press, 1960); James McPherson, "Antebellum Southern Exceptionalism: A New Look at an Old Question," *Civil War History* 29 (1983): 242; Roland, *Improbable Era*, 192; Degler, "Thesis," 5.

8. John Blassingame, *The Slave Community*, rev. ed. (New York: Oxford University Press, 1979), 49.

1

Alvar Núñez Cabeza de Vaca
Conquistador and Sojourner

Peter Stern

For many years, the influence of the dominant British heritage on the United States dictated the views of students about the nation's early history. The standard texts usually stressed how "America" had been established with settlements at Jamestown in 1607 and at Plymouth in 1620. However, that history often ignored the influence and role of the French and Spaniards, among others. Ponce de León, for example, landed in Florida in 1513 and St. Augustine was founded in 1565—forty-two years before the English colony in Virginia. Spanish explorers crisscrossed the South, reaching as far north as present-day Virginia.

Spanish aid helped the United States achieve its independence, but that support did not translate into security for Spanish New World possessions. In 1800, France gained Louisiana from Spain; twenty-one years later the United States secured Florida. Following Mexico's independence, the Mexican-American War brought what had been other parts of the Spanish empire into U.S. hands. However, if Spain lost its lands, its influence continued, particularly in the Southwest. In the twentieth century, a new Hispanic presence would once more remind the South of the longtime Spanish dominance in the region.

One of the first Europeans to see parts of this New World was Alvar Núñez Cabeza de Vaca, who traveled through what is today Florida, Alabama, Texas, and New Mexico. His story reveals much about the mindset of the early conquerors, the lives of the Indians they encountered, and the ability of individuals to grow, learn, and change.

Peter Stern is a Latin American specialist at the University of Massachusetts, Amherst, and the author of numerous articles on Spanish borderland history.

Alvar Núñez Cabeza de Vaca was a conquistador, one of an audacious breed of men who embarked from Spain to win their fortunes in the New World that Christopher Columbus had discovered only thirty-five

This essay originally appeared in Ian K. Steele and Nancy L. Rhoden, eds., *The Human Tradition in Colonial America* (Wilmington, DE: Scholarly Resources, 1999), 1–19.

years before. Shipwrecked on the coast of Texas, nearly naked, starving, and freezing, he and a small group of companions set out to find their way back to friendly Spanish territory in Mexico. They walked for nearly three thousand miles through what is today west Texas, New Mexico, and Sonora, meeting many Indian tribes along the way and becoming healers and medicine men. They were the first Europeans to reach the valley of the Río Grande, and they ultimately brought tragedy to the peoples who lived in the Southwest. Their journey produced the first "captivity narrative" in the Americas and the first written account of the Southwest of the United States. Above all, Cabeza de Vaca was a man of his time—bold and courageous, but also greedy, narrow-minded, and prejudiced.

Alvar Núñez Cabeza de Vaca was born in the Spanish city of Jerez de la Frontera around 1490, although the exact year is uncertain. His surname, Cabeza de Vaca, literally means "head of a cow"; and although this sounds absurd to us today, it actually represented a great honor for his family. During the Reconquista, the seven-hundred-year-long struggle of the Christians to push the Moors (a generic term that the Spaniards used for all Muslims in Iberia, whether they were Berbers or Arabs) out of Spain, the Christian army reached the Sierra Morena north of Seville in 1212. The Moors held all the mountain passes, and the Spanish army was stymied. But a peasant offered to show the Spanish king an unguarded mountain pass that would allow the Christians to attack their enemies from the rear. The peasant marked the pass with the skull of a cow, and the Christian army was able to surprise the Muslims and defeat them. After the battle, King Sancho ennobled the peasant, who was an ancestor of Alvar Núñez, and gave him and his descendants the title Cabeza de Vaca.

In 1492, Columbus sailed westward, in search of the Great Khan of the Indies, and discovered a new world instead. But by 1519 bright hopes for that New World had turned to despair. The Spaniards, eager to find gold, had used the native peoples of the Caribbean for slave labor, abused and maltreated them, and had unknowingly passed on to them many of the common diseases of Europe—measles, smallpox, mumps, and even the common cold—to which the Indians had no immunity or resistance. Within the space of thirty years, the native population of the Caribbean had been reduced to a tiny fraction of its numbers in 1492. Spanish greed and, more important, European microbes had created a wasteland out of paradise.

In 1521 everything changed again. In that year, Hernándo Cortés, with a few hundred men, completed his conquest of the empire of the Aztecs, making the Spaniards lords of all Mexico and fabulously rich. Adventurous young Spanish men eagerly sailed for the New World in the hopes of enlisting in another great venture, the next Mexico.

Young Cabeza de Vaca was born into a household of adventurers; his grandfather had taken part in the conquest of the Canary Islands, far out in the Atlantic Ocean. Cabeza de Vaca grew up listening to the stories and songs of the Guanche servants in his grandfather's household; the Guanches, natives of the Canaries, had been enslaved by Spanish conquistadores. In 1511, when he was twenty-one, he sailed as part of an expedition sent by King Ferdinand to Italy, where Pope Julius II was fighting French invaders. Cabeza de Vaca fought in battles at Bologna and Ravenna, and was rewarded for his bravery by being promoted to the rank of *alférez*, or ensign. When he returned to Spain in 1513, he was made a steward in the household of the Duke of Medina Sidonia. As a steward, or *camarero*, he was both household manager and soldier; he helped to put down an internal revolt of *comuneros* in Spain and was again promoted for bravery. Cabeza de Vaca went on to fight the French again in Navarre, earning for himself more honors and the reputation of a man of courage and dedication. Serving in the household of a royal duke, he may well have met conquistadores returning from their campaigns in America.

Little is known about the next years of Cabeza de Vaca's life. He married, although the records of his marriage have been lost. In 1527 he joined Pánfilo de Narváez's expedition to the West Indies to conquer an unknown land called La Florida. Narváez was an experienced conquistador, a veteran of fighting in both the Caribbean and Mexico, which makes his subsequent follies harder to comprehend. Cabeza de Vaca was made treasurer of the expedition, a key position requiring a great deal of trust, as the treasurer collected the king's *diezmo*, or royal tenth, of any gold or other treasure found by this *entrada*, or military incursion. In order to carry out this task, Cabeza de Vaca was also made provost marshal, in charge of military discipline for the expedition. To ensure his loyalty, he posted a bond of two thousand pieces of gold before leaving Spain.

Narváez sailed in June 1527 with five ships and six hundred men (accompanied by at least ten wives). Horses and dogs were loaded onto the ships as transportation and offensive weapons of war; cattle and pigs would provide meat "on the hoof" in Florida. Five Franciscan monks went along to convert the Indians whom the Spaniards were sure to encounter. The trip to the Caribbean took two months, and the journey was an awful one. Crammed into tiny, leaking wooden ships and fed a monotonous diet of biscuit, with a little wine, meat, salt fish, and olive oil, many of the men were sick of the whole business by the time the fleet reached the island of Hispaniola (today the Dominican Republic and Haiti). One hundred and twenty deserted as soon as the ships reached port. Narváez managed to pick up a few men in Cuba, his last stop before the mainland, to replace those who had already fled. Bad weather kept the fleet in Cuba for the entire winter and part of the spring, but on April 12, 1528, the ships of the Narváez expedition reached the southwest coast of Florida, landing at what is today Tampa Bay.

By the spring of 1528, Florida had already been visited by the expeditions of Juan Ponce de León and four other conquistadors. Thanks to the cruel way in which the Spaniards treated the natives, seizing them as slaves and torturing them to obtain gold, the Indians of Florida were very wary of the strangers. When Narváez's ships anchored in a beautiful bay, they could see over the dunes huge mounds of oyster shells and, beyond them, an Indian village.

Their first contacts with the Indians were not very promising. An emissary of Narváez was rowed ashore to assure the Indian chief, or cacique, of the Spaniards' good intentions. The chief gave the man a gift of venison and fish, but when the emissary left, the entire village fled into the forest. The rest of the Spaniards went ashore to find that the Indians had left behind nothing—in particular, no food. But they did find a gold rattle in one hut. This discovery excited them enormously; they reasoned that if the Indians could give an infant a rattle made of gold, then surely they must have huge quantities of the precious metal.

The party raised the flag, and Narváez took possession of the land in the name of the king of Spain. He then read aloud the *requerimiento*— a long statement that informed the Indians that they were now subjects of the Crown and, furthermore, that they were to be baptized Christians and give up their "heathen" ways. (The reading of the *requerimiento* was a legal necessity, but, as one historian wryly noted, it was sometimes read out of arrow shot of the natives.) That there were no Indians in sight to hear this proclamation mattered not at all—the forms had been observed, and from that moment the natives had to obey all Spanish civil or religious laws. If they did not, they could be legally enslaved and sold. Thus the Spaniards dealt with the natives of their new land of Florida. The rest of the day was spent in getting the horses ashore; of the eighty horses with which the Spaniards had left Cuba, only forty-two were still alive by the time the ships reached Florida.

The next day was Easter Sunday. The Franciscans held Mass for the entire expedition, but the solemn occasion was marred when a party of Indians approached the Spaniards and angrily gestured at them to go away. On Monday, the serious business of exploration began. Governor Narváez took forty men, including Cabeza de Vaca, off to the north to see if they could find more people and, of course, more gold. They ran across a few Indians, whom they immediately made prisoners, and showed them some ears of corn, asking in sign language where more were to be found. The Indians took them to a village where corn was growing. The Spaniards found a few more bits of gold among the natives; and, when asked about this metal, the Indians pointed to the north, saying "Apalachen." The Spaniards and the Indians could not understand one another, but the former chose to convince themselves that this "Apalachen" was where more precious gold was to be found.

This incident exemplifies a common occurrence in relations between the Spaniards and the Indians of the Americas. The Europeans, always convinced that gold would be found in great quantities just around the next bend, were ready to read the presence of precious metals into the most innocent of statements by the Indians. In fact, small amounts of gold could be found in West Florida and Georgia and were collected by the Apalachee Indians—the "Apalachen" to whom the natives around Tampa Bay, who were Timucan, were referring. But there was no gold where they were at the moment, nor much in the way of food. There was an urgent need for them to move on or starve to death because, to the Spaniards, there was nothing edible growing in the flats of northwest Florida.

Governor Narváez held a council with some of his trusted men, including Cabeza de Vaca. Narváez proposed that the expedition march inland, following the coast, in search of a great bay that all of his pilots insisted was just a short distance away. The Spaniards had no idea that they were almost two thousand miles from Mexico; they assumed that it was just a few days' sail until they reached friendly territory again, at Pánuco (today's Tampico). In the meantime, the ships would sail up the coast directly to this great harbor. Cabeza de Vaca argued against splitting up the party:

It seemed to me, I answered, that under no circumstances should we forsake the ships before they rested in a secure harbor which we controlled; that the pilots, after all, disagreed among themselves on every particular and did not so much as know where we then were; that we would be deprived of our horses in case we needed them; that we could anticipate no satisfactory communication with the Indians, having no interpreter, as we entered an unknown country; and that we did not have supplies to sustain a march we knew not where. . . . I concluded that we had better re-embark and look for a harbor and soil better suited to settle, since what we had so far seen was the most desert and poor that had ever been discovered in that region.[1]

But the majority accepted the pilots' declaration that they were just ten to fifteen leagues (about twenty-five to forty miles) from Mexico, and the governor agreed with them. Narváez turned to Cabeza de Vaca and proposed that, since he seemed to be afraid of marching inland, he should go with the ships and establish a settlement in case the flotilla reached a harbor before the column. Cabeza de Vaca felt insulted by this suggestion and refused. That night the governor came to him once more, this time with less scorn in his voice, and asked him to reconsider; he needed someone whom he could trust to go with the ships. Once again, Cabeza de Vaca refused. He was determined to share the dangers with the rest of the men.

On May 1, three hundred men and forty horses set out for the interior. Each man's rations consisted of two pounds of biscuit and one-half pound of bacon, all of the food left to the expedition. Swamps and creeks constantly hampered their march; they saw no villages, no tilled fields, and no other people. After two weeks, they came to a river, which they crossed on makeshift rafts constructed on the spot. On the other side they encountered a band of several hundred Indians, who made menacing gestures with their weapons. The Spaniards seized a few as hostages; the captured Indians led the party to a village, where the corn stood ripe in the fields for harvesting. The ravenous Spaniards immediately stripped the fields of the entire crop.

A few days later the party crossed the Suwanee River; entering another village, they found once again that the natives had fled at the sight of them. Finally, on June 25, they reached their goal, the village of Apalachee. Cabeza de Vaca was ordered to take fifty men and nine horses and storm the town. The Spaniards had marched for weeks and suffered privations in order to conquer a new Indian empire like that of the Aztecs. Instead, in Cabeza de Vaca's words, "We found a large stand of corn ready to pick, and a lot more already dried and stored; also many deerskins, and, with them, some small, poor-quality shawls woven of thread. The women partially cover their nakedness with such garments. We also noted the bowls they grind corn in. . . . The village consisted of forty low, small thatch houses set up in sheltered places for protection from the frequent storms. It was surrounded by dense woods and many little lakes, into which numerous big trees had fallen to become effective obstructions."[2] This, then, was the mighty Apalachee that they had sought for so long! There were no gold, no jewels, no mighty palaces, and no empire. They had been seeking a phantom kingdom.

There were only women and children in the village. While the Spaniards were milling about, the native men returned and began shooting arrows at the Europeans, killing one horse. They then fled, but came back two hours later and asked for a truce. Narváez agreed, but seized the cacique as hostage (a tactic that Cortés had used in dealing with Emperor Moctezuma in Mexico). The Indians responded by attacking the Spaniards the next morning. Over the next few days, the Indians ambushed them several more times, attacking and retreating so quickly that the Spaniards could not respond effectively to these guerrilla tactics.

Narváez and his men stayed in the village for almost a month. Several reconnaissance trips showed that the surrounding countryside was sparsely populated and difficult to traverse because of the swamps, woods, and lakes. The natives indicated that Apalachee was the biggest town in the area; to the north the villages were smaller and more scattered, and in the interior were only immense forests and lakes, with no precious metals or powerful native kingdoms. The Indians were telling the Spaniards the absolute truth: there were no Mexicos in the forests of northern Florida and southern Georgia. The Spaniards were disappointed, ready to quit and return home: "Taking everything into consideration—the poverty of the land and unfavorable reports of the people . . . the constant guerrilla tactics of the Indians, wounding our people and horses with impunity from the cover of the lakes whenever they went for water . . . we decided to strike for the sea."[3] Cabeza de Vaca then wrote at length about the natives' skill at warfare, which he could not help but admire: "All the Indians which we had seen so far in Florida had been archers. They loomed big and naked and from a distance looked like giants. They were handsomely proportioned, lean, agile, and strong. Their bows were as thick as an arm, six or seven feet long, accurate at 200 paces."[4] The Spaniards' steel armor could not deflect the Indians' arrows; Cabeza de Vaca swore that he had seen an arrow buried half a foot in a poplar trunk. (While fighting the Aztecs, the Spaniards had observed how their steel breastplates were penetrated by native arrows and had switched to the quilted cotton armor that the Indians wore.)

The Spanish, marching to the Gulf of Mexico, passed through a big town (Aute) that had already been deserted and burnt by its inhabitants; the Indians, however, had left behind corn, beans, and squash, which the starving Spaniards seized and devoured. By the time the party reached Apalachee Bay, many were sick, including Governor Narváez. Cabeza de Vaca, although slightly wounded in an Indian ambush, took sixty men to try to find a harbor. For several days they marched over salt flats and sand dunes, eating oysters from the bay, but found no secure landing spot and no sign of the ships. The whole expedition was in a desperate plight, and dissension broke out among the men; the expedition's horsemen plotted to abandon the rest of the weak, sick, and starving party and strike out for Mexico on their own. They were dissuaded from this shameful act, but the fact remained that the fleet was nowhere to be seen, and most of the party was in terrible condition (more than forty died from hunger and disease), stranded on a bleak shore and menaced by hostile Indians. The desperate expedition then decided to build boats and try to make it to Mexico by sea, although no one knew how to navigate.

Somehow the Spaniards managed to build five boats out of materials that they found on the shore or had with them, and on September 22, 1528, the two hundred and forty-seven surviving men of the Narváez expedition, which had set out to conquer the territory of Florida for the king of Spain, cast off on their voyage of desperation. For weeks the leaky crafts, crammed with too many men, slowly made their way to the north and west, constantly running aground on the sandbars and shallows of the coastal waters. Once they encountered some Indians in canoes, who fled from the strange, bearded skeletons. The party went ashore at a small village, which was abandoned, and ate up the dried mullet that they found there. They also seized the native canoes and used them to reinforce their boats.

Onward they sailed, occasionally spotting a distant canoe. After a month had passed, they found shelter on a small island, where they huddled for six days as a terrible storm lashed the Gulf of Mexico. They had no fresh water with them; some of the men became so desperate that they drank salt water and died in agonies of thirst. Finally, the Spaniards reached the end of their rope: "Rather than succumb right there, we commended our souls to God, and put forth into the perilous sea as the storm still raged."[5] They headed in the direction where they had seen a solitary canoe, rounded a point of land, and found themselves in a great bay (Pensacola Bay).

Here their luck seemed to change for the better; they came across a large Indian settlement, where the inhabitants were friendly and invited the starving Spaniards to eat and drink. They gave the Europeans water and fish; the cacique invited the governor into his hut. Narváez responded with courtesy, presenting the chief with some parched corn. But that night the Indians turned hostile and fell upon the men. Narváez was hurt, and several men killed; most of the rest clambered aboard one of the boats and pulled out to sea. Cabeza de Vaca and fifty men stood on the beach to cover their comrades' retreat. Three times during the night the Indians attacked, but were driven back. At dawn, Cabeza de Vaca burned the Indians' canoes, and he and the remainder of his men reembarked on their boat.

When the party reached what is now Mobile Bay, they encountered a fleet of Indian canoes, and once again relations between the Spaniards and the Indians turned hostile. After some Spaniards and a black slave went ashore with the Indians for water, they were never seen again; the Spaniards then seized some Indian chiefs in retaliation. Finally, the bedraggled flotilla reached a mighty river, clearly the Mississippi. Here the expedition literally broke up; the boats started to drift apart in the strong current, and Governor Narváez's craft, with the strongest and fittest men, began to row ahead of the rest. Cabeza de Vaca yelled for them to throw him a rope, but Narváez shouted back that each man must make for home as best he could. Narváez was clearly abandoning the remnants of his expedition; neither he nor his men were ever seen again. On November 6, 1528, Cabeza de Vaca's boat ran aground on an island (Galveston Island), and he and his surviving handful of explorers were marooned.

It is from this point onward that the tale of Alvar Núñez Cabeza de Vaca fundamentally changes. Until his shipwreck, he had been a conquistador; he had come, along with other Spaniards, to conquer and to take from the native people what was not his. But on Galveston Island, he became a supplicant, asking others (the Karankawa Indians) to save his life. The Indians on the island reacted to Cabeza de Vaca and his men with sympathy, giving them food and water in return for a few bells and beads that the Spaniards had with them. When the Spaniards tried to relaunch their craft, a wave swamped it and three men drowned. As they had put their clothing on board, the survivors were now naked as well as cold and hungry. The Indians actually began to weep when they found out what had happened, a sympathetic reaction that the Europeans had never seen before: "The Indians, understanding our full plight, sat down and lamented for half an hour so loudly they could have been heard a long way off. It was amazing to see these wild, untaught savages howling like brutes in compassion for us."[6] Cabeza de Vaca asked the Indians to take his party to their village. Some of the veterans of Mexico warned that they would all be sacrificed, but necessity made them accompany the Indians to their settlement. The Spaniards huddled together, fearing their imminent death as the Indians danced in celebration, but the night passed, and the men relaxed as it became apparent that no such fate awaited them.

The Spaniards called the island on which they were marooned *la isla malhadada*—the island of doom—and it and the Texas coastal plain nearby were to be their home for the next six years. One last attempt to relaunch their boat ended in failure. Cabeza de Vaca later wrote: "With most of us naked and the weather discouraging walking or swimming across rivers and coves—also with no food supply or even anything to carry one in—we resigned ourselves to remaining where we were for the winter."[7] The Spaniards decided that four of their most robust men should try walking to Pánuco (which they believed was nearby) to report their presence and bring back rescuers. These four set out and were never seen again. "Within a few days of the departure of the four Christians," wrote Cabeza de Vaca, "the weather turned so cold and stormy that the Indians could not pull up roots; their cane contraptions for catching fish yielded nothing; and the huts being open, our men began to die."[8] Many of the Spaniards died from exposure; a few marooned on the mainland nearby were reduced to cannibalism as their comrades died—a practice that profoundly disturbed the Indians. Cabeza de Vaca reported that "five Christians quartered on the coast came to the extremity of eating each other. Only the body of the last one, whom nobody was left to eat, was found unconsumed. . . . The Indians were so shocked at this cannibalism that, if they had seen it sometime earlier, they surely would have killed every one of us."[9]

Cabeza de Vaca reported in his narrative that of the ninety Spaniards who had survived the shipwreck of the various boats on the island and the nearby mainland, only sixteen were alive "in a very short while." Then, as happened so often when Europeans and Native Americans met in the New World, the Indians began to die; they came down with "a disease of the bowels," possibly dysentery caught from the soldiers. Some of the Indian survivors came to kill the Spaniards, blaming them for the many deaths, but one Indian stopped them, ascribing to the foreigners the power of sorcery.

Eventually, Cabeza de Vaca began to act as a trader and go-between among the various tribes (mostly Karankawa and Attakapa Indians) who lived on the island and the nearby mainland. His travels as a trader took him deep into Texas (some scholars believe that he got as far as Oklahoma). Cabeza de Vaca, tiring of his lowly status as a laborer, described his own metamorphosis:

> I set to contriving how I might transfer to the forest-dwellers, who looked more propitious. My solution was to turn to trade. . . . The various Indians would beg me to go from one quarter to another for things they needed; their incessant hostilities made it impossible for them to travel cross-country or make any exchanges. But as a neutral merchant I went into the interior as far as I pleased. . . .
>
> My principal wares were cones and other pieces of sea-snail, conchs used for cutting, sea-beads and a fruit like a bean [mesquite] which the Indians value very highly, using it for a medicine and for a ritual beverage in their dances and festivals. This sort of thing I carried inland. By barter I got and brought back to the coast skins, red ochre which they rub on their faces, hard canes for arrows, flint for arrowheads, with sinews and cement to attach them, and tassels of deer hair which they dye red.
>
> This occupation suited me; I could travel where I wished, was not obliged to work, and was not a slave. Wherever I went, the Indians treated me honorably and gave me food, because they liked my commodities. They were glad to see me when I came and delighted to be brought what they wanted. I became well known; those who did not know me personally knew me by reputation and sought my acquaintance. This served my main purpose, which all the while was to determine an eventual road out.[10]

Cabeza de Vaca must have acquired enough fluency in the native languages to facilitate his work as neutral go-between and trader.

He and several of the other Spaniards also became, almost involuntarily, medicine men to the Indians: "The islanders wanted to make physicians of us without examination or a review of diplomas. Their method of cure is to blow on the sick, [with] the breath and the laying-on of hands supposedly casting out the infirmity." Cabeza de Vaca and the other Spaniards blessed the sick people, blew upon them, and recited a Pater Noster and Ave Maria over them. When the patients got well, they ascribed their miraculous recovery to the "magic" of the Spaniards, and in this way Cabeza de Vaca and his companions acquired a reputation as healers. "In consequence," he wrote later, "the Indians treated us kindly. They deprived themselves of food to give to us, and presented us skins and other tokens of gratitude."[11] Cabeza de Vaca and his companions scoffed at the natives' belief in their healing powers and initially refused to practice their "medicine," but the Indians withheld food from them until they finally yielded. He does not say what happened when their "patients" did not recover, but he admitted that the Spaniards were occasionally nervous about failing to work their miracles.

Meanwhile, about a dozen other Spaniards lived with various Karankawa bands along the coast. The survivors later called themselves slaves of the Indians, but they were not captives. The Indians, tired of feeding loafers, sometimes drove out the Europeans, and they wandered until they found a new band with whom to live. Andrés Dorantes wrote years later that "they were treated as slaves, and used more cruelly than by a Moor, naked and barefoot on a coast that burns like fire in summer . . . and since they were *hidalgos* [gentlemen] and men of standing and new to such life it was necessary to have patience as great as their labors."[12] However, a famous colonial chronicler noted wryly: "Those Indians, in whose company these few Christians were, tired of giving them [food] to eat, as always happens when the guest stays longer than the host wishes and in particular if they have not been invited nor contribute anything."[13] These *hidalgos* had few skills to offer to the well-being of the Indian tribes, and so were reduced to fetching water and wood and digging roots for their hosts, and they were sometimes taunted and abused. They thought of themselves as slaves of the Indians and dreamed continually of escape.

Finally, there were only a few Spaniards left alive, scattered among the various bands of the coast; and in the summer of 1534, Cabeza de Vaca was joined by Andrés Dorantes, Alonso del Castillo Maldonado, and Estevánico, or Esteban, a Moorish slave belonging to Dorantes. In September or October they conferred on how best to escape and headed west. Thus began the quartet's epic journey.

We begin to see in Cabeza de Vaca's *Relación* a change in attitude toward the Indians. Until this point, he had nearly always been at the mercy of Indian bands, often in peril of his life, and his writing about them is either contemptuous or detached. From this point onward, in his manuscript (written eight years later), he began to refer to the natives with sympathy, even warmth. Cabeza de Vaca was undergoing a remarkable conversion, from haughty conquistador to sympathetic and engaged observer. Almost immediately, the Spaniards began to assume their role as healers: "The very evening of our arrival [the day they decided to escape the coast], some Indians came to Castillo, begging him to cure them of terrible headaches. When he made the sign of the Cross over them and commended them to God, they instantly said that all pain had vanished."[14] The Indians rewarded the party with venison and some tuna cacti (a type of prickly pear).

Now other Indians began to approach the men, bringing them sick people whom they begged the Spaniards to cure. The men made the sign of the Cross and prayed over the afflicted. While it always seemed to work, Castillo, for one, was afraid that they would fail and the Indians' admiration would turn deadly. When a call came for help from an Indian camp, the Spaniards arrived to find a man without a pulse, apparently dead. Still, they prayed for his recovery; that night, Indians returned to tell the Spaniards that the "dead" man had indeed recovered! Now all four began to practice healing; said Cabeza de Vaca, "We all came to be physicians." The Indians believed that the strangers were "truly sons of the sun," as they began to call the Europeans. The quartet lived with one band of natives, the Avavares, for eight months. Cabeza de Vaca became the boldest and most adventurous in trying to cure anything: "With no exceptions, every patient told us he had been made well. Confidence in our ministrations as infallible extended to a belief that none could die while we remained among them."[15]

Cabeza de Vaca's writing was often anthropologically descriptive, as he related how the Indians he encountered lived their material and spiritual lives. The Avavares, for instance, among whom the Spaniards had dwelt so long, were not especially prosperous. All went naked, covering themselves with deerskins only at night. The Indians had no corn, acorns, or pecans. They had little fish either, and so they were hungry most of the time; only when the prickly pears ripened did the Indians have enough to eat. When the Spaniards passed from the land of the Avavares to that of the Maliacones on the coast, their privations were even more acute. Cabeza de Vaca's narrative refutes the idea, widely held in popular contemporary culture, that America was an absolute Eden when the Europeans arrived. In nontemperate, arid zones such as west Texas and many other parts of the West, geography, climate, and the scarcity of water made for a harsh environment in which hunger often afflicted Native Americans.

In fact, Cabeza de Vaca related that "all these tribes are warlike, and have as much strategy for protection against enemies as if they had been reared in Italy in continual feuds. . . . All these nations, when they have personal enmities and are not related, assassinate at night, waylay, and inflict gross atrocities on each other." Yet he also praised their physical endurance: "I believe that these people see and hear better and have keener senses in general than any in the world. They know great hunger, thirst, and cold, as if they were made for enduring these more than other men, by habit and nature."[16]

Within weeks after starting their trek, Cabeza de Vaca and his companions were accompanied by a large retinue of Indians as they traveled from one village to the next, still in search of other Europeans. To avoid the Indians of the coast, they turned north and west. After wandering along the Colorado, Pecos, and Peñasco Rivers, they turned south and crossed the Río Grande at El Paso, but again turned northwest and headed into what is today New Mexico. News of their coming went before them, and large crowds of natives turned out to greet them: "Since the Indians all through the region talked only of the wonders which God our Lord worked through us, individuals sought us from many parts in hopes of healing."[17] But the Spaniards were disturbed by a new phenomenon: "Those who accompanied us plundered our hospitable new hosts and ransacked their huts, leaving nothing. We watched this with deep concern, but were in no position to do anything about it; so for the present had to bear it until such time as we might gain greater authority. Those who lost their possessions, seeing our dejection, tried to console us. They said they were so honored to have us that their property was well bestowed—and that they would get repaid by others farther on, who were very rich."[18]

Cabeza de Vaca's attitude toward the people of the region had turned from fear and dislike to admiration and sympathy, but he also started to think once again like a conquistador. He began to speculate about returning some day with authority to rule over the natives, and to behave like an explorer, turning to the north, toward the distant mountains, to see what lay in the interior of the country.

One day, as the party continued to travel westward toward distant mountains, they encountered two women who were carrying heavy packs. The women offered the Spaniards some cornmeal; the four had not seen maize since they had left Florida years before. A few days and a few villages onward, they were presented with some more gifts: a copper rattle and some cotton shawls. Where did these things come from? The Indians pointed to the north, where, they said, strange people lived; almost certainly they were referring to the Pueblo Indians of northern New Mexico, although metals such as copper were rare among Native Americans.

Finally, the Spaniards and their enormous retinue of Indians descended into the valley of the Río Grande. By now their companions no longer looted each village as they entered it; rather, the natives offered the newcomers all that they possessed. The four continued to bless and "heal" the sick Indians; indeed, Cabeza de Vaca described how he performed an operation in the "mountain country," opening up a man's chest with a flint knife and extracting an arrowhead from an old wound. The patient survived; and, as Cabeza de Vaca wrote, "This cure so inflated our fame all over the region that we could control whatever the inhabitants cherished."[19]

The Spaniards and their retinue continued journeying westward, telling the natives that they wished to go where the sun sets. They reached the land of the Cow People, so called because the Indians there were skilled buffalo hunters. In what is now New Mexico, in the Río Grande Valley, the natives lived in huts of mud and cane, raised cotton and wove cloth from it, and cultivated corn, beans, and squash. In one town of the Pima Indians, the party was presented with six hundred deer hearts as food and gifts.

All flocked to the famous healers to be cured of their illnesses. Cabeza de Vaca and his companions spoke of their God and Christian faith to the masses as well, although with little effect. The Indians were convinced that the visitors came from Heaven. To better maintain their authority over the Indians, the Spaniards gradually stopped communicating with them and made Esteban the Moor their intermediary.

One day, probably in early January 1536, when they were in the country of the Opata Indians in what is now Sonora, in northwest Mexico, Castillo saw a native wearing around his neck a sword-belt buckle; stitched next to it was a horseshoe nail. "We asked the Indian what it was. He said it came from Heaven. But who had brought it? He and the Indian with him said that some bearded men like us had come to that river from Heaven, with horses, lances, and swords, and had lanced two natives."[20] Casually, the Spaniards asked what had become of the men from Heaven. They had traveled across the water, came the reply. "We gave many thanks to God our Lord," wrote Cabeza de Vaca. "Having almost despaired of finding Christians again, we could hardly restrain our excitement."[21] Now the party began to travel more quickly, and each day they heard more tales of these strangers.

They hurried through an empty land, the natives having fled to the mountains in fear of Spanish soldiers clearly on a slaving expedition from Mexico. "With heavy hearts we looked out over the lavishly watered, fertile, and beautiful land, now abandoned and burned, the people thin and weak, scattering or hiding in fright."[22] By this time, Cabeza de

Vaca, treasurer of an expedition to conquer La Florida, had made an inner journey as well as a physical one, from arrogance to compassion, from conquistador to emissary of peace. When he had first set foot in America, his purpose was to loot and enslave; now he was intent upon stopping his fellow countrymen from doing so. In his *Relación* to the Spanish king, he remarked that the only certain way to bring the Indians to Christianity and subjection to the Crown was through kindness.

The day of meeting arrived at last; in late January 1536, near the Río Sinaloa in Mexico, Cabeza de Vaca and Esteban encountered a party of four mounted Spaniards, who stared at the bearded vagabonds in astonishment. Curiously, Cabeza de Vaca said little about the momentous, long-deferred reunion: "We gave thanks to God our Lord for choosing to bring us out of such a melancholy and wretched captivity. The joy we felt can only be conjectured in terms of the time, suffering, and peril we had endured in that land."[23] Diego de Alcáraz commanded the slave-hunting party. Cabeza de Vaca asked for a certificate stating the year, day, and month in which he had at last encountered his countrymen.

Within a few days, after Dorantes and Castillo had joined Cabeza de Vaca and Esteban, along with six hundred Indians who accompanied them, the quartet found themselves at odds with the Spaniards under Alcáraz. These men wanted to make slaves of all the Indians, but Cabeza de Vaca and his companions argued with Alcáraz and ordered the Indians to return home. The Indians insisted that it was their obligation first to deliver Cabeza de Vaca and his party into the hands of other tribes, as custom demanded, which aroused the jealousy of the Spanish slavers:

> Alcáraz bade his interpreter tell the Indians that we were members of his race who had long been lost; that his group were the lords of the land who must be obeyed and served, while we were inconsequential. The Indians paid no attention to this. Conferring among themselves, they replied that the Christians lied: We had come from the sunrise, they from the sunset; we healed the sick, they killed the sound; we came naked and barefoot, they were clothed, horsed, and lanced; we coveted nothing but gave whatever we were given, while they robbed whomever they found and bestowed nothing on anyone.[24]

To the last, said Cabeza de Vaca, he could not convince the Indians that he and his companions were of the same people as the Christian slavers, but he did induce them to return to their homes. The slavers sent the quartet under escort to Culiacán, in Sinaloa, the nearest Spanish settlement, where the *alcalde*, or mayor, tried to convince the four that the greatest service they could do the Indians was to persuade them to come out of hiding and settle down as farmers under Spanish "guidance."

Cabeza de Vaca and his companions finally reached Mexico City in the summer of 1536 to a tumultuous welcome. They had walked about twenty-eight hundred miles from the coast of Texas, and had been out of touch with other Europeans for almost nine years. Viceroy Antonio de Mendoza was interested in sending the Spaniards back into the wilderness to bring the barbarian Indians (in his words) to submission, but Cabeza de Vaca was intent upon returning to Spain to seek an audience with the king. He had two goals in mind: to persuade the monarch that kindness and charity, rather than enslavement, would ultimately bring more native souls to God and Spanish authority; and to get himself named governor of Florida.

In this effort he failed, for Charles I had already named Hernando De Soto as the new governor. Although Cabeza de Vaca talked with De Soto before he left for the West Indies, that gentleman repeated every mistake of Pánfilo de Narváez and more besides, by alienating an already suspicious and fearful people and enslaving and killing the Indians of Florida and Alabama, until he died of fever in 1542. The only difference between De Soto's expedition and that of Narváez is that a few hundred Spaniards from the De Soto *entrada* managed to reach Pánuco, empty-handed and in rags, four years after leaving Havana.

Cabeza de Vaca continued to follow his dreams of glory in America; named governor of the province of Río de la Plata (now Argentina), he tried to put into effect his rather advanced ideas about treating the native peoples of the interior with respect and fairness. For this, he lost his office and was arrested and imprisoned by Spanish settlers and royal officials whom he had alienated. The settlers hated him because he had forbidden concubinage between Spaniards and unwilling Indian women, seized for that purpose by conquistadores. The royal officials who complained about him to the king resented his curbs on their abuse of the powers of taxation. In 1546 he was seized by rebellious Spaniards in Asunción (today the capital of Paraguay) and sent back to Spain in chains. He spent years arguing his case before the Council of the Indies, but in vain; the entrenched power of rapacious conquistadores, power-hungry missionaries, and corrupt royal officials was too strong to resist. In 1551 the Council ruled against him, stripped him of his royal offices, and banished him from the Indies for life. From this point on, the historical sources are unclear. One story has him dying penniless; another states that the king gave him a pension. He apparently died sometime around 1559.

His Spanish companions in the great trek fared better. Both Castillo and Dorantes married wealthy widows and lived prosperously in Mexico. Esteban the Moor came to a bad end: sent back to the far north by Viceroy Mendoza along with a Franciscan monk to report on the natives, he collected an escort of Indians as in the old days, forging far ahead of the missionary in his eagerness to be the first discoverer of the pueblos of the Río Grande. But Esteban became overconfident and self-important, demanding that each village furnish him with turquoises and women. When he arrived at Háwikuh Pueblo in the Zuñi country, the Indians there killed him. Fray Marcos, the Franciscan, turned back. When he returned to Mexico City, he embellished his story, telling the viceroy that he had seen from afar the Seven Cities of Cíbola, fabulous cities of gold. The Spaniards mounted a huge expedition, headed by Francisco de Coronado, to conquer these kingdoms. Even though Coronado failed in his objective, the long road to occupation and bitterness for the Pueblo Indians of New Mexico had begun.

Alvar Núñez Cabeza de Vaca was very nearly unique in the bloody annals of Spain's "encounter" with the New World. He was a rare conquistador, and one of a mere handful of Spaniards, who believed that the way of the conqueror was morally wrong and practically inefficient. He came to these beliefs through a remarkable empathetic transformation wrought from hardship, hunger, fear, and pain. He discovered a common humanity between Europeans and Native Americans, and for these beliefs he ultimately sacrificed his own career. The thousands-mile trek of Cabeza de Vaca wrought a bridge between two peoples—an ephemeral one that, once it was sundered by the human follies of ignorance and greed, could never be rebuilt.

Notes

1. Alvar Núñez Cabeza de Vaca, *Cabeza de Vaca's Adventures in the Unknown Interior of America*, trans. and annotated by Cyclone Covey, with a new Epilogue by William T. Pilkington (New York: Collier Books, 1961), 33–34.
2. Ibid., 39.
3. Ibid., 41.
4. Ibid., 42.
5. Ibid., 48.
6. Ibid., 57–58.
7. Ibid., 59.
8. Ibid., 60.

9. Ibid.

10. Ibid., 66–67.

11. Ibid., 64–65.

12. Carl Ortwin Sauer, *Sixteenth-Century North America: The Land and the People as Seen by the Europeans* (Berkeley: University of California Press, 1971), 111.

13. Gonzalo Fernández de Oviedo y Valdés, *Historia general y natural de las Indias,* book 35 (Madrid, 1851–1855), as quoted in Sauer, 111–12.

14. Cabeza de Vaca, *Cabeza de Vaca's Adventures,* 85.

15. Ibid., 89.

16. Ibid., 96–97.

17. Ibid., 88.

18. Ibid., 103.

19. Ibid., 110.

20. Ibid., 122.

21. Ibid.

22. Ibid., 123.

23. Ibid., 125.

24. Ibid., 128.

Suggested Readings

Two primary source narratives were written after the journey of Alvar Núñez Cabeza de Vaca and his companions. Cabeza de Vaca himself wrote the *Relación y comentarios del Gobernador Alvar Núñez Cabeza de Vaca de lo acaescido en las dos jornadas que hizo a las Indias,* published in 1542. Many editions in Spanish have appeared under the title *Naufragio y comentarios.* A number of English translations have been made of the *Relación;* the most widely read is *Cabeza de Vaca's Adventures in the Unknown Interior of America,* trans. and annotated by Cyclone Covey (New York: Collier Books, 1961).

The three survivors—Cabeza de Vaca, Dorantes, and Castillo—also presented a joint report in 1537 to the Audiencia of Santo Domingo. This report, principally made by Dorantes, was excerpted and condensed by the historian Gonzalo Fernández de Oviedo y Valdés in book 35 of his *Historia general y natural de las Indias,* partially published in 1535 and 1547, but not published in a full edition until 1851–1855 in Madrid.

The secondary literature on Cabeza de Vaca's journey is immense. Fanny Bandelier, along with her husband Adolph, not only translated Cabeza de Vaca's account but also retraced the route of his party through Texas and the Southwest. The result was published as *The Journey of Alvar Núñez Cabeza de Vaca and His Companions from Florida to the Pacific, 1528–1536* (New York: Allerton Book Co., 1905). In 1940, Cleve Hallenbeck made his own calculation of the Spaniards' route across the Southwest, published as Cleve Hallenbeck, *Alvar Núñez Cabeza de Vaca: The Journey and Route of the First European to Cross the Continent of North America, 1534–1536* (Glendale, CA: The Arthur H. Clark Co., 1940).

Two noteworthy scholarly examinations are Carl Ortwin Sauer, *Sixteenth-Century North America: The Land and the People as Seen by the Europeans* (Berkeley: University of California Press, 1971); and David A. Howard, *Conquistador in Chains: Cabeza de Vaca and the Indians of the Americas* (Tuscaloosa: University of Alabama Press, 1997). Donald E. Chipman, "In Search of Cabeza de Vaca's Route across Texas: An Historiographical Survey," *Southwestern Historical Quarterly* 91 (1987): 127–48, is a review of the many attempts (including one made by James Michener in the novel *Texas*) to retrace the party's journey.

If in recent decades historians have overlooked Cabeza de Vaca in their pursuit of more cutting-edge topics, literary scholars have more than made up the difference. The number of articles examining Cabeza de Vaca's *Relación*, even in English, is impressive. Among the most interesting are Rolena Adorno, "The Discursive Encounter of Spain and America: The Authority of Eyewitness Testimony in the Writing of History," *William and Mary Quarterly* 49 (1992): 210–28; idem, "Peaceful Conquest and Law in the *Relación* (Account) of Alvar Núñez Cabeza de Vaca," in *Coded Encounters: Writing, Gender, and Ethnicity in Colonial Latin America*, ed. Francisco Javier Cevallos-Candau et al. (Amherst: University of Massachusetts Press, 1994), 75–86; idem, "The Negotiation of Fear in Cabeza de Vaca's *Naufragio*," *Representations* 33 (1991): 163–99; Juan Francisco Maura, "Truth versus Fiction in the Autobiographical Accounts by the Chroniclers of Exploration," *Monographic Review/Revista Monográfica* 9 (1993): 28–53; Jacqueline C. Nanfito, "Cabeza de Vaca's *Naufragio y comentarios*: The Journey Motif in the Chronicle of the Indies," *Revista de Estudios Hispánicos* (Puerto Rico) 21 (1994): 179–87; Lee H. Dowling, "Story vs. Discourse in the Chronicle of the Indies: Cabeza de Vaca's *Relación*," *Hispanic Journal* 5 (Spring 1984): 89–99; and Mary M. Gaylord, "Spain's Renaissance Conquests and the Retroping of History," *Journal of Hispanic Philology* 16 (Winter 1992): 125–36.

2

Eliza Lucas Pinckney
Vegetables and Virtue

Gary L. Hewitt

The settlement of the English colonies in America came in different forms and at different times, often accompanied by high death rates. Non-Native American women first came to this new land in roles as varied as African slaves or as indentured servants or as members of the elite.

Eliza Lucas Pinckney was one of those immigrants. She lived most of her life on a plantation, as one of the upper class. In her era, a patriarchal system of authority often dictated what role women like her would play. Spheres of activity began to intensify, with women's spaces being increasingly separated from men's in areas such as public life and business. That world often provided women with little economic independence, limited educational access, and restricted opportunities.

Eliza Lucas Pinckney broke free of those accepted norms. Necessity, her own will and personality, and other factors shaped her response, but the world she crafted for herself would be very different from that of other women of her class and era. She engaged in business, experimented in indigo dye production, and generally controlled her own life.

During the Revolutionary War period in which she lived, Enlightenment thought stressed liberty and the will of the people. The idea of equalitarianism grew stronger. Yet, in the end, the American Revolution had little immediate impact on women's legal standing. They might be—like Eliza Lucas Pinckney—mothers of patriots, educating their sons to be virtuous citizens of the Republic, and be indirectly involved in civic affairs that way. Yet continuity of past ways still persisted. Nevertheless, Eliza Lucas Pinckney has shown that other futures could exist—and would exist—for southern women.

Gary L. Hewitt, an American historian at Grinnell College, Iowa, has completed a book-length study of the political economies and plantation systems of South Carolina and Georgia in the early eighteenth century.

This essay originally appeared in Nancy L. Rhoden and Ian K. Steele, eds., *The Human Tradition in the American Revolution* (Wilmington, DE: Scholarly Resources, 2000), 39–60.

E liza Lucas Pinckney's young son Tom once observed that "Mama
loves long letters."[1] Despite her earlier fears that she might not
have enough "matter to support an Epistolary Intercourse," Eliza's surviving letters span nearly half a century.[2] Her extensive correspondence
has proved a blessing for modern historians, who have found in those
long letters a tantalizing window into the world of a woman of striking
intelligence, vivacity, and charm. While Eliza did not quite write her
"waking and sleeping dream,"[3] as she threatened one friend, her letters
touched on topics as diverse as the prices of agricultural products, local
politics, neighborhood romance and marriage, and the latest novels.
Her mail was directed around the globe to friends, relations, and business associates from London to New England to the West Indies, and it
was accompanied by gifts to cement these cosmopolitan friendships.
Eliza Lucas Pinckney's world was as far-flung as the sprawling British
Empire of the eighteenth century, and she tied it together with her letters.

Eliza was from the very circumstances of her life an extraordinary
woman. Her education, wealth, and status all made her decidedly atypical
for Carolinians of the mid-eighteenth century. Eliza read voraciously in
literature and philosophy and wrote numerous long letters during an
age when a minority of Carolinians, whether male or female, free or
enslaved, was literate. She was born in the West Indies, educated in
England as a girl, and returned for an extended stay there after her marriage. Although most Carolinians during this era, like Eliza, had been
born outside the colony, most had not experienced her wide travels. She
enjoyed the leisure and comforts that came with being a member of one
of the wealthiest families in the colony: not only a library filled with
books but also gardens, music lessons, and a constant round of visits
and entertaining. Her father was a colonel in the British army and lieutenant governor of the wealthy colony of Antigua, her husband was a
prominent South Carolina politician, and her two sons were leaders of
the patriot cause during the American Revolution in South Carolina—
both as generals in the state militia, and one as the state's delegate to the
Constitutional Convention in 1787.

Eliza Lucas Pinckney's story is noteworthy but not simply because
she was a wealthy and privileged lady. Her accomplishments were unusual for a woman of her wealth and status, or perhaps for any woman
in the eighteenth-century Anglo-American world. Eliza directed important family business as she managed the Lucas family's three plantations
from 1739 to 1745. She possessed a keen interest in the life of the mind,
as her wide-ranging and frequent letters attest. She was also an amateur,

though talented, scientist. Eliza was, as she put it once, "fond of the vegetable world," and for several years she was engaged in horticultural experiments that eventually led to the successful commercial cultivation of indigo in South Carolina—a crop that quickly became a major contributor to the wealth of the colony's plantation economy.[4]

Despite Eliza Lucas Pinckney's unusual level of activity and wealth, she helps to illuminate some of the central themes of revolutionary-era American life. Her education and thinking reflect the intellectual currents of the eighteenth century. Her travels from colony to colony and two sojourns in England illustrate the interlocking sinews of the British Empire. Her management of the family plantations and agricultural innovation depict a desire for success and profit among the planters of South Carolina. As a whole, Eliza Lucas Pinckney's life helps demonstrate how fluid women's roles could be in the eighteenth century. Her opportunities were tremendous, and she took good advantage of them to participate in the world of business and of the mind. Yet, Eliza was constrained by her sex as well. She was conscious that, as "a girl," her ideas were valued differently from those of her brothers. More profoundly, Eliza's horizons shrank after her marriage and the birth of her three children. Eliza moved easily into a new role of wife and mother and left some of the intellectual vivacity of her youth behind in favor of a more sober didactic sensibility, in which the education—especially moral—of her children was most important. Her desire to instill "virtue" into her sons' breasts stands out in her numerous letters—virtue that served both Eliza and her sons well when the Revolution came to South Carolina.

Eliza Lucas had lived a cosmopolitan life before she was out of her teens. Born on the British island colony of Antigua in December 1722, Eliza spent a few years in an English girls' school and briefly returned to her birthplace before moving to South Carolina in 1738 with her father and mother, George and Anne Lucas, and her younger sister Mary (her younger brothers, George and Thomas, remained in England at school). Her far-reaching travels were the consequence of her family's wide-ranging set of transatlantic connections. Her father was an important man on Antigua: he was heir to a large sugar estate and son of an assemblyman, and by 1733 he sat on that colony's Royal Council. George Lucas also had a promising military career. Beginning as a captain of a local militia in 1722, he had purchased a major's commission in the British army by the time the family moved to South Carolina.

The Lucas family was no less important in their new home. Here, too, the Lucases were closely connected to the wealthy and powerful planters and merchants who ran South Carolina by the 1730s. These connections were hardly accidental, since Carolina had a long-standing relationship with the Caribbean. From South Carolina's beginnings in the late seventeenth century, West Indian planters had invested heavily in its colonization. The islands had gotten crowded after a half-century-long sugar boom, and opportunities for planters' sons were declining. Sugar plantations needed food, too, and Carolina was close enough to provide a reliable and cheap supply of grain and meat that many West Indian planters, in pursuit of sugar profits, refused to grow for themselves. The Lucases followed this pattern. As early as 1713, Eliza's grandfather John Lucas had acquired substantial amounts of land in South Carolina, and his holdings had grown over the years. When the Lucases arrived in South Carolina in 1738, the family owned three thriving plantations on the Wappoo, Combahee, and Waccamaw Rivers, as well as several lots in the thriving provincial capital and port city of Charles Town (now called Charleston).

Major Lucas's status within the British Empire called him to the king's service when war broke out between England and Spain, only a year after his family's arrival in South Carolina. He was promoted to the rank of colonel and appointed lieutenant governor of his native island colony of Antigua, and so was forced to leave his wife and daughters behind in the comparative health and safety of the mainland. His departure, combined with Anne Lucas's chronic illness, left his family and affairs largely in the hands of his sixteen-year-old daughter Eliza, who made the most of this opportunity to exercise her considerable talents.

The most striking aspects of Eliza's life in South Carolina was her restless activity, both mental and physical. Many days she spent on the plantation, busy from before dawn to after dark. Perhaps the best illustration of her level of activity is her description of the course of a typical day to her friend, Miss Bartlett, niece of Eliza's close friends Elizabeth and Charles Pinckney. "In general," Eliza wrote, "I rise at five o'Clock in the morning, read till Seven, then take a walk in the garden or field." After breakfast, she spent an hour practicing music, then an hour reviewing French or shorthand. Then two hours were devoted to teaching her younger sister and the two slave girls who, she hoped, would teach the rest of the family's slaves. More music followed lunch, with needlework until dark, after which time she would "read or write." Yet her life was not all fancywork and modern languages. Thursdays were reserved entirely for "the necessary affairs of the family"—which meant writing letters, either on the "business of the plantation" or to her friends. Mixed into this schedule were variations: music lessons, entertaining visitors from neighboring plantations, and on Fridays going "abroad" to visit neighbors.[5]

Although Eliza chose to live "in the Country" after her father's departure, she was by no means socially isolated on their Wappoo River plantation. In her own neighborhood, she reported, there were six "agreeable families" with whom she socialized, and she frequently visited Charles Town, just seven miles away by water. Almost all political and business affairs were settled in the provincial capital, so most prominent families had houses in town, and Charles Town became the center of social life in the colony. By the time of Eliza's arrival, it was a bustling town of almost seven thousand inhabitants and boasted a literary society, a theater, and a weekly newspaper, as well as horse races, balls, and an endless round of informal visits among the elite. Eliza, as a single, wealthy, and attractive young woman, found herself at home in Charles Town society, where she developed intimate friendships with several families with whom she stayed while enjoying "all the pleasures Charles Town affords."[6]

Charles Town was not the limit of Eliza's social circle. She maintained a broad set of correspondents far beyond South Carolina. Her letters were directed across the empire in a sort of female counterpart to her father's imperial web of connections. She could not boast a commission in the army or a governorship, but Eliza still maintained in her letters the cosmopolitan flair of her youth, corresponding with her hostess during her youthful sojourn in England, a cousin in Boston who had been a companion in both Antigua and South Carolina, and a friend from school in England, who was the daughter of the governor of Pennsylvania. Even in South Carolina, Eliza's connections had a transatlantic feel: one of her closest friends, Miss Bartlett, was a visitor from England. Many early letters described the Carolina countryside and local news to her curious correspondents. Since Eliza's family was separated across the globe—her brothers were in England, her father in Antigua, and her mother and sister with her in South Carolina—much time was spent soliciting and passing along family news.

Eliza accompanied her letters with gifts. The variety of these gifts displays not merely a generous spirit made possible by great wealth; it also helps to illustrate aspects of colonial life as diverse as young ladies' activities and the commercial needs of the British Empire. To Miss

Thomas in Philadelphia, she sent a tea chest that she had lacquered; to her father she sent one of her lacquered butler's trays. Ornamental work was one employment that occupied the time of many well-to-do young ladies in London and South Carolina and, not surprisingly, Eliza participated. Eliza's other gifts reveal more. Often she sent food across the sea: "a kegg of sweetmeats"[7] and turtle meat (for turtle soup, a delicacy) to England, or potatoes to New England. She also sent larger quantities of beef, rice, and even pickled eggs to her father in Antigua. Unlike her gifts of turtle or sweetmeats, these were profitable commodities in the Atlantic world. She even hoped to establish a lucrative market in eggs in Antigua. Thus, Eliza's correspondence reflected more than young ladies' crafts: she was a messenger on the outposts of a vibrant and dynamic English commercial empire. With the public world of imperial life largely closed to her sex, Eliza Lucas created around herself a different kind of personal empire—a social circle of family and female friends, brought together with friendly moral advice and gifts of turtle meat and japanned boxes, yet also tied together by the practical sinews of commerce and business.

The most striking aspect of Eliza's letters is her constant intellectual energy. Her two hours of reading a day were spent on books as diverse as John Locke's *Essay Concerning Human Understanding*, Samuel Richardson's novel *Pamela*, and Latin pastoral poems—all of which served as the basis for a lively commentary. Eliza's thoughts, so far as her letters reveal them, appear at first glance to have traveled along fairly conventional eighteenth-century paths. Alongside the everyday sociability of her letters is a fairly commonplace concern for duty to parents, adherence to moral principles, and following the principles and observances of the established church. Yet behind this conventionality lurked Eliza's realization that her attention to the life of the mind was unusual for one her age, especially unusual for a young woman. Shadowy figures of older women appear in her letters, chiding her for getting up too early, for working too hard, for reading too much (one woman threw Eliza's book into the fire), and perhaps even for thinking too much. Since women's roles were not so confined in eighteenth-century South Carolina as they would become a century later, Eliza did not self-consciously transgress beyond women's "proper" sphere. She was not a rebel, but she lived on the fuzzy boundaries between the world of women and the world of men.

Another characteristic of Eliza's thinking was a concern for self-discipline and self-reflection, concepts that infused eighteenth-century standards of virtue and manliness. Several times she commented on the propriety of the amusements that Charles Town had to offer: card games, promenades, balls, and the theater. She believed it was acceptable to indulge, at least in moderation, in these pleasures, but still feared the consequences that overindulgence would have on her own character. When she returned from lively Charles Town to the slow-paced life of her plantation and found it "gloomy and lonesome," she gazed inward, and wondered why her isolation could no longer "sooth my . . . pensive humour." Had home changed, or had she changed? She "was forced to consult Mr. Locke" on the question of "personal Identity." Evidently, Eliza was pleased when her reading helped return her to her former "love of solitude."[8]

Yet underneath this self-reflection ran a current of lightness and self-effacement, not ponderous philosophizing and self-aggrandizement. She hoped that her correspondent (her Charles Town friend, Elizabeth Pinckney) would not "conclude me out of my Witts" or "religiously mad" because she was "not always gay."[9] Her thoughtfulness would turn neither to morbid self-reflection nor to a religious enthusiasm that led to events such as the suicide of Mrs. Le Brasures, who had killed herself to get to Heaven sooner. In addition, Eliza's moral comments were also part of the more important process of tying her social world together. This lighter side was most evident when one of Eliza's friends designed a cap for her, and named this new pattern a "whim." Eliza feared that the cap was ill-named, since she already had "so many whims before, more than I could well manage." "Perhaps," Eliza punned, the designer "thought the head should be all of a peice [*sic*], the furniture within and the adorning without the same"—that is, a whim on the head to match the whims within.[10] Nevertheless, Eliza sent the pattern along with her comment to her friend Miss Bartlett, who, Eliza thought, had not so many whims.

Eliza was as happy to give advice as patterns for caps, at least to those younger than herself. Miss Bartlett received a few moral and religious lectures, which Eliza usually turned in humorous directions. When a local planter had religious delusions, Eliza lectured on the importance of rationality in religious life, but finished her discourse with the jocular question of whether Miss Bartlett would "wish my preachment at an End."[11] Eliza changed the subject to the appearance of a comet in the Carolina sky, but quickly returned to the contemplation of whether this comet portended the end of the world, meditations on the "shortness of life," and finally the consolation regarding death that "the Christian religion affords the pious mind."[12] In general, Eliza's advice ran along less sober lines: the two exchanged poetry (and Eliza gave helpful criticism of Miss Bartlett's verses) and commentaries on the propriety of the heroine's behavior in the tremendously popular English novel *Pamela* (1741). Throughout Eliza's writings, a moral sensibility predominated; after Miss Bartlett returned to England, she asked Eliza to "write a poem on Virtue."[13] Eliza disclaimed any ability on that score—she was as likely to read ancient Greek, she said, as write a good poem on any subject— but Miss Bartlett's request says much of the relationship between the two young women and Eliza's character.

Eliza's two younger brothers, who had remained in England to complete their education, were the recipients of more sober moral lessons. The younger brother, Thomas, was gravely ill while Eliza was in South Carolina, a fact that elicited both cheerful encouragement and long meditations on mortality from his sister. George, on the other hand, was healthy and had entered the British army as an ensign at only fifteen years of age. Eliza feared the dangers her brother would encounter in the military, especially the violent passions provoked by the heat of battle and the company of soldiers. Instead, she counseled a "true fortitude," in which "rational principles" would provide him with the necessary courage to fight with honor, but not lead him to take unnecessary chances. A "composed state of mind" was what she recommended.[14] She understood that "Victory and conquest must fire your mind" as a soldier, but reminded George that "the greatest conquest is a Victory over your own irregular passions."[15] True virtue, for Eliza, allowed the rational mind to overcome desires for glory or revenge, while following the dictates of religion and conscience. While Eliza's image of man's virtue at war with his passions was by no means unusual for her era, she extended her concern for reason and virtue to both men and women. It seems, however, that she believed the stakes of male virtue were higher, even as the threats were stronger.

"But to cease moralizing and attend to business," Eliza punctuated one of her letters to her father (after describing her sisterly advice to George on the subject of virtue).[16] That Eliza would think of morality and business as separate pursuits indicates something about eighteenth-century political thought. Hers was an era before Adam Smith argued that an "invisible hand" could make individuals' pursuit of self-interest yield a public good. Rather, in her era, "irregular passions," including self-interest, threatened the virtue of Eliza's brother. For this reason, Eliza's business correspondence has a matter-of-fact quality quite distinct from her breezy social exchanges or her sober moral lessons. To be sure, Eliza paid close attention to the management of her family's South Carolina estates. She continually wrote to her father and her business associates in Charles Town about the day-to-day business of rice planting and international commerce. But Eliza usually did not make the effort to copy the text of these matters verbatim. She preferred simply to write memoranda into her letterbook noting the general subjects of her letters, or perhaps she copied them elsewhere or sent them to her father. In any event, the point remains that she considered business a separate realm, one of memoranda and ledger entries, not of personal relationships that merited word-for-word copies of letters. Of course, Eliza also had close personal attachments to most of the recipients of these letters: her father, the Pinckneys, and the other members of South Carolina's merchant elite who were also her friends. Thus Eliza might bring together these two worlds with her awkward transition from a moral concern for her brother to "attend to business."

That junction represented the outer limits of what Eliza could do as a woman in the British Empire. There were, however, times when Eliza carved a further breach in the masculine world of business, or at least exploited the blurry lines between women's and men's roles. From time to time, as she reported to her friend Miss Bartlett, she provided legal services for her "poor Neighbors" who could not afford the services of a lawyer. Eliza had a copy of an English legal handbook and used it to draw up wills for neighbors on their deathbeds. But Eliza knew when she was out of her depth—even when "teazed intolerable," she refused to draw up a marriage settlement (a sort of eighteenth-century prenuptial contract, intended to allow a bride to retain control of the property she brought to the marriage). She did finally serve as a trustee of the bride's property in that instance; this role was not an unheard-of one for a woman, but it was unusual for anyone as young as Eliza. The "weighty affairs" Eliza had on her hands led her to wonder whether she would become "an old woman before I am well a young one." Eliza understood that her attention to business and the world of "affairs," like her self-described "pensive humour" and her love of books, set her apart from most young women.[17] Perhaps for this reason, Eliza wanted Miss Bartlett to keep her lawyering a secret from her aunt and uncle, the Pinckneys.

Eliza Lucas's most famous activity during her first years in South Carolina was her agricultural experimentation on her father's plantations. "I

love the vegitable world extremely," she told one friend, and her horticultural work was constant as long as she lived in South Carolina.[18]
Within a year of her arrival in the colony in 1738, she began planting
numerous crops in an effort to determine which ones might grow well
in her new home. Many of them were common to her native West Indies:
indigo, ginger, cotton, lucerne (a kind of alfalfa), and even cassava, a
root crop originating in Brazil that became a staple for Caribbean slaves.
None of these had been commercially successful in South Carolina, and
Eliza did not always succeed. Her first crops of cotton and ginger were
destroyed in a frost, and her lucerne, she reported, was "dwinderling."[19]
She also experimented with Mediterranean crops and tried an orchard
of fig trees. Not all of her horticultural efforts were directed toward
commodities. While reading Virgil, she was struck by his descriptions
of Roman gardens, which she thought might suit her own colony. So
Eliza's busy mind immediately contemplated the "beauties of pure nature, unassisted by art" on her plantation.[20] She also considered how
she might improve on nature, by planting a cedar grove as well as gardens of flowers and fruit trees.

Still, profit was never far from Eliza's active thoughts either. Her
future husband, Charles Pinckney, accused her of having a "fertile brain
at scheming," by which he meant schemes to make money.[21] Indeed, in
most of her agricultural experiments, Eliza was interested in making
them pay off, or at least hoped that they might "provid[e] for Poster-
ity."[22] Her fig trees were planted "with design to dry and export them,"
and she carefully calculated the expenses and profits of that project.[23]
She planted oaks in the hopes that they could be sold to shipbuilders.
She even pickled eggs and sent them to the West Indies, hoping they
might provide another source of income. In each venture, she looked
for commodities that would serve as articles of trade in the dynamic
commercial empire that Great Britain had created in the early eighteenth century. Just as Eliza's letters circulated around the empire, so
too, did her produce.

In this context of searching for profitable export commodities, Eliza's
most famous experiment developed. Indigo, a blue dye extracted from
the *Indigofera anil* plant, was the object of Eliza's highest hopes and
most diligent efforts. The dye had been produced in the first years of
South Carolina's settlement in the late seventeenth century, but the production of rice and naval stores had quickly taken over the colony's
economy. The drawbacks to these new staples had become evident by
1740. South Carolina's naval stores were of low quality and therefore

price. Rice, which dominated the economy after 1730, was bulky in relation to its value, and many ships were needed to carry away the annual crop. With hostilities heating up after 1739, these ships were in danger from privateers, and insurance rates skyrocketed. War also cut off the colony's primary European markets for rice, and prices therefore dropped dramatically. By 1744, the colony was in deep recession from this squeeze on rice profits—something which, one imagines, went through Eliza's mind as she reviewed her plantation business each Thursday, or while she calculated the profits to be earned from her fig orchard. Indigo solved these problems: it was much more valuable per pound, and a year's product could be carried on a few well-armed ships. England's growing textile industry needed dyes, and so prices were high.

No wonder that Eliza, together with her father and her neighbors, invested so much time and effort in producing indigo. A great effort was necessary, since a number of logistical problems had to be overcome if indigo was to be produced profitably. South Carolina's climate was just barely suited to growing the plant, and Eliza's first crop was destroyed by frost before the plants were mature, and the second by worms. Her father sent different strains of seeds repeatedly to restart the process. More problematic, however, was the high level of technical expertise required to oversee the production of the dye itself. Turning the gold leaves of the indigo bush into cakes of almost-black dyestuff required a series of stages of fermentation, stirring, and drying, all of which needed to be closely monitored in order to produce a high-quality dye. Colonel Lucas sent a series of indigo experts to help instruct the Carolina slaves in the processing of indigo, but these experts were more interested in keeping their secrets than in sharing their knowledge. One, Eliza thought, had deliberately ruined a batch of indigo by dumping too much lime into the vat of fermenting leaves. Eventually, however, the joint efforts of Eliza, her neighbors, and their slaves succeeded; in 1744 a small amount of dye was produced, along with a sufficient quantity of seed to sell to other Carolinians eager to find a secondary crop.

Indigo cultivation spread rapidly across South Carolina after 1745, a testament to the collective efforts of Eliza and her neighbors in developing the crop. Eliza's friend and neighbor (and future husband) Charles Pinckney helped promote indigo, publishing articles in the *South Carolina Gazette* that lauded it as the answer to South Carolina's economic problems. And indigo was not just a profitable export commodity; it was also well suited to the colony's existing economy. It complemented rice planting and slavery. By 1740 the colony's economy depended utterly on slaves to do the backbreaking work of planting rice. The production of indigo, especially, fit into this slave economy. Indigo cultivation and rice cultivation could coexist on the same plantation—they demanded different kinds of land and labor at different times of the year. Rice planters could easily move into the production of indigo, and they did so. One of Eliza Lucas's legacies to South Carolina was the revitalization of plantation slavery during a decade of hard times for the colony's key crop, rice. By the end of the 1740s the value of indigo exports approached that of rice exports, and the slaves who tended both found themselves busier than ever.

Slavery, it should be remembered, was an important part of Eliza Lucas's life in South Carolina. By 1739 about two-thirds of the colony's population was enslaved and of African descent, although this fact is nearly invisible in Eliza's letters, in which she rarely mentions her family's slaves. Slaves sometimes delivered her frequent messages to her friends in Charles Town, since she referred to "Mary Ann," "Togo," and "David" as conveyors of messages. Thus, slaves both produced Eliza's wealth and helped tie together her social world. Slavery drew Eliza's attention more often because of the possibilities of slave rebellion. This focus is not surprising: the Lucases arrived in South Carolina just before the Stono Rebellion erupted there in September 1739, the largest slave rebellion to occur in that colony or all of colonial North America. About one hundred slaves, crying "Liberty," rose up against their masters and fought their way toward Spanish St. Augustine, killing about twenty white Carolinians in the process. Although the rebellion was suppressed in a few days, and far more slaves were executed than whites had perished, white society was hardly calmed. The nearly simultaneous onset of war with Spain, and the Spanish offer of freedom to Carolina's slaves that had contributed to the rebellion, only made white Carolinians more nervous about the threat that their enormous numbers of slaves posed to their dominance and safety. Fears of slave rebellion echoed for the rest of the 1740s. Eliza Lucas noted several suspected slave conspiracies early in that decade, including one that implicated one of her family's slaves.

While the South Carolina Assembly responded to the Stono Rebellion by passing a strict slave code in 1740, restricting slaves' freedom of movement and ability to congregate, it does not appear that Eliza Lucas cracked down on her family's slaves. Indeed, Eliza may have had a more humanitarian notion of how to treat her slaves, although she could not have lived on her plantation without witnessing the daily brutality of slavery. In 1741, Eliza mentioned a "parcel of little Negroes whom I have undertaken to teach to read," and later she told her father of another one of her "schemes": she wished to teach two slave girls to read, so that they could in turn serve as "school mistres's [*sic*] for the rest of the Negroe children."[24] Her purpose in educating her slaves remains unclear. Perhaps teaching her slaves was yet another outlet for her seemingly boundless energy; perhaps she had some other plan. (Slave education would not be outlawed in South Carolina until a later rebellion in 1822.)

It seems possible that Eliza was less fearful of her slaves than many Carolinians, a feeling that her account of a strange event in 1742 helps illustrate. In March a wealthy planter, Hugh Bryan, in the religious enthusiasm of the Great Awakening, began to prophesy slave rebellions and cast himself in the role of Moses in leading slaves to freedom. His attempt to part the waters of a creek, however, failed—he nearly drowned—and Bryan quickly recanted his prophecies. Many white Carolinians feared the "consiquence [*sic*] of such a thing being put in to the head of the slaves," as Eliza put it, but, for her own part, Eliza seems to have appreciated the ridiculousness of the entire story more than its danger.[25] The lesson she drew from it concerned the perils of religious enthusiasm and the importance of following natural reason even in contemplating religious matters. It is characteristic of Eliza Lucas that her mind turned quickly from the threat of slave rebellion to a didactic lesson, from fear to hope. It is also characteristic that Eliza opposed the Great Awakening's religious fervor and followed instead the mainstream Anglican theology of her friend Dr. Alexander Garden, commissary of the Church of England and opponent of religious revivalism.

In January 1744, Eliza Lucas's good friend, Mrs. Elizabeth Pinckney, died after a long illness. Four months later, Eliza Lucas married the widower, Colonel Charles Pinckney. Twenty-four years Eliza's senior, Charles Pinckney was an important man in South Carolina. In the 1730s he had served actively in the colony's Commons House of Assembly, and in 1736 he was elected speaker of the Commons House, a testament to his importance within the colony's political structure. The Pinckneys had been among Eliza's first friends in South Carolina. A close, even affectionate relationship between Eliza and Charles had emerged alongside the female friendship of Eliza, Elizabeth Pinckney, and the Pinckneys' niece, Miss Bartlett. It was Charles who lent Eliza books, assisted in her indigo experiments, and accused her of having a fertile mind for scheming. The two exchanged a continuous friendly correspondence, the breeziness and intimacy of which is striking between a single woman and a married man. Perhaps Charles was a father figure to Eliza, as he was about her father's age. Charles also may have substituted as a social companion for his increasingly ill wife—certainly, Eliza wrote far fewer letters to Elizabeth Pinckney than to Charles. In fact, Charles appears to have been the only man not a relative with whom Eliza cultivated a close correspondence.

Charles Pinckney was not the first man to fall for Eliza Lucas, although none of the earlier suitors gained her favor. When Eliza was only eighteen, two men conveyed their interest in Eliza to her father, who passed on these sentiments to the young lady. She refused them absolutely, and in characteristic form. As for the first, "the riches of Peru and Chili . . . could not purchase a sufficient Esteem for him"; the second she did not know well enough to consider.[26] She preferred to remain single. Indeed, she seemed to spend little thought on matters of the heart: "As to the other sex, I dont trouble my head about them. I take all they say to be words. . . ."[27] Matters had not changed the next year. Eliza reported a romantic "Conquest" of an "old Gentleman" to her friend Miss Bartlett several years later, but refused to provide details in her letter. Indeed, Eliza promised that Miss Bartlett's uncle (Charles Pinckney himself!), who was "much pleased" with the entire affair, would provide a "full account."[28]

On the other hand, in 1741, Eliza signed her copy of one of her letters to Charles Pinckney oddly—"Eliza Pinckney"—which was three years later to be her married name.[29] Perhaps this was a slip of her pen when she copied her letter over in her letterbook, though one must speculate in that case as to whether her subconscious was busily at work. Regardless of Eliza's thoughts that day, it is clear that Eliza and her future husband had developed a close friendship before the death of Elizabeth Pinckney. There is something in the tone of these letters that betrays a high degree of affection and intimacy between the two. The rapidity of their marriage following Elizabeth Pinckney's death was hardly unusual in the eighteenth century, but it occurred soon enough that local gossips wondered whether Eliza had denied Mrs. Pinckney medical care as she was dying. Eliza was shocked by the implication that she would do away with her friend—but Eliza's marrying one of South Carolina's wealthiest and most important men probably made envious aspersions inevitable.

Marriage in May 1744 marked a basic transformation in Eliza's life. While she still looked after her father's plantations after moving to Belmont, the Pinckney plantation north of Charles Town, her activities on that score were necessarily reduced now that she had a husband (and her own household) to attend to. This transformation was surely magnified when Eliza became pregnant within a month of their marriage, and gave birth to her first son, Charles Cotesworth, in February 1745. Three more births followed over the next six years: a son, George, in 1747 (who died two weeks after his birth); a daughter, Harriott, in 1748; and a son, Thomas, in 1750. In short order Eliza had become a wife and a mother, and her inclinations toward religious and moral instruction—already evident in her relationship with her brothers—quickly rose to the occasion. Charles apparently was of one mind with Eliza, and together they worked to educate their sons and daughter. Charles Cotesworth reputedly knew his letters before he could talk. The children memorized passages from the Bible and attended church regularly. Eliza's ample energies were now focused, it seems, on her children's education and her husband's happiness, "even in triffles."[30] Her energies were not limitless, on the other hand: with three living infants, and a bout of depression following the death of George, Eliza ceased writing in her letterbook for five years.

South Carolina, despite its wealth and vibrant social life, was still a province, and Charles Pinckney believed that his sons would be best educated at "home"—that is, in England. Eliza, of course, had herself been educated in England, and since the birth of Charles Cotesworth she had hoped that the family would be able to make an extended stay in the mother country. Charles Pinckney's hopes for appointment as chief justice in South Carolina put off the trip for several years, but the position eventually went to another, and Charles put his financial affairs in order for the long visit to England. He also was appointed by the South Carolina Commons House of Assembly as the colonial agent to the Board of Trade in London, providing the family with social and professional contacts in England, as well as more financial support. With these preparations done, in late April 1753 the family of five boarded ship for the voyage across the Atlantic and arrived twenty-five days later in England.

For Eliza, this move was both gratifying and unsettling. She very much desired to return to England. Although her brothers had since departed, she still had friends from her first stay there as a girl. Yet she also "gave a wistful look" at Charles Town as she left.[31] Eliza was now thirty-two years old, and had lived about half her life—all her adult life—in South Carolina. Soon after arrival the family settled near London, and Eliza set about the task of entering English society. Friendships from her earlier stay in London were quickly renewed, and the large community of Carolinians in London supplemented Eliza's lively social scene. At the same time, Eliza maintained her connections across the Atlantic and wrote long letters to women in South Carolina, full of the news from London. With her sons deposited in boarding school and her husband busy in London, Eliza entered the social world with all her energy—with winters at Bath, frequent attendance at the theater, and visits to and from her friends.

While London offered more social opportunities than South Carolina, the narrowing of Eliza's horizons that had begun with her marriage continued in England. Certainly, Eliza's letters ceased to show the kind of vivacity and energy that they had during her single life. Perhaps the variety of social connections in England available to Eliza allowed her to show her wit and charm in drawing rooms instead of in her letters. Yet this change in the tone of her letters also reflected a change in what she herself had to do. Her activities no longer included horticultural experiments, and her moralizing was restricted while her sons were at school. Although her sons' occasional illnesses demanded a mother's attention, socializing occupied most of Eliza's time.

Charles Pinckney became homesick soon after the family's arrival in London, but it is clear that Eliza did not share this feeling and, in fact, opposed returning to Carolina. Perhaps Eliza was less tied to the New World; the only sign that Eliza might have felt attached to America was her close attention to American affairs after the French and Indian War broke out in 1754. Her letters to South Carolina reveal no pining for that distant land. The outbreak of war, however, did dramatically change the Pinckney family's circumstances. Charles feared that South Carolina was in peril from French attack and desired to return to the colony so he could liquidate his plantations. The children would remain in the safety of English schools. Eliza was not enthusiastic about this plan. She feared the dangers of travel during wartime (her father had died in 1747 after being captured during the last war) and did not particularly want to return to South Carolina herself. Most important, she did not want to be separated from her children for the two or three years it would take for Charles to settle his Carolina affairs. Yet she submitted to her husband's wishes for the most part: Eliza and Charles left their sons in England and embarked for South Carolina in the early spring of 1758, but they took their ten-year-old daughter Harriott with them.

Separation from her sons was only the first of Eliza's trials that year. Less than a month after the couple's arrival in Charles Town, Charles Pinckney contracted malaria, lingered for three weeks, and died on July 12, 1758. Over the next month, Eliza buried her husband, began to arrange for the disposition of his estate, and went about the melancholy task of informing her sons and her family of Charles's death. In these letters, Eliza displayed her characteristic strength of character and moral sensibility, as well as her affection for her husband of fourteen years.

One can imagine how difficult it was to break this news by letter to her sons, only seven and thirteen years old. Not surprisingly, Eliza drew a potent moral and religious lesson from the untimely passing of Charles at fifty-nine years of age. His family more than ever had to depend on the strength of God, whose will was most clearly expressed in the unhappy event. She told her sons that their father's death was an exemplary one: "His sick bed and dying moments were the natural conclusion of such a life," and he "met the king of terrors without the least terror or affright," and "went like a Lamb into eternity." Eliza promised that she, as widow and mother to Charles Pinckney's children, would devote the rest of her life to honoring their father's memory by serving them. She concluded with an exhortation that her sons be "worthy [of] such a father as yours was."[32] To her mother, who had returned to Antigua after Eliza's marriage, Eliza repeatedly described the virtues (she used the word four times in her letter) of her husband and her hopes to meet Charles in eternity.

More pressing practical business included the settlement of Charles's estate and providing for the education of the children still in England. For Eliza, both were familiar territory. She had no problem assuming the management of Charles's affairs: paying debts, arranging for probate of the will, and maintaining the family plantations, which were run down after the Pinckneys' four-year absence. One imagines that Eliza's return to the world of business must have been unhappy at first, but that, with time, planting gardens and directing affairs were pleasant tasks. "I love a Garden and a book," Eliza wrote a friend in England five years after her husband's death, "and they are all my amusement" except for raising her daughter.[33] Eliza also renewed the vivacity and charm of her youth during these years, as she continued to build and maintain the friendships that she had made across the globe and sent more potatoes, limes, and beets around the world.

Yet managing these worldly matters demanded that Eliza remain separated from her sons; Charles Cotesworth did not return to South Carolina until 1768, and Thomas not until 1772. Eliza's direction of their education accordingly had to take place across the Atlantic. Here, too, Eliza gave the same counsel as she had to her brothers: she emphasized virtue, independence, and Christian morality to her sons. She gave advice on a wide variety of subjects, from proper treatment of servants to the importance of restraining one's passions. While Eliza feared that "the morals of Youth are taken little care of" at public schools and university and she knew that London offered "temptations with every youthful passion," she had faith in her sons' ability to maintain "moral Virtue, Religion, and learning."[34]

Her counsels were given to sons who followed a typical English gentleman's education—attendance at elite boarding schools, followed by a stint at, if not a degree from, Oxford or Cambridge University, and perhaps legal training at the Inns of Court in London. The next generation of planter-aristocrats received an English liberal education. It is ironic, then, that both Charles Cotesworth and Thomas Pinckney came of age in England and partook of an English gentleman's education just as the first stirrings of Anglo-American conflict appeared. Both sons identified with their native soil from the earliest phases of this conflict, with Thomas being known as the "Little Rebel" by his English friends and Charles Cotesworth in 1766 having a portrait painted of himself declaiming against the Stamp Act of 1765.

During the convulsions preceding American independence, Eliza saw her daughter Harriott married to Daniel Horry in 1768, and her two sons return to South Carolina, marry, and take their place on Pinckney family plantations. These domestic transformations did not leave Eliza alone or idle, since she still maintained the easy sociability of the South Carolina low country, and her new son- and daughters-in-law merely expanded her social circle. Eliza spent long periods with Harriott at Hampton, the Horry family estate. It must have gratified Eliza to see Harriott follow her mother's interest in gardening and to assist in the moral and intellectual training of her grandchildren, who were born with some regularity in the years following 1768. Eliza also appears to have become something of a medical practitioner in middle age; ailments and treatments played an increasing role in her correspondence with her South Carolina acquaintances.

Eliza Lucas Pinckney had spent her life enmeshed in a web of empire-wide connections. Her father was a colonial official, she had spent long periods of time in England, and her family had even at one point planned to settle in the mother country. Her friendships extended around the Atlantic, mostly among correspondents who were also connected with imperial administration. It is ironic, then, that her family would be so closely identified with the movement for American independence in South Carolina. While Eliza made few references in her letters to the crises leading to that independence, her sons, especially Charles Cotesworth, were intimately involved with the political storms that developed during the 1770s and usually favored a vigorous colonial response to the actions of the British ministry. Soon after the battles of Lexington and Concord in April 1775, Charles Cotesworth led a raid on the colony's armory that secured the government's weapons for the patriots, and later that year he was elected a captain in the South Carolina militia. Thomas soon followed his brother into the patriots' service, and both ended the war as high-ranking officers in the Continental army, with Charles Cotesworth becoming a brigadier general.

The Pinckney sons' deep support of the patriot cause is not altogether surprising, even considering their close connections with the British Empire. Their father had been central in the development of a distinctive political rhetoric in South Carolina in the 1730s, one that emphasized the necessity of virtue and independence in government. South Carolinians repeatedly decried attempts by royal governors to limit the prerogatives of the elected assembly, either by overt action or by insidious acts of "corruption": for instance, providing government offices to assemblymen friendly to the government. Charles Pinckney Sr. had experienced corruption firsthand just before the family's trip to England, when he was denied the office of chief justice of South Carolina in favor of a better-connected man. Even after their father's death, Eliza's consistent reminders to her sons to follow the paths of virtue and independence reinforced this basic understanding of politics. When the British ministry's acts began to look corrupt in the escalating crises following the Stamp Act, the Townshend Duties, and finally the Intolerable Acts, men such as the Pinckneys were willing to put aside their loyalty to the king and follow the path that they had been taught was virtuous.

During these crises, Eliza could not be virtuous in the same way as her sons. As a woman, her political role was restricted to the sidelines. When war came to South Carolina in 1778, however, women such as Eliza had to make choices about what to do, choices that indicated their loyalty and could also provoke reprisals from the partisan forces at war. With the British occupation of Charles Town and a bitter civil war raging over the countryside, there was no neutrality. Eliza, caught in the midst of these struggles on her son-in-law's plantation outside Charles Town, chose to support the patriot cause in her way. Much of the low country where Eliza's family lived was occupied alternately by British and American troops, leaving her subject to depredations from both sides, but mostly from the British. Since Eliza would not proclaim loyalty to the king, her houses in Charles Town were occupied by British troops who paid no rent, while her stock was carried off her plantations and her slaves ran away or were captured, leaving her plantations to produce no income at all. In 1779, Eliza complained of her "losses" and the "almost ruined fortunes" of her sons, and two years later she found herself incapable of paying a debt of £60 sterling—an amount that would have been a trifle just five years earlier.

Eliza suffered more than economic losses. Both her sons were soldiers in the cause of independence, and she was daily concerned with their health and welfare. Thomas was injured and captured by the British in 1780, leaving her quite distraught with worry. Charles Cotesworth quickly offered to share his own estate with his brother and mother after these disasters, but both refused. For Eliza, what was most grievous was the loss of her independence, her ability to be free from obligation to others and to shower her own benevolence on her children and grandchildren. Here, Eliza shared in the ideas of virtue and independence that she had impressed upon her sons: she wanted to be dependent on no one, to provide for herself.

Following the war, times did not immediately improve. The War of Independence in South Carolina had become a bitter civil war among the colony's inhabitants, and this animosity persisted well beyond the coming of peace in 1783. Independence had thrust many poorer Carolinians into political activity, an unaccustomed phenomenon for the low-country planter oligarchy who had maintained the upper hand for so long. Sizable numbers of low-country planters had been loyal to the king or tepid in their patriotism, which made their property attractive targets for angry patriots, who pushed for bills confiscating loyalist estates and heavily taxing those whose support for the cause was less than fervent. Perhaps because Eliza Lucas Pinckney herself had no public political position—as a woman she had no formal political voice, and her husband's politics had been in the grave for nearly a quarter century—her estates (damaged as they were) could not be seized. In fact, the damage that Eliza's property received at the hands of the British probably helped demonstrate that the British did not consider her a friend. Finally, her two sons' conspicuous service in the patriot cause ensured that they would not be punished (Charles Cotesworth, indeed, sat in the state legislature). Eliza's son-in-law Daniel Horry was less lucky—his estate was punitively taxed, and a friend of the family believed that only the Pinckneys' "many Virtues" prevented it from being confiscated.[35]

Eliza spent most of the postwar years at the Horry plantation, where she continued her agricultural labors and helped oversee the education of her grandchildren. She even entertained President George Washington during his visit to South Carolina in 1791. A single letter to her grandson, Daniel Horry Jr., survives, in which she reprised for a third generation the moral and religious advice she had given her brothers and sons. A "liberal Education," a proper restraint of emotions and passions, and industriousness were the virtues she urged upon twelve-year-old Daniel, whom she saw as part of a "rising generation" whose "abilities and improved Talents" would raise the newly independent South Carolina in its "Second Infancy."[36] Eliza's basic message had not changed: virtue, restraint of passions, and self-control. To this, however, Eliza added a new message of service to one's nation. Historians have called this moral emphasis "Republican motherhood"—the notion that women, as mothers and grandmothers, could instill in their children the virtue needed to guide a nation. Eliza had been doing this job for three generations, but the political context of this work had changed in the meantime, from the world-spanning British Empire, to the independent State of South Carolina, and now to the new United States of America.

Eliza Lucas Pinckney was diagnosed with cancer in 1792, at seventy years of age. A year later she traveled to Philadelphia to consult with a famous physician, who failed to cure her. She died on May 26, 1793, and was buried the next day, with President George Washington serving as a pallbearer. (Washington had sought out Eliza during his visit to South Carolina two years earlier; he had wanted to meet the famous agriculturalist and the mother of two such conspicuous South Carolina patriots.) Eliza had lived a long and varied life. She had been the epitome of the cosmopolitan British Empire, and the mother of American patriots. She had been a society belle with extraordinary wit, charm, and manners, and had also been a devout Christian, a moralist, and an agricultural innovator. She was a vivacious single woman, a devoted wife and mother, and an industrious widow, but her life was never entirely defined by her connections to men. Her legacies lived long after her death—her descendants continued to experiment with new crops such as sugar and cotton, and the Pinckneys remained politically prominent in South Carolina. Eliza Pinckney is well remembered as the mother to this famous family; she should be remembered also in her own right.

Notes

1. Eliza Lucas Pinckney (hereafter, ELP) to Mrs. Evance, June 19, 1760, in Elise Pinckney, ed., *The Letterbook of Eliza Lucas Pinckney, 1739–1762* (Chapel Hill: University of North Carolina Press, 1972), 151. Hereafter cited as *Letterbook*. All dates before 1752 are Old Style, except that the year is taken to begin on January 1.
2. Eliza Lucas (hereafter, EL) to Miss Bartlett (hereafter, Miss B.), January 14, 1742, *Letterbook*, 26.
3. Ibid.
4. ELP to C. C. Pinckney, September 10, 1785, quoted in *Letterbook*, xxv.
5. EL to Miss B., ca. April 1742, *Letterbook*, 34–35.
6. EL to Mrs. Boddicott, May 2, 1740, *Letterbook*, 7–8.
7. EL to Mrs. Boddicott, June 29, 1742, *Letterbook*, 42.
8. EL to Mrs. Pinckney, ca. July 1741, *Letterbook*, 19.
9. Ibid.
10. EL to Miss B., ca. April 1742, *Letterbook*, 31.
11. EL to Miss B., ca. March 1742, *Letterbook*, 29.
12. Ibid., 29–30.
13. EL to Miss B., ca. May 1743, *Letterbook*, 62.
14. EL to George Lucas, June 1742, *Letterbook*, 45.
15. EL to dear Brother, July 1742, *Letterbook*, 52–53.
16. EL to Father, February 10, 1743, *Letterbook*, 59.
17. EL to Miss B., ca. June 1742, *Letterbook*, 41.
18. EL to Miss B., ca. April 1742, *Letterbook*, 35.
19. EL to Father, June 4, 1741, *Letterbook*, 15.
20. EL to Miss B., April 1742, *Letterbook*, 36.
21. Ibid., 35.
22. EL to Miss B., May 1742, *Letterbook*, 38.
23. EL to Miss B., April 1742, *Letterbook*, 35.
24. EL to Charles Pinckney, February 6, 1741, *Letterbook*, 12; EL to Miss B., April 1742, *Letterbook*, 34.
25. EL to Miss B., March 1742, *Letterbook*, 29–30.
26. EL to Colonel Lucas, ca. April 1740, *Letterbook*, 6.
27. EL to Miss B., January 1742, *Letterbook*, 27.
28. EL to Miss B., May 1743, *Letterbook*, 62.

29. EL to Charles Pinckney, February 6, 1741, *Letterbook*, 12.

30. ELP to Gov. George Lucas, ca. 1745, quoted in Marvin R. Zahniser, *Charles Cotesworth Pinckney: Founding Father* (Chapel Hill: University of North Carolina Press, 1967), 8.

31. ELP to Mary W. Wragg [?], May 20, 1753, *Letterbook*, 75.

32. ELP to Charles and Thomas Pinckney, August 1758, *Letterbook*, 94–95.

33. ELP to Mr. Keate, February 1762, *Letterbook*, 181.

34. ELP to Charles Pinckney, February 7, 1761, *Letterbook*, 158–59; ELP to Charles Pinckney, April 15, 1761, *Letterbook*, 167.

35. Edward Rutledge to Arthur Middleton, February 26, 1782, quoted in Zahniser, *Charles Cotesworth Pinckney*, 73.

36. ELP to Daniel Horry Jr., April 16, 1782, in Elise Pinckney, ed., "Letters of Eliza Lucas Pinckney, 1768–1782," *South Carolina Historical Magazine* 76 (1975): 167.

Suggested Readings

Baskett, Sam S. "Eliza Lucas Pinckney: Portrait of an Eighteenth Century American." *South Carolina Historical Magazine* 72 (1971): 207–19.

Chaplin, Joyce E. *An Anxious Pursuit: Agricultural Innovation and Modernity in the Lower South, 1730–1815.* Chapel Hill: University of North Carolina Press, 1993.

Coon, David L. "Eliza Lucas Pinckney and the Reintroduction of Indigo Cultivation in South Carolina." *Journal of Southern History* 42 (1976): 61–76.

Kerber, Linda. *Women of the Republic: Intellect and Ideology in Revolutionary America.* Chapel Hill: University of North Carolina Press, 1980.

Pinckney, Elise, ed. *The Letterbook of Eliza Lucas Pinckney, 1739–1762.* Chapel Hill: University of North Carolina Press, 1972.

———. "Letters of Eliza Lucas Pinckney, 1768–1782." *South Carolina Historical Magazine* 76 (1975): 143–70.

Ravenel, Harriott H. *Eliza Pinckney.* New York: Scribner's, 1896.

Woloch, Nancy. "Eliza Pinckney and Republican Motherhood." In *Women and the American Experience*, 51–64. New York: Alfred A. Knopf, 1984.

Zahniser, Marvin R. *Charles Cotesworth Pinckney: Founding Father.* Chapel Hill: University of North Carolina Press, 1967.

3

William McIntosh
The Evolution of a Creek National Idea

Michael D. Green

When the words "the South" are mentioned, the popular imagination likely forms an image of a place peopled by blacks and whites. But before either of those groups walked the region, another population lived there for thousands of years. American Indians left their imprint on the South for centuries. Exactly when the first human stepped on the land called the South is unknown to history, but that action began the process of habitation that continues today.

For thousands of summers, American Indians hunted and fished; over time they developed an agricultural base and expanded trade routes. Some groups built sizable towns, significant earthen pyramids, and massive burial mounds. Dominant tribes rose and fell; commerce ebbed and flowed; wars sprang up and died out. But then the greatest change came, when new groups intruded into that world.

The first legacy of European contact was disease. Great epidemics depopulated Indian towns and villages, and estimated death tolls range as high as 80 percent. The "Great Dying" was a catastrophe of such proportions that nothing would again be the same. By the time traders and then settlers made contact in that middle ground between cultures, the Indian population represented a very different one than had been there only decades before. A revolution in ethnic identities had emerged, and tribes such as the Cherokee, Chickasaw, Choctaw, Creek, and Seminole faced the European colonials.

Indians struggled to determine their place in this new cultural and economic world. Missionaries sought their conversion, whiskey sellers encouraged their addiction, and military men from different parts of Europe wanted their firepower. Internally, tribal nations debated whether their future should include accommodation, assimilation, or rejection of the white man's ways.

Michael D. Green tells of one of those struggles, among the Creeks. He shows how differing concepts of governance within that nation evolved and grew bitter. After that story ended, the Indian saga would include the lengthy guerrilla-style Second Seminole War in Florida from 1835 to 1842, and the deadly "Trail of Tears" of 1830–1838, where disease and scarcity resulted in distress and death before Oklahoma was reached. Yet in the twentieth and twenty-first centuries, victories would be won for the Native American cause in a struggle that still continues.

Michael D. Green is author of numerous articles on Native American history and has written *The Creeks* (1990) and *The Politics of Indian Removal* (1982). Coauthor of *The Cherokee Removal* (1995) and *The Columbia Guide to American Indians of the Southeast* (2001), he is professor of American studies at the University of North Carolina, Chapel Hill.

Nationalism and centralized government, at least as Europeans understood them, were foreign to the cultures of native North America. But the challenges presented by aggressive European and American neighbors forced many Indian tribes to adapt their traditional institutions of politics and government in order to resist and survive. For the Creek Indians of the southeastern United States, nationalism and centralized government represented such adaptations. The execution of William McIntosh for "treason" in 1825 is the dramatic evidence of Creek political change.

By noon on the first day of May 1825, William McIntosh, fifth-ranked chief of the Creek Nation, commanding officer of the Creek police force (called Lawmenders), and former commander and major general of the Creek auxiliaries in the army of Andrew Jackson, lay dead in the yard of his Chattahoochee River plantation. Behind him his two-story house was a pile of smoldering ashes. The Georgia press heralded McIntosh as a fallen martyr, Georgia governor George M. Troup pledged to avenge the slain hero, even if it meant an invasion by the state militia, and historians ever since have used his murder to document nearly everything from savage blood lust to pitiful primitivism to intense political factionalism. Politicians, journalists, and scholars cried "bloody assassination" and "foul murder," but the Creek National Council, which ordered McIntosh's death, called it the legal execution of a criminal who had violated council law and betrayed his nation for money.

Students of Creek political history have tried to understand how the Creeks modified their legal and governmental institutions in the early nineteenth century in order to respond more effectively to the intense pressures from outside to give up their lands and move west of the Mississippi River. That research has inexorably led to McIntosh, his execution, and the justification offered by Creek leaders to explain what they had done. In short, William McIntosh's dead body, lying riddled with bullets in the grass, can tell us something extremely important about how the Creek conception of nation, government, and law evolved.

William McIntosh. From Thomas L. McKenney and James Hall, *History of the Indian Tribes of North America, with Biographical Sketches and Anecdotes of the Principal Chiefs* (Philadelphia: D. Rice and J. G. Clark, 1842–1844), opposite p. 129. *Courtesy of the Rare Book Collection, University of North Carolina, Chapel Hill*

The decision to execute McIntosh was more important than the execution itself. The scholarly, as well as popular, perception of Indians has long been that they were stubbornly conservative, their cultures were brittle and static, and their refusal to change in response to new circumstances was virtually absolute. Nothing could be further from the truth.

The story of William McIntosh and his execution provides a powerful example of the kind of creative adaptation that really characterizes Native American history. It illustrates how Creek leaders took foreign concepts of government and nation and refashioned them to serve their unique purposes.

Ancestors of the Creeks dwelt in the Southeast centuries before any Europeans came. They were a culturally, linguistically, and historically mixed people who identified themselves as members of a large number, perhaps as many as fifty, of separate and distinct autonomous tribal groups. Legends tell of the coming together of the four original tribes into a kind of military alliance, of the eastward march of conquest of these allies, and of the absorption into the alliance of both conquered tribes and refugee groups from elsewhere seeking security in numbers. More recent scholarly analysis suggests that their roots lay in the Mississippian cultural tradition that dominated the Southeast from the ninth to the sixteenth centuries. Marked by hierarchical political and ranked social organizations, the Mississippian chiefdoms had developed a complex belief system that linked their chiefs to the power of the sun and had constructed ceremonial centers around large, flat-topped mounds. Politically fragile, Mississippian chiefdoms rose and fell with sometimes surprising speed, but the explorations of Hernando de Soto and other Spaniards in the sixteenth century, and the foreign diseases they carried, killed both staggering numbers of people and the cultural tradition that they had developed. Straggling refugees, survivors of the devastation, formed new arrangements. Many of the southern tribes, including the Creeks, emerged from them. Prior to the late eighteenth century, the growing collection of tribes, called by English-speaking observers the Creek Confederacy, was characterized by tribal autonomy with intertribal cooperation limited to the normal functions of an alliance system.[1]

Increasingly intimate relations with the English, Spaniards, and French during the eighteenth century brought about at least one significant political alteration. Representatives from the allied tribes (called towns in the ethnographic literature) began meeting more frequently and formally to make foreign policy decisions collectively. These decisions were not binding—autonomous allied towns were free to pursue their own self-interests—and the executive leadership that Europeans thought they saw could best be described as only a modification of the traditional political relations between the towns. But nevertheless the Confederacy had shaped a council. It was important because it provided a more or less regular forum for intertown communication and consultation within the Confederacy, thereby systematizing an identity that transcended the towns.

There is no evidence that this council concerned itself with the domestic affairs of the allies. Each town governed itself with a council of civil and war chiefs, old and honored men, and various other officials. Theirs was a rule of law, but it was customary law enforced by social pressure and kinship groups—clans. Among other things, clans protected the welfare of their members and guided and taught their young. Clansmen avenged wrongs done their kin, thereby preserving social order. And the clans regulated the use of land, all of which was communally owned. To the Creeks, law was interpersonal relations, government's primary task was to settle disputes, and order was the chief social good.[2]

During the eighteenth century, a small but growing number of Europeans, mostly Scotsmen and Englishmen, entered the Creek country. Primarily traders, they settled in, married high-placed Creek women, and fathered children who grew up with the cultures of both parents. Alexander McGillivray was the son of such a union. Educated in Charleston and Savannah before the American Revolution, Tory McGillivray served as a British agent among the Creeks during the war. In the first decade of peace, until his death in 1793, he emerged as an enormously influential and innovative Creek leader. His diplomatic legerdemain in the Southeast is well known but his role as a Creek nationalist and political revolutionary is less well understood. McGillivray believed that hostile and dangerous powers surrounded the Creeks and put their survival as a free and independent people in jeopardy. But he also believed that their survival was possible if they followed his prescription for change. They needed, he thought, a sense of national identity that transcended town autonomy and a centralized national government that could formulate domestic as well as foreign policy, enact and execute laws, and maintain political discipline and command universal loyalty as well as preserve social order.

Eneah Miko (Fat King) and Tallassee Miko (Tame King), chiefs of two of the allied towns, represented two of McGillivray's most relentless opponents. They showed their resistance to his revolutionary ideas in various ways, including their agreement to three separate land cession treaties with Georgia in the 1780s. McGillivray was outraged by their willingness to deal independently with Georgia and part with large portions of the Creek land base, but he could do nothing. "They have long been in the American interest," he complained, "forwarding their

Views against this Country, on which account I lament that our Customs, (unlike those of Civilized people) Wont permit us to treat [them] as traitors by giving them the usual punishment."[3]

McGillivray's charge that Eneah Miko and Tallassee Miko were traitors working in the "American interest" arose from the sale of lands claimed by Cusseta and Tallassee, the towns of the two chiefs. McGillivray argued that the lands in question rightfully belonged not to those two towns but instead to the Creek Nation collectively. In his book *Imagined Communities*, political scientist Benedict Anderson defines a nation as "an imagined political community." It is imagined, Anderson says, "because the members of even the smallest nation will never know most of their fellow-members, meet them, or even hear of them, yet in the minds of each lives the image of their communion." Eneah Miko and Tallassee Miko could imagine their own tribal political communities; they could not imagine one that embraced all the towns of the alliance and incorporated all the lands claimed by each as a Creek national domain. McGillivray argued for just such a national idea. He imagined a political community that encompassed all the towns of the confederacy, and more, he imagined the emergence of a government and a body of law that would give that community the strength to defend itself in a world filled with aggressive enemies.[4]

The act for which William McIntosh was executed in 1825 was identical to what Eneah Miko and Tallassee Miko got away with three times in the 1780s. But between the 1780s and the 1820s many Creeks had begun to "imagine" a nation. Federal policy initiated the imagining. U.S. Indian Agent Benjamin Hawkins believed that a centralized Creek government under his influence would enhance his efforts to transform the Creeks into "civilized," market-oriented plow farmers who could one day be assimilated into American society. He designed a national council popularly elected from electoral districts that would enact laws for the nation. To enforce the laws, Hawkins encouraged the development of a national police force, called Lawmenders because they repaired laws that had been broken. Hawkins convinced reluctant chiefs to accept the innovations by arguing that if the Creek government did not punish lawbreakers, especially horse thieves and murderers, the United States would hold the entire nation responsible. Rather than unite the Creek Nation, however, Hawkins's idea of a centralized government exacerbated existing factional divisions. But two important Creek towns, Tuckabatchee and Coweta, supported the scheme.[5]

William McIntosh was a Coweta. Born in the mid-1770s, he was the son of William McIntosh, a trader born in Georgia and an officer in a Loyalist Georgia regiment during the Revolution, and a Creek woman, perhaps named Senoia, of the Wind clan. At war's end, McIntosh's father left the Creek Nation and settled near Darien, Georgia, where he married and raised a family. McIntosh family legend claims that he maintained contact with his Creek family, which would explain how William McIntosh grew up in Coweta as a bicultural and bilingual young man.

The first documented evidence of McIntosh occurs in 1797, when he sold beef worth twelve dollars to Benjamin Hawkins. McIntosh returns to the record in 1805. In that year he was one of six Creek chiefs sent to Washington to negotiate the sale of a strip of land between the Oconee and Ocmulgee Rivers. He made the principal reply to President Thomas Jefferson and his was the second signature on the treaty document. The Creeks had a history of elevating young men with special skills, like literacy in English, into positions of prominence usually reserved for elders. Like McGillivray before him, McIntosh seems to have been similarly singled out. By the end of the decade, McIntosh commanded the Lawmenders, and during the Creek civil war of 1811–1814 he played a significant role as a supporter of the group that embraced Hawkins's efforts to "civilize" the Creeks. After the war, McIntosh led a force of Creek warriors in alliance with General Andrew Jackson during the First Seminole War. At that time, Jackson appointed McIntosh a major general.[6]

The Creek civil war was complicated, with many causes and complex divisions, but cultural questions lay at its heart. Many Creeks had responded to the "civilization" program administered by Hawkins by adopting various of its elements. Market values, an interest in the accumulation of property, even selfishness at the expense of community well-being became important to some. Hawkins's efforts to centralize the nation's government went along with these new economic interests. A growing body of Creeks concluded, however, that American cultural influences, accompanied by domestic political and economic corruption, threatened the nation's future. The result was that cultural conservatives, variously called "nativists" and "fundamentalists" by recent scholars, attempted a forceful reorganization of Creek life. American interference in this civil conflict transformed it. American armies and allied Creek opponents of the "nativist" cause destroyed the power of the conservatives, at the time called "Red Sticks," but at the price of the devastation of the nation. McIntosh's role as the leader of the allied Creek warriors guaranteed that at war's end he would assume a powerful leadership position in the nation.[7]

By 1820, McIntosh was clearly the best-known Creek in the United States. His exploits with Jackson had won him military honors. But he had also won the applause of Georgians. In 1818 he was guest of honor at a public dinner hosted by the citizens of Augusta. According to press coverage, he was "prepossessing . . . dignified . . . entirely devoid of the wild, vacant, unmeaning stare of the savage. . . . We have seen him in the bosom of the forest, surrounded by a band of wild and ungovernable savages—we have seen him too, in the drawing room in the civilized walks of life, receiving that meed of approbation which his services so justly merit. In each situation we found him the same, easy and unconstrained in his address, and uniform in his conduct."[8] This reporter unwittingly identified what made McIntosh invaluable to the Creeks. Comfortable in American society, at ease with American cultural values, and articulate in English, he represented what many Creeks had come to believe was the future. His wisdom, judgment, and experience could guide the Creeks there.

During the decade between the end of the Creek civil war and his death, McIntosh occupied some of the most important political posts in the nation. A citizen of Coweta, he became one of its spokesmen in the council and held the important position of council speaker. The mouthpiece of the chiefs, the speaker held enormous responsibility. He explained council decisions, spoke for the chiefs in diplomatic conferences, and served as the voice of the Creek National Council to the outside world. Three times between January 1817 and January 1820 McIntosh led delegations of Creek chiefs to Washington on official business with the government. In 1818 and again during the winter of 1820–1821 he was a principal in treaties of land cession negotiated in the nation.

McIntosh also became deeply involved in business. He opened at least one trading post that employed both Creek and American agents and traders, developed an inn at a mineral spring of local repute on a main road through Georgia, and built a plantation staffed by one hundred slaves on the banks of the Chattahoochee River, the site of one of his ferries across that river. A partnership with David B. Mitchell, former governor of Georgia and Creek agent between 1817 and 1821, smoothed the way for McIntosh's ambitions and opened a host of additional possibilities, many of which involved swindling the Creek people out of much of the income gained from land sales.[9]

It is not clear how much of Hawkins's governmental reforms actually came into being. There is no evidence that the Creeks ever divided their nation into electoral districts for the purpose of choosing delegates to the National Council. But the police force of Lawmenders survived and gained substantial influence. Hawkins almost certainly also encouraged the council to draft a written law code. When it began to do so is unknown, but in 1818 the chiefs mailed a copy of their code to Washington, perhaps as evidence of their movement toward "civilized" government. The first five laws in the code undermined traditional legal forms by outlawing clan vengeance for murder. No longer could the clan of the victim claim the life of any member of the clan of the perpetrator. Rather, only the killer could be punished, and only by the Lawmenders. In other words, the code defined individual guilt and asserted the right of a national institution to administer justice. A powerful centralist impulse, the code gave government the responsibility to protect the lives of its citizens. The balance of the laws related to the protection of personal property rights. This emphasis indicates that accumulating and securing personal property had become important and that those with property interests looked to government to intervene on their behalf in its defense.[10] Clearly, many in the nation believed that a powerful and centralized government benefited their interests.

McIntosh was intimately involved in the drafting of this code. An additional law, not included in the code sent to Washington but reputedly enacted at the same time, defined the land within the boundaries of the Creek Nation as a tribal domain that could be sold only by the National Council. Punishment for the violation of the law was death. This change reversed the claim, cited by Eneah Miko and Tallassee Miko in the 1780s, that the many autonomous towns of the nation had control over the land they used. By asserting a national right to all the land, the council claimed authority as a government to act in the name of the people to protect and defend national territory. As speaker of the National Council, McIntosh proclaimed the law against land sales. His duty as commanding officer of the Lawmenders was to execute it.[11]

In addition to his other public responsibilities, McIntosh served as an ambassador to the Cherokees. He attended meetings of the Cherokee National Council and participated freely in discussions. In October 1823 the Cherokees agreed to entertain a delegation of government commissioners sent by President James Monroe to arrange for the purchase of some Cherokee land. David Meriwether and Duncan Campbell, Georgians known to McIntosh, headed the commission. They could get nowhere with the Cherokees, who refused to sell any land. With the talks on the verge of breaking down, McIntosh arrived. Immediately he began to argue in favor of the sale and in private offered bribes of several thousand dollars to key Cherokee leaders. When asked to explain himself, McIntosh told the Cherokees that Commissioners Meriwether and Campbell authorized the bribes. He also told how he had accepted bribes in the past for selling Creek lands. The Cherokees threw McIntosh out of the councilhouse and wrote to the Creek chiefs warning that "you as Brothers [should] keep a strict watch over his conduct, or if you do not he will ruin your Nation."[12] McIntosh rode his horse to death in his haste to get home safely.

Under suspicion, McIntosh tried to regain his standing in the Creek Nation by posing as champion of the Creek national domain. In a particularly dramatic incident at a ball game at Coweta in August 1824, he climbed into the bed of a wagon, spread his feet, and shouted: "Any man who should offer to sell the first bit of land as large as that between [my] feet, should die by the law; the National Council [has] made the law, and a man who violates it should die by the law."[13] The timing of McIntosh's pronouncement was crucial. One month before, President Monroe had appointed the same Meriwether and Campbell to convince the Creeks to sell all their land located within the borders claimed by Georgia and agree to move west of the Mississippi.

The Creek National Council took seriously the warning of the Cherokees. The chiefs knew that the federal government would ask again for land and they recognized the danger McIntosh represented. Meeting at Tuckabatchee in May 1824, in McIntosh's absence, they drafted a policy statement that affirmed the law against unauthorized land sales. "On no account whatever will we consent to sell one foot of our land, neither by exchange or otherwise," they announced. "We have a great many chiefs and head men but, be they ever so great, they must all abide by the laws. We have guns and ropes: and if any of our people break these laws, those guns and ropes are to be their end." Five months later, having learned about the appointment of Meriwether and Campbell, the chiefs prepared a second document. Drafted and signed in the house of William Walker, an agency official, this "Law of Pole Cat Springs" affirmed the law prohibiting unauthorized land sales and announced: "We deem it impolitic and contrary to the true interest of this nation to dispose of any more of our country."[14] The chiefs ordered that both of these documents be published in the local newspapers. Together, they stood as the will of the council and represented an unmistakable assertion of centralized council control over the Creek national domain.

Meriwether and Campbell arrived at Broken Arrow, the Creek town designated as the site for the negotiations, in late November 1824. Having seen the papers, they had read the Tuckabatchee and Pole Cat Springs statements and knew the Creek National Council was united against their demands. Both the Georgians were well placed in state politics and convinced that the continued growth and prosperity of their state depended on the expulsion of the Indians. Fearing failure, they arrived prepared to be generous with bribe money. Indeed, throughout the talks, relatives and friends of the commissioners offered bribes to virtually everyone they saw who might have some influence on the outcome.

Talks lasted more than a week, but after the second day the outcome was clear. The Creek chiefs rebutted every argument, citing treaty guarantees to support their right to refuse to sell, and no one was willing to suggest that removal might be acceptable. When Meriwether and Campbell tried to sweeten the deal with more money, Opothle Yoholo, the speaker for national chief Big Warrior, announced that "he would not take a house full of money for his interest in the land."

Private talks, held in the middle of the night in the woods, supplemented these negotiations. In these sessions, Meriwether, Campbell, and McIntosh hammered out a deal. McIntosh had made it clear long before that he could be bribed, and the Georgians were willing to pay. Furthermore, McIntosh was embittered because the council chiefs learned of his private conversations and "broke" him as their speaker. But McIntosh would say nothing in public. Fearful of the law, he knew that if he signed a treaty of cession in violation of the will of the council, he would forfeit his life. Thus, Meriwether and Campbell closed the negotiations and made preparations for a second meeting, to be held at McIntosh's Indian Springs tavern some sixty miles outside the Creek Nation in Georgia. There, McIntosh believed, he would be safe from Creek law.[15]

Negotiations began at Indian Springs on February 10, 1825. Over four hundred council chiefs, their minds unchanged, attended. The proposal Meriwether and Campbell presented included an exchange of most of the Creek national domain for a tract of similar size in the West plus a payment of $500,000 for abandoned improvements and the costs for transporting the Creeks to their new homeland. Through Opothle Yoholo, the council speaker, the chiefs explained that they had no authority to sell the land. They recognized the right of individual Creeks to move west if they desired, but they denied such persons the right to sell their interests in the land they left behind. This conversation lasted two days, at the end of which the highest-ranking council chiefs left Indian Springs and returned home. Opothle Yoholo stayed behind and on February 12 heard the treaty, drafted in secret by the Georgians and McIntosh, read to the crowd. As McIntosh stepped to the table to sign it, Opothle Yoholo approached him and said: "My friend, you are about to sell our country; I now warn you of your danger." Fifty-one other men signed.[16] Later investigation revealed that except for McIntosh, fifth-ranked chief of the nation, none of the signers had political stature. Despite protests from the National Council and John Crowell, the Creek agent, that the treaty was a fraud signed without council authorization by men who had no standing, the U.S. Senate ratified it and on March 7, President John Quincy Adams proclaimed the Treaty of Indian Springs the law of the land.[17]

Between mid-February and late March 1825 the council met twice to discuss what had happened. The law was clear and McIntosh was obviously guilty of its violation, but he was also a powerful man, a respected chief, and the darling of influential Georgians. Depending on the protests sent to Washington and assuming a treaty so obviously fraudulent would never be ratified, they stripped McIntosh of his rank and offices and deferred a decision on his crime.

Georgia governor Troup, McIntosh's cousin, was overjoyed by the treaty. It not only assured his reelection, but it also paved the way for his state's future growth and prosperity. But an impatient Troup wanted to ignore the stipulation that gave the Creeks eighteen months to vacate the land and sought to send in men immediately to survey it. He pressured McIntosh to approve his scheme, which brought the hapless chief once again to the attention of the National Council, now aware that the Senate had ratified the treaty. Under its terms, they had to be out of the country by September 1, 1826.

On April 19, 1825, Agent Crowell called the council together to receive the first payment authorized by the treaty. The chiefs refused to accept the cash. They had sold no land, they explained. If they took the money, it would look as if they had. Then they ejected Crowell from the councilhouse and had a long private meeting. In the end, they passed the death sentence on McIntosh, Etomme Tustunnuggee, and Samuel and Benjamin Hawkins, sons-in-law of McIntosh. All had signed the treaty. The other forty-eight signers, too insignificant to notice, they forgave. The council then authorized the creation of a special posse of Lawmenders, composed of warriors from throughout the nation and representing all the clans, under the command of Menawa, the council chief from Okfuskee, to carry out the sentence.

On the night of April 30–May 1, 1825, McIntosh and Etomme Tustunnuggee were at McIntosh's Lokcha Talofa (Acorn Town) plantation on the banks of the Chattahoochee River in what is now Carroll County, Georgia. Like most southern plantations, it resembled a village. Sprawled around the big two-story house was a guesthouse for travelers, various outbuildings, cabins for one hundred slaves, and a public ferry across the river. Menawa and the Lawmenders, variously numbered at from 120 to 200 men, arrived after dark and surrounded the place. They set fire to an outbuilding to light the yard, then fired the house to force out its occupants. Two of McIntosh's wives and their children escaped. McIntosh and Etomme Tustunnuggee appeared at the doorway. Gunfire downed Etomme Tustunnuggee. McIntosh ran upstairs and opened fire from a second-story window. As the flames advanced, he retreated to the first floor, threw open the door, and fell to a volley from the Lawmenders, who ran to the porch, dragged McIntosh into the yard, and stabbed and shot his body for several minutes. Then, according to some accounts, one of them scalped him. If true, it was to show the council that the deed had been accomplished. The repeated stabbings and shootings were probably done to involve everybody, thus spreading the act to all and denying McIntosh's Wind clan kin a claim to seek vengeance on individuals. After the execution, the Lawmenders confiscated McIntosh's slaves, livestock, and valuables, burned his orchard and farm equipment, and generally destroyed the place. When they learned that McIntosh was dead, another group of Lawmenders who had captured Sam Hawkins hanged him. They later wounded Ben Hawkins, but he escaped.[18]

Several threads tie this story together: Americans thought of the allied towns as a nation and held it politically responsible for the actions of its members, no matter to which town they belonged; U.S. and Creek diplomats in a series of treaties beginning in 1790 defined the nation with fixed and precise boundaries; and frontierspeople and their political agents struggled relentlessly to get rid of the Creeks and possess the lands within those bounds. The Creeks wove these threads into an ideological fabric of response. If the Americans considered the allies a nation responsible for the actions of its citizens, then the Creeks needed a national government that could control, through law, such actions. If the nation had specific boundaries defined in the treaties, then its government must possess the power to defend them. And if the Americans aggressed against the land and people of the nation, then the government could never conceive of the two as separate.

The evolution of this ideology was both more and less complicated than it seems, for these were as much mutations of old ideas as they were radical new concepts. But in the form it took, this ideology of resistance was a conscious response to outside threats and represents the Creek version of the virtually universal phenomenon of Native adaptation of European ideas to serve their own particular needs.

Rennard Strickland documents a somewhat similar history of the Cherokees. The written code of 1818 was like the Cherokee codes described by Strickland in that they rejected the right of the clans to exact vengeance and protected the rights of private property in goods, livestock, slaves, and improvements to the land. Further, they provided for a police force to execute the laws outside the traditional framework of the clans. This wording was crucial, because the codes also defined the difference between accidental death and murder, excused the former from the certainty of clan vengeance, and made the latter punishable by the police rather than by the clan kin of the victim. In other words, the codes asserted a theory of law that aimed to achieve the traditional goal of maintaining social order but through governmental action rather than through the workings of the ancient kinship network of the clans.

As Strickland argues for the Cherokees, the driving force behind these changes in Creek law came from the growing group of bicultural people. The significance of their actions goes far beyond their economic interests, however. In drafting these laws, they presented traditional Creeks with a European theory of interventionist national government possessed with the power to enforce national law. It was a short step further to promulgate the law that forbade, on pain of death, any sale of Creek lands to the United States without the prior authorization of the National Council. While not written into the 1818 code, this law was repeatedly affirmed in public gatherings and by 1825 council chiefs called it an old and well-known law.[19]

The meaning of the law seems clear. Benedict Anderson's definition of "nation" focused on people, but the Creeks conceived of their nation differently. It meant the people, to be sure, but it also embraced the land. Those who found McGillivray's imagination compelling in the

1820s could not conceive of the Creek Nation as a people distinct from the land. In their view, the nation could not exist without the land. A threat to the land was a threat to the nation; to safeguard the land was to safeguard the nation. Without saying so specifically, the law McIntosh violated was a treason law—one drawn to throw up a legal barrier around the nation—and in deciding to execute the law by executing McIntosh the National Council judged him a traitor. The English law of treason evolved in medieval times from a crime against the king to a crime against the kingdom. Among the Creeks, the history was different, but the result was the same. The nation was the kingdom and the land was the nation's most tangible reality.

This process had a system to it. "The great revolutionary political accomplishment of complex societies was the creation of a form of social cohesion other than kinship," wrote sociologist Eli Sagan in his *At the Dawn of Tyranny.*[20] A defining characteristic of kinship societies is communal land ownership. When Anderson wrote of an "imagined community," he described kinship transcended. Eneah Miko and Tallassee Miko functioned within traditional kinship societies that were small, circumscribed, and autonomous. Alexander McGillivray's protonationalist activities and the codes that substituted law and police for clan retaliation delivered heavy blows to the clan system and threatened the survival of kinship society. The irony of the Creek story, where it diverges from Sagan's model, is that the Creek National Council asserted Creek nationhood in order to preserve intact the Creek national domain. The council's theory of nationhood extended the kinship society model of communal ownership of land by redefining the community as the nation. The council imagined a community by extending the concept of kinship to embrace nation. From this perspective, the treason law was little more than the ancient principle of clan retaliation writ large.

William McIntosh was well acquainted with this treason law. He had proclaimed it in public himself, many times, and was fully aware of the danger he faced when he and a small group of associates signed, against the clearly stated orders of the National Council, the Treaty of Indian Springs. Why he engineered the deal to dispose of approximately 80 percent of the Creeks' national domain is not clear. Some believe he read the future, saw no hope for the survival of the Creek Nation in the Southeast, and agreed to the deportation as being in the best interests of his people. Others argue that he was handsomely bribed to betray his countrymen. Evidence supports both interpretations. In any event, he took elaborate precautions to safeguard his life and was no doubt chagrined to learn he had failed.

So we end where we began, with the bloody corpse of William McIntosh, and we ask it to tell us what happened. It would say, surely, that treason is risky business. But it would also say that treason is impossible if there is no nation to betray. Treason cannot exist if there is no government to define it, outlaw it, and prescribe a punishment for it. And treason cannot be dangerous if that government lacks the power to punish. The corpse of McIntosh would tell us, in other words, that a process of adaptation had occurred in which the Creeks blended tradition and innovation to imagine a nation with a central government with a plan and a will to survive. It might also tell us that at that moment it seemed to be working quite well.

Notes

1. Michael D. Green, *The Politics of Indian Removal: Creek Government and Society in Crisis* (Lincoln: University of Nebraska Press, 1982), 96–97. Vernon James Knight, "The Formation of the Creeks," in Charles Hudson and Carmen Chaves Tesser, eds., *The Forgotten Centuries: Indians and Europeans in the American South, 1521–1704* (Athens: University of Georgia Press, 1994), 373–92, discusses the emergence of the Creek Confederacy from the ashes of the Mississippian cultural tradition.

2. Green, *Politics of Indian Removal*, 4–16.

3. Michael D. Green, "Alexander McGillivray," in R. David Edmunds, ed., *American Indian Leaders: Studies in Diversity* (Lincoln: University of Nebraska Press, 1980), 41–63; Alexander McGillivray to Vicente Manuel de Zespedes, November 15, 1786, in John W. Caughey, *McGillivray of the Creeks* (Norman: University of Oklahoma Press, 1938), 139.

4. Benedict Anderson, *Imagined Communities: Reflections on the Origins and Spread of Nationalism* (London: Verso, 1983), 15.

5. Benjamin Hawkins to Thomas Jefferson, March 1, 1801, in C. L. Grant, ed., *Letters, Journals, and Writings of Benjamin Hawkins*, 2 vols. (Savannah, GA: Beehive Press, 1980), 1:351–52; Duane Champagne, *Social Order and Political Change: Constitutional Governments among the Cherokee, the Choctaw, the Chickasaw, and the Creek* (Stanford, CA: Stanford University Press, 1992), 113–17.

6. James C. Bonner, "Tustunugee Hutkee and Creek Factionalism on the Georgia-Alabama Frontier," *Alabama Review* 10 (1957): 111–25; Bonner, "William McIntosh," in Horace Montgomery, ed., *Georgians in Profile: Historical Essays in Honor of Ellis Merton Coulter* (Athens: University of Georgia Press, 1958), 114–43.

7. For the Creek civil war see H. S. Halbert and T. H. Ball, *The Creek War of 1813 and 1814* (Chicago, IL: Donohue and Henneberry, 1895; reprint Tuscaloosa: University of Alabama Press, 1969); Joel W. Martin, *Sacred Revolt: The Muskogees' Struggle for a New World* (Boston, MA: Beacon Press, 1991). Gregory Evans Dowd, *A Spirited Resistance: The North American Indian Struggle for Unity, 1745–1815* (Baltimore, MD:

Johns Hopkins University Press, 1992), calls the Red Sticks "nativists." Champagne, *Social Order and Political Change,* calls them "fundamentalists."

8. *Niles' Weekly Register* 15 (November 7, 1818): 176.

9. Green, *Politics of Indian Removal,* 56–59.

10. Records of the Secretary of War Relating to Indian Affairs, Letters Received, 1800–1823, "Laws of the Creek Nation Proclaimed at Broken Arrow," June 12, 1818, Microcopy M271, 2:772–75, RG 75, National Archives (hereafter NA).

11. Green, *Politics of Indian Removal,* 74–75.

12. U.S. House, William McIntosh to John Ross, October 21, 1823, 19th Cong., 2d Sess., H.Rept. 98, serial 161, 638–39; Office of Indian Affairs, Letters Received, Creek Agency, Path Killer and Cherokee National Council to Big Warrior and Little Prince, October 24, 1823, Microcopy M234, 219:1082–85, RG 75, NA.

13. U.S. House, *Affidavit of William Lott,* June 28, 1825, 19th Cong., 2d sess., H. Rept. 98, serial 161, 432.

14. Published in the local papers, *Niles' Weekly Register* picked them up and published them nationally on December 4, 1824.

15. U.S. House, *Journal of the Proceedings of the Commissioners Appointed to Treat with the Creek Indians,* July 16–December 18, 1824, 19th Cong., 2d sess., H.Rept. 98, serial 161, 98–113.

16. U.S. House, *Proceedings of the Negotiations at Indian Springs,* February 12, 1825, ibid., 130; *Testimony of Thomas Triplett,* July 20, 1825, ibid., 392.

17. Green, *Politics of Indian Removal,* 78–89.

18. Ibid., 89–97.

19. Rennard Strickland, *Fire and the Spirits: Cherokee Law from Clan to Court* (Norman: University of Oklahoma Press, 1975), especially 77–102. A revised version of the Creek codes compiled in 1825 has been published in Antonio J. Waring, ed., *Laws of the Creek Nation,* University of Georgia Libraries Miscellanea Publications No. 1 (Athens: University of Georgia Press, 1960). See Waring's "Introduction," 5–6, for a discussion of the history of the law prohibiting land sales. Strickland, *Fire and the Spirits,* 52, 77–78, discusses a similar policy enacted by the Cherokees.

20. Eli Sagan, *At the Dawn of Tyranny: The Origins of Individualism, Political Oppression, and the State* (New York: Alfred A. Knopf, 1985), 225.

Suggested Readings

Michael D. Green, *The Creeks, A Critical Bibliography* (Bloomington: Indiana University Press, 1979), introduces readers to the history and literature on the Creeks. Two general histories of the Creeks are Angie Debo, *The Road to Disappearance* (Norman: University of Oklahoma Press, 1941), and Michael D. Green, *The Creeks* (New York: Chelsea House, 1990). Creek legendary history is discussed in Albert S. Gatschet, *A Migration Legend of the Creek Indians, With a Linguistic History, and Ethnographic Introduction* (Philadelphia, PA: Daniel G. Brinton, 1888). The standard ethnographic source is John Swanton, "Social Organization and Social Usages of the Indians of the Creek Confederacy," *42nd Annual Report of the United States Bureau of American Ethnology* (Washington, DC: Government Printing Office, 1928), 25–472. The best recent interpretation of the Creeks in the eighteenth century is Claudio Saunt, *A New Order of Things: Property, Power, and the Transformation of the Creek Indians, 1733–1816* (New York: Cambridge University Press, 1999). The major biographies of William McIntosh are George Chapman, *William McIntosh: A Man of Two Worlds* (Atlanta, GA: Cherokee Publishing Company, 1988), and Benjamin W. Griffith Jr., *McIntosh and Weatherford: Creek Indian Leaders* (Tuscaloosa: University of Alabama Press, 1988). The story of William McIntosh and his family is found in Harriet Turner (Porter) Corbin, *A History and Genealogy of Chief William McIntosh, Jr. and His Descendents* (Long Beach: n.p., 1967).

4

James O'Kelly
Father of Christian Fundamentalism in America

Ellen Eslinger

The role of religion in shaping the mind and actions of the American South has been pervasive. While the rough backwoods often eschewed formal religion, a certain sense of sin and piety swept across the South in the late eighteenth and early nineteenth centuries, as the evangelicalism of the Great Revival, or Second Great Awakening, was formed from southern religious streams. The republicanism of the Revolutionary era spread to religious circles and, as Ellen Eslinger demonstrates, fostered splits in established churches. The resulting antiauthoritarian tradition would continue into the present.

Out of that came what one author called "denominational diversity and religious homogeneity." New churches—the Christian, various Pentecostal groups, and others—grew from southern origins, yet at the same time the region kept an orthodox Protestant core of beliefs. By the beginning of the twenty-first century, 90 percent of white southerners identified themselves as Protestant, half of them Baptist. An evangelical Christianity stressed the Bible as the guide for beliefs and practices, emphasized individual salvation through open access to a higher being, and focused on informal, less ritualistic, methods of worship. As other parts of the country moved toward a more pluralistic, secular religion, influenced by the Social Gospel movement, the South remained the Bible Belt, a place of more fundamentalist views.

The "old-time" religion found new adherents across the nation as more people sought some sense of community and identity as words of change echoed around them. Beginning in the 1980s tent and television preachers with southern accents introduced a broader audience to the traditional part of the South's religious experience. Of course, as throughout the region's history, other elements in other churches continued to offer alternative versions of religion as well.

Dr. Eslinger looks at a person she calls the father of fundamentalism, and shows how that aspect of Christian conservatism grew out of strong republican ideals. In examining the origins of beliefs—and of religious conflicts—that still remain a part of southern life, she demonstrates how one man's efforts set the stage for a much greater mass religious movement.

Ellen Eslinger currently serves as associate professor of history at DePaul University in Chicago. In addition to numerous articles, Dr. Eslinger is the author of *Citizens of Zion: The Social Origins of Camp Meeting Revivalism* (1999).

One of the hallmark characteristics of the American South as an enduring cultural region is the prominent role of religion and, in particular, Christian fundamentalist belief. This fundamentalism has been strong and concentrated enough in recent generations to influence public policy, usually toward socially conservative ends. Almost forgotten is any memory that Christian fundamentalism in America began quite differently.

In the course of reconstituting civil government, the American Revolution led many people to consider the basic nature of human society. How could the new nation inculcate the morality and virtues necessary for sustaining a fragile republic? Christianity seemed the most obvious place to begin, not only for its religious principles but also as a model for society. Early Christian fellowship bore a remarkable, and some people believed providential, resemblance to the egalitarian and harmonious ideals of republicanism. Many religious leaders therefore believed that the New Testament could provide Americans with a social as well as a spiritual blueprint. This "Restoration Movement" proved especially strong in the southern states where the Anglican Church had previously enjoyed established status and the break with Britain was not only political but also religious.

One of the earliest expressions of the Restoration Movement occurred within Methodism, which had originated during the late colonial period as a pietistic expression of the Episcopal or Anglican Church. Initially it was unclear what effect, if any, political independence might have on religious ties with Britain. But for some American Methodists, the hierarchical institutional structure, headed by John Wesley in Britain and administered through his appointed superintendents, smacked of "ecclesiastical monarchy." If monarchy was dangerous in civil government, was it any less so in religious government? Although the man who emerged as American Methodism's first national leader, Bishop Francis Asbury, seemed a person of unimpeachable character—dedicated and able—some American Methodists worried that he perhaps exercised too much power. The most serious challenge to Asbury's growing authority came from an itinerant preacher named James O'Kelly and a small group of colleagues centered in southern Virginia along the border with North Carolina.[1]

In the nearly two centuries since O'Kelly's death in 1826, Methodism's denominational historians have usually sought to minimize the significance of the "O'Kelly Schism" in 1792, dismissing O'Kelly as disloyal and paranoid, and ultimately insignificant.[2] The schism held little interest except for its denominational significance. But scholars now studying American religious history recognize James O'Kelly's break with Methodism and his leadership in the Restoration Movement as part of an important democratizing trend in American Protestantism.[3]

James O'Kelly was born around 1735, probably in Ireland, and died in 1826 at age ninety-two. He came from modest beginnings, yet his later writings indicate that he benefited from some access to education. As a young man he settled in Surry County, Virginia, and married Elizabeth Meeks around 1760. He later relocated his family across the state line to Chatham County, North Carolina, where he is buried. Little is known about O'Kelly's life prior to his adoption of Methodism in 1774, around age forty. That this life change occurred at a mature age and was preceded by the conversion of his wife and son William suggests that O'Kelly had not previously been religiously disposed. Few other details are known about what proved to be the defining event of his life.

O'Kelly was soon traveling as an itinerant lay preacher throughout southern Virginia. He continued his work during the War for Independence, when many Methodist preachers returned to Britain or adopted pacifist positions, and by 1778 had an assignment to New Hope Circuit in North Carolina. As O'Kelly proudly attested later, he also served on two military campaigns and obtained a substitute for another. When not serving in a military capacity, O'Kelly continued to preach the Gospel, which also exposed him to personal danger. In the course of traveling as a civilian preacher in a region subject to brutal guerrilla warfare, O'Kelly was briefly captured by local Tories, and on another occasion by a contingent of the British army. Despite these potentially life-threatening encounters, he refused to deny his patriot sympathies. Methodist records show that O'Kelly was sent to Tar River Circuit in North Carolina in 1780 and over the next decade served in the neighboring circuits of Mecklenburg, Brunswick, and Sussex.[4]

James O'Kelly established a strong regional reputation during these years. Perhaps because his spiritual awakening had occurred rather late in life, O'Kelly spoke with particular urgency to all who would hear him. His ministry proved very successful among both whites and blacks. Younger preachers found him an inspiring, generous mentor. By the end of the War for Independence, the south side of the James River in

Virginia and the adjacent section of North Carolina emerged as major strongholds of Methodism, with O'Kelly as its leading voice. He did not hesitate to use his growing influence, speaking out against slavery and publishing a bold essay urging an end to it in 1788.[5]

James O'Kelly's stature was confirmed at the 1784 "Christmas Conference" in Baltimore, the meeting in which American Methodists established their separation from Anglican Methodists. He was among the first ministers selected to serve as a presiding elder. In this new position, from 1785 to 1792, O'Kelly supervised about two dozen preachers in the South District of Virginia, a region that encompassed his home and the circuits he himself had served. Francis Asbury, the acknowledged leader of the American Wesleyans, named him to the church's elite Council in 1789. These distinctions demonstrated that James O'Kelly was one of the new nation's most prominent Methodists, a member of the inner circle.[6]

O'Kelly's break with Methodism occurred in 1792, at the first quadrennial General Conference. Seeking to place a check on Francis Asbury's new powers as the American bishop, O'Kelly proposed a resolution that preachers could appeal the bishop's assignments to particular circuits before the conference, "and if the conference approve his objections, the bishop shall appoint him to a different circuit." Methodist preachers were extremely dedicated, but at times in a man's life he might have found it unduly burdensome to be sent far from family or friends. Asbury, recognizing how the motion so directly involved his own actions, absented himself, but not without a statement averring that he had always made assignments according to his best judgment as a "trembling, poor preacher," and had "never stationed a preacher through enmity, or as a punishment."[7] Most Methodist preachers would have agreed that problems occurred with rarity. O'Kelly himself had been assigned a district conveniently encompassing his home for the past decade. His resolution seems to have originated solely from a principled opposition to concentrated power in a bishop for the same fears that the new American government restricted the powers of the Executive branch.[8]

The conference members thoroughly debated O'Kelly's motion, which was quickly refined into two questions. The first was whether the bishop held the power to appoint preachers to circuits, which was answered in the affirmative. The second, whether a preacher might appeal, became the subject of a painful debate extending across two days. According to one of the preachers in attendance, John Kobler, the right to an appeal "seem to ly [*sic*] heavy on the minds of many." Numerous arguments arose both for and against. Kobler, for one, "was struck with fear that some of the brethren was rather too warm, & by the delivering their arguments, was giving way to a false zeal."[9]

Kobler was not unique in feeling that O'Kelly exaggerated the danger of placing power in the hands of Bishop Asbury. According to another preacher, "For myself, at first I did not see anything very objectionable in it; but when it came to be debated, I very much disliked the spirit of those who advocated it, and wondered at the severity in which the movers, and others who spoke in favor of it, indulged in the course of their remarks." Specifically, "Some of them said that it was a shame for a man to *accept* of such a lordship, much less to *claim* it; and that they who would submit to this absolute dominion must forfeit all claims to freedom, and ought to have their ears bored through with an awl, and to be fastened to their master's door and become slaves for life." These were harsh words for colleagues.

Observers described Asbury's defenders, by contrast, as being "more dispassionate and argumentative." They pointed out that no similar objection had ever been made to John Wesley's more extensive exercise of episcopal authority. Furthermore, permitting aggrieved preachers to appeal their annual appointment would create serious practical problems.[10] O'Kelly's simple resolution was debated for nearly two days in an earnest but ultimately futile effort to achieve consensus. When the vote was taken, "a very large majority" of preachers joined in voting down the right to appeal.[11]

O'Kelly, however, believed that he could not yield. After an agonizing night of private deliberation, he sent the conference a declaration of his withdrawal from their association. As John Kobler recorded in his private journal, O'Kelly submitted his withdrawal with "the overflowings of a ful [*sic*] heart," but was compelled by a sincere fear that Bishop Asbury was "on a stretch for power." O'Kelly's withdrawal shocked the body of ministers. According to Kobler, "tears flowed from every face." In the words of another witness, "His wound was deep, and apparently incurable."[12] As O'Kelly walked away, accompanied by a small core of preachers, most of whom had served under him in the South Virginia Conference, one Methodist colleague commented, "I was sorry to see the old man go off in that way, for I was persuaded he would not be quiet long; but he would try to be head of some party." The conference sent emissaries to plead with O'Kelly to return, but they could not prevent American Methodism's first major schism.[13]

Asbury quickly attempted to control the damage. At his behest, the General Conference agreed to allow the disaffected preachers to continue speaking from Methodist pulpits. This generous offer also created a possibility that the break would not become institutionalized and final. In addition, Asbury requested that O'Kelly's annual stipend be continued, provided he did not act to exacerbate the division. This effectively tempered the critique expressed by O'Kelly's withdrawal. O'Kelly could have used the funds, but he interpreted the offer as an insulting effort to silence him with money. Somewhat later, O'Kelly did accept a small amount of money from Asbury, but mistakenly understood it to be a gift. The Methodists capitalized on this error immediately. When word spread that O'Kelly had seemingly capitulated and was back on the Methodist payroll, he angrily returned the sum. O'Kelly and his supporters did, however, avail themselves of the Methodist pulpits.[14]

James O'Kelly's withdrawal in 1792 was the culmination of a long personal campaign to establish republican forms of church governance. He feared that the Episcopal hierarchy that Methodism had inherited from its parent church dangerously paralleled the British monarchy. Too much power in the hands of a single individual offered an invitation to eventual tyranny. O'Kelly therefore had opposed the continued influence of John Wesley, Methodism's British primary founder, as well as Asbury's desire to establish a strong position of bishop as head of the American church. He had consistently worked for broad participation in church governance and a decentralized structure at every opportunity, years before his departure from Methodism in 1792.

The first hint of James O'Kelly's readiness to challenge Methodist church authority dates to 1779, at a Methodist conference held in his home region, at Brokenback Church in Fluvanna County, Virginia. This meeting voted to disregard the well-known position held by both Wesley and Asbury and allow lay preachers to administer the sacraments. Previously, as a movement within the Anglican Episcopal Church, the Methodists had always relied upon the local clergy for baptism and the Lord's Supper. Anglican clergy were not numerous in America, however, and ordination required travel to a bishop in Britain. The lengthy war had made the issue critical, as most Episcopal clergy returned to Britain. The simplest solution was to ordain the American lay preachers. The Tory sympathies of John Wesley and the men he sent to superintend the colonial adherents made this unlikely. Believing that if God had called them to preach, He had also called them to perform the other duties of spiritual ministry, the Methodist preachers who met at Brokenback in

1779 proceeded to ordain each other. Returning to their circuits, they began administering the sacraments. Their action in effect constituted a religious declaration of independence.[15]

Despite popular pressure for access to the sacraments, the unilateral decision at Brokenback seemed precipitate to Methodist leaders elsewhere, particularly Francis Asbury, the American movement's acting head. Asbury, who had not attended the meeting, promptly called his own meeting in Baltimore where it was decided to send emissaries to insist that the southern colleagues suspend any further administration of the sacraments. Recognizing the need to avoid schism and resolve the problem through some regular, united means, Asbury proposed a full conference for the following year in Baltimore. James O'Kelly remained an "unreconciled dissenter," but agreed to let the problem be submitted to John Wesley in Britain for resolution. The ongoing war, however, delayed Wesley's reply. The Christmas Conference of 1784, where the American Methodists were established with Wesley's blessing as independent and able to conduct ordination, finally brought closure.[16] Throughout this time, as one of the older and most articulate of the Virginia preachers, O'Kelly's had been a conspicuous voice for reform. Most significant for later events, it was in the course of dealing with the ordination problem that O'Kelly began to examine the nature of church authority.

Although John Wesley had granted independence to American Methodists, he continued to be actively involved in American affairs. From the American side, the people had a great fondness and high regard for Wesley. At the Christmas Conference, the ministers had expressed their gratitude for his leadership by pledging continued submission to him in matters of church governance. When it came to specific issues, however, the Americans were not so easily controlled, especially as time went by. Thus, Wesley's appointment of Richard Whatcoat as joint superintendent with Asbury in 1786 encountered resistance. The main opposition came from James O'Kelly's Virginia Conference. It opposed Whatcoat's appointment on the grounds that it came from the "European heads" of the Methodist Church. Contributing factors were Whatcoat's youth, his newness to America, and the danger of having two executives. O'Kelly contended that the American preachers could conduct their own affairs and that if a second superintendent was indeed necessary, then they could handle the problem without interference from Wesley. Although Asbury accepted Wesley's appointment of Whatcoat, he referred the controversial matter to an upcoming conference in

Baltimore. Not only was Whatcoat rejected by a vote of the assembled preachers there, but Wesley's name was stricken from the minutes. An important point had been clarified.[17]

Further conflict surfaced in 1789, when Bishop Asbury established a ruling council of bishops and appointed presiding elders. O'Kelly was among those selected as an elder but opposed the idea of a council almost immediately because he believed the organizational design contained flaws.[18] Particularly disturbing to O'Kelly was the bishop's power to override the council's resolutions with a veto. A single man could thus resist the collective wisdom of the church's best leaders. "Instead of counsellors, we were his tools," wrote O'Kelly.[19] The arbitrary exercise of executive power by the bishop, moreover, was not a remote danger but evident almost immediately. In order to get the new plan of government approved in South Carolina, Asbury agreed to a few minor modifications. In North Carolina a different issue impeded endorsement, and Asbury entered into yet another modification. O'Kelly decried Asbury's readiness to alter the council's work, pointing out that it not only put multiple plans of church government into operation but it also demonstrated Asbury's dangerous appetite for ecclesiastical power.

O'Kelly's loud and persistent opposition troubled Francis Asbury. In his private journal, Asbury wrote that O'Kelly "makes heavy complaints of my power" and had threatened to "use his influence against me."[20] Exasperated by the entrenched, seemingly irrational opposition of O'Kelly and most of the other ministers in the South Virginia Conference, Asbury briefly expelled them all from the church.[21] This, of course, was exactly the kind of arbitrary exercise of power that O'Kelly had feared. Though Asbury soon reversed himself, O'Kelly remained disaffected and refused to participate in further meetings of Asbury's council. He also corresponded with other Methodists to explain his opposition and gain their support for a more open governance body. Asbury eventually conceded by calling the General Conference in 1792. The idea of an appointed council quietly disappeared.[22]

James O'Kelly framed all of these ecclesiastical struggles within the ideology of the American Revolution. Francis Asbury was "born and nurtured in the land of kings and bishops," wrote O'Kelly, "and that which is bred to the bone, is hard to be got out of the flesh."[23] During the war years, Asbury had been forced to leave Maryland because of his pacifist beliefs, taking up residence with Thomas White, a magistrate of Kent County, Delaware. There, too, he narrowly avoided arrest as a suspected Loyalist. O'Kelly, by contrast, had continued his ministry at considerable personal risk and did not shirk his military responsibilities. His later struggles with Asbury never centered upon theology but rather church governance. At a time when America's civil governments were characterized by a weak Executive branch for fear of political tyranny, creating a strong bishop seemed as if it might lead directly to religious tyranny. Moreover, the General Conference, although better than a council, was not elected by the church members. "Neither do they consider themselves accountable to the people, because they do not derive their legislative authority from them." O'Kelly believed that liberty, whether civil or religious, could only be "guarded, and preserved by representation," a new concept of religious liberty.[24]

O'Kelly's withdrawal in 1792 was a personal decision, but most of the preachers who had served under his leadership as presiding elder soon followed. They still regarded themselves as Methodists, however, and regretted the need to take an opposing stand. O'Kelly insisted he had "no intention of a separate party."[25] He therefore called a meeting for early 1793, at Piney Grove Meetinghouse in Chesterfield County, Virginia, to discuss the "present distress." The resulting letter to Asbury asked him to call a meeting and reopen the issue of appealing appointments. Asbury, however, claimed that he was absolutely powerless to grant their request. Thus, "the door to negotiation was shut," declared O'Kelly.[26] A second meeting, in December 1793, at Manakin Town, Virginia, considered Asbury's answer. Faced with rejection and the prospect that any further appeal would meet the same response, O'Kelly's group of about thirty preachers reluctantly decided to form a new religious body. The theology continued to be Methodist in content; they differed in the adoption of a republican governance structure. They called their new group the "Republican Methodist Church."

The process of separation generated new questions and problems, necessitating a second meeting in 1794 at Lebanon Church in Surry County, Virginia. A special point was made to open the doors to all adherents, not just preachers. Although the participants were united in principle, a satisfactory consensus for a practical yet just system of church governance proved elusive. "At length it was proposed that we should lay aside every manuscript and take the word of God as recorded in the Scriptures," recalled O'Kelly. "We were much delighted to find that the true hierarchy, or primitive church government, which came down from heaven, was a republic." Thus, according to O'Kelly, "We formed our ministers on an equality; gave the lay-members a balance of power in the legislature; and left the executive business in the church collectively."[27]

The emphasis upon Scripture not only for doctrine but also for governance led O'Kelly's group to soon gain a second name and become widely known as the "Christian Church."[28]

When James O'Kelly withdrew from the Methodist connection in 1792, his old Methodist colleagues believed that he would endeavor to defend his decision publicly. They did not have long to wait. "The mischief has begun," Asbury recorded in his private journal shortly after O'Kelly walked away from the General Conference. "Brother O'Kelly called here and vented his sorrows, and told what the General Conference had done."[29] As Devereux Jarratt, an Episcopal clergyman in Virginia who knew O'Kelly, commented at the time, "O'Kelly does great things in the divisive way and I daresay he will make Asbury's mitre set very uneasy on his head."[30] Not only was the initial impact serious, but O'Kelly continued to cause trouble. When Asbury returned to Virginia two years later in early 1794, he commented: "there is sad work with those who have left us, and who are now exerting themselves to form as strong a party as they can." He singled out O'Kelly, their ringleader.[31] The following year, O'Kelly was reportedly "now preaching through the neighborhood while multitudes from every quarter flock to hear him."[32] Methodist classes throughout Virginia and North Carolina, especially where O'Kelly had preached for nearly two decades, suffered division and loss of members. In 1796, for example, Asbury noted that the congregation at Lane's Chapel had lost twenty members, about one-third of the total.[33]

Methodist records confirm that O'Kelly's departure constituted a major setback, evident for the rest of the century.[34] The Virginia Methodists in 1793 numbered 17,605, and by 1799 this number had dropped to 13,288, white and black members. Not until 1800 did the number of Methodist adherents begin to recover. Meanwhile, an estimated thirty ministers and perhaps some 20,000 members cast their lot with O'Kelly by 1810.[35] O'Kelly's influence was strongest in those sections of Virginia and North Carolina where he was known personally, but Christians were also to be found in other southern states and the parts of the Ohio Valley settled by southerners. The denominations's loose, decentralized structure, however, later proved a major obstacle to growth.

The worst point from Asbury's perspective probably came in 1798 when O'Kelly "hath now published to the world what he hath been telling to his disciples for years," a 120-page work entitled, *The Author's Apology for Protesting against the Methodist Episcopal Government*.[36] But even this did not mark the final round. According to Asbury in 1805,

O'Kelly was reportedly still ranting against "government, monarchy, and episcopacy; occasionally varying the topic by abuse of the Methodists, calling them aristocrats and Tories."[37] O'Kelly kept dissent alive, injuring the Methodist cause well beyond the immediate impact of 1792.

Most of James O'Kelly's influence was concentrated within the region of Virginia and North Carolina where he had so long ministered, but through published essays he sought to reach wider audiences. *The Author's Apology for Protesting against the Methodist Episcopal Government* recounted the controversies preceding the General Conference in 1792, the proceedings of that momentous meeting, and the ensuing separation. Asbury's defense was penned by a lieutenant, Nicholas Snethen, in *Reply to an Apology* (1800). Another round in the feud led to O'Kelly's *A Vindication of an Apology* and Snethen's *An Answer to James O'Kelly's Vindication of His Apology*. The struggle with Asbury, however, did not constitute O'Kelly's sole reason to write. He had taken a bold and controversial stand against slavery in 1788, with his widely read *Essay on Negro Slavery*, in which he used Scripture and natural rights philosophy to attack the institution. Later works expounded upon principles for church governance and practice as revealed in Scripture. These titles include *An Address to the Christian Church* (1801), *The Divine Oracles Consulted* (1820), *Letters from Heaven Consulted* (1822), and O'Kelly's last major work for publication, *The Prospect Before Us by Way of Address* (1824). O'Kelly also provided his followers with liturgical material, including *Hymns and Spiritual Songs Designed for the Use of Christians* (1816), some of which he claimed to have authored. Unfortunately, none of his personal papers, including an incomplete autobiography, survive.[38]

Despite an impressive collection of titles, O'Kelly presented ideas that were not particularly distinctive for their subtlety or learned quality. His influence probably owes more to the power of a straightforward, plain style of expression. Asbury's defenders and other opponents attempted to smear O'Kelly with charges of heterodoxy (about the Trinity, for example), but the peculiarities in his beliefs appeared to be more a product of O'Kelly's limited education than true theological error. His ideas about God, salvation, and sin were fairly conventional. Likewise, little if anything was original in his ideas about government and power. Thus, O'Kelly's prominence can be attributed largely to the familiarity of his message and the force of his personality, which apparently was considerable.[39] His main contribution to southern religion was to bang the drum against "ecclesiastical monarchy"—to work toward a system of worship in keeping not only with early Christianity but also more appropriate for a country where, within living memory, popular notions of power and leadership had become much more democratic.

James O'Kelly might stand as merely another religious eccentric, but similar efforts to restore American Christian belief and polity to its original base in the New Testament were soon occurring elsewhere as well. One such initiative was among a small number of Baptists in New England, under the leadership of Elias Smith and Abner Jones. Smith published an influential newspaper, *The Herald of Gospel Liberty*. Another movement began among some evangelical Presbyterians in central Kentucky in the aftermath of the Great Revival, nationally famous for a massive camp meeting at Cane Ridge in August 1801. Cane Ridge's pastor, Barton Warren Stone, had been amazed by the sight of some thousands of sinners crying out in repentance. He, along with a small band of other western clergymen, soon abandoned Calvinism and embraced the Scripture as his sole guide.[40] This branch of the Restoration Movement later combined with a parallel development, also based in the Upper South, led by Alexander Campbell.

The work of the Republican Methodists, New England Baptists, and Stonites shared a common interest in resurrecting an apostolic Christianity, and after much correspondence they decided to explore those similarities further in a General Conference meeting held in New Hampshire in 1808. Coming from independent traditions rooted in different sections of the country, these groups developed a shared governance structure only slowly. The result, in keeping with the primitive spirit of early Christianity, kept directives to a minimum. Not until 1834 did the various branches begin meeting as the General Conference on a regular quadrennial basis. Dispersed and always independent, the Christian Church continued to operate as a loose confederation. Unfortunately, the divisive issue of slavery came to trouble the American Christians as it did most other denominations. A split occurred in 1854 that was not repaired until 1894. Another major problem during this period—the lack of formally trained clergy—contributed toward the founding of Elon College in North Carolina in 1890. Further organizational changes occurred in the twentieth century. The Christian Connection, as it was termed, united with the Congregational Church in 1931 to form the Congregational Christian Church; and, merging in 1957 with the Evangelical and Reformed Church, it now calls itself the United Church of Christ.[41]

James O'Kelly played only a minuscule role in these efforts to unite with similar believers. Perhaps the biggest impediment to a greater leadership role was his stubborn adherence to the old Methodist practice of baptism by sprinkling rather than by full immersion, as depicted in the New Testament. The controversy about baptism erupted into heated debate in 1810 and led to a deep rift. The majority of the congregations in Virginia left O'Kelly's leadership and formed their own Virginia Conference. It was primarily this group that connected with the Christians in New England. The O'Kellyites, as they were called, organized the North Carolina Conference. The two groups finally reunited with other southern Christians in 1854, more than a quarter-century after O'Kelly's death.

All of this splintering ran, ironically, contrary to a key concern in the Christian movement, that of unity. O'Kelly lamented, "The house of God is now distinguished by *names* and parties, as though christians differed like the birds of the air!"[42] James O'Kelly, Barton W. Stone, Alexander Campbell, and numerous others who identified with the Christian movement ardently hoped that a return to Christian fundamentals in both belief and polity would bring a final end to denominational differences. O'Kelly publicly urged American Baptists, Episcopalians, and Methodists to finish the Reformation. They needed to abandon modern peculiarities of doctrine and polity, created by humans rather than God, and return to original apostolic practice.[43] Unity proved futile, of course, even within the Restoration Movement.

The O'Kelly Schism remains an important event in American religious history. James O'Kelly's withdrawal from the Methodist Church in 1792 had a devastating effect on what had been a stronghold of support. Although Methodist numbers eventually recovered, contemporaries viewed the O'Kelly Schism as a genuine crisis, and decades later it was still regarded as such. Although O'Kelly and his followers achieved limited success in denominational strength, they were far from alone in their hope to restore Christianity to its original apostolic condition, in both doctrine and governance, as described in the New Testament. The idea of a simple Christian fellowship modeled after the Apostles resonated with many citizens of the new American republic. O'Kelly and his followers might well be described as the Restoration Movement's shock troops, at the radical forefront of a much larger phenomenon.

The O'Kelly Schism holds significance for another, less recognized reason. The recent scholarship on religion during the early national period emphasizes the "democratization of American Christianity" and the demise of Calvinism.[44] The idea of an exclusive, predestined spiritual fate was rejected in numerous sectors of the United States and replaced by a belief that salvation was open to all people. A new era of evangelicalism followed. Yet, the story of James O'Kelly suggests that perhaps theology should be seen as less an engine of change and more a product. O'Kelly's crusade for a republican governance structure in religion originated from his political experience and preceded any substantial theological shift. Thus, the challenge to Calvinism and other hierarchical elements in American religion only became possible once common people gained access to church governance structures. James O'Kelly helped make this possible.

Notes

1. Charles Franklin Kilgore, *The James O'Kelly Schism in the Methodist Episcopal Church* (Mexico City: Casa Unida de Publicaciones, 1963); Frederick A. Norwood, *The Story of American Methodism* (Nashville, TN: Abingdon Press, 1974); John J. Tigert, *A Constitutional History of American Episcopal Methodism* (Nashville, TN: Publishing House of the M. E. Church, South, 1894).

2. See, for example, Abel Stevens, *History of the Methodist Episcopal Church*, 3 vols. (1867; reprint ed., New York: Hunt and Eaton, 1889); William W. Bennett, *Memorials of Methodism in Virginia* (Richmond, VA: W. Bennett, 1871); Matthew Simpson, *A Hundred Years of Methodism* (New York: Nelson and Phillips, 1876).

3. Nathan O. Hatch, *The Democratization of American Christianity* (New Haven, CT: Yale University Press, 1989), 69–71; Russell E. Richey, *Early American Methodism* (Bloomington: Indiana University Press, 1991), 88–90; John H. Wigger, *Taking Heaven by Storm: Methodists and the Popularization of American Christianity* (New York: Oxford University Press, 1998); Christine Leigh Heyrman, *Southern Cross: The Beginnings of the Bible Belt* (New York: Alfred A. Knopf, 1998), 102; Dee E. Andrews, *The Methodists and Revolutionary America, 1760–1800: The Shaping of an Evangelical Culture* (Princeton, NJ: Princeton University Press, 2000), 196–207.

4. Wilbur E. MacClenny, *The Life of Rev. James O'Kelly and the Early History of the Christian Church in the South* (1910; reprint ed., Indianapolis, IN: Religious Book Service, 1950); Kilgore, *James O'Kelly Schism*, 4–5.

5. James O'Kelly, *Essay on Negro Slavery* (Philadelphia: Pritchard and Hall, 1788). O'Kelly, interestingly, utilized both natural rights philosophy and Christian principles in his antislavery argument.

6. William Warren Sweet, *Virginia Methodism: A History* (Richmond, VA: Whittlet and Shepperson, 1955), 128; Norwood, *The Story of American Methodism*.

7. Elmer T. Clark, ed., *The Journal and Letters of Francis Asbury*, 3 vols. (Nashville, TN: Abingdon Press, 1958), 1:737.

8. The origins of O'Kelly's unrelenting opposition to tyranny and support of democratic principles is unknown. His writings upon abuses of power follow the main currents of popular thought. He seems unusual only in his unyielding demand for a

decentralized, participatory church structure. Neither was O'Kelly's Virginia neighborhood, the south side of the James River, remarkable for radical politics. O'Kelly is not known to have held any public office in either Virginia or later in North Carolina. His son William, however, became a North Carolina state representative early in the nineteenth century. O'Kelly presents the fullest explanation of his ideas in *The Author's Apology for Protesting against the Methodist Episcopal Government* (1798). See also Frederick Abbott Norwood, "James O'Kelly: Methodist Maverick," *Methodist Magazine* 189 (1966): 14–28.

9. Sweet, *Virginia Methodism*, 129–30; Norwood, "Methodist Maverick," 16–17; "John Kobler's Account of the General Conference," in Clark, *Journal and Letters of Francis Asbury*, 3:560.

10. Thomas Ware, quoted in John J. Tigert, *A Constitutional History of American Episcopal Methodism* (Nashville, TN: Publishing House of the M. E. Church, South, 1894), 260.

11. Clark, *Journal and Letters of Francis Asbury*, 1:734.

12. O'Kelly, *Author's Apology*, 39; "John Kobler's Account," in Clark, *Journal and Letters of Francis Asbury*, 1:560; Nathan Bangs, ed., *The Life of Freeborn Garrettson, Compiled from His Printed and Manuscript Journals and Other Authentic Sources* (New York: J. Emory and B. Waugh, 1832), 237.

13. Jesse Lee, *A Short History of the Methodists in the United States of America* (1810; reprint ed., Rutland, VT: Academy Books, 1974), 180.

14. Kilgore, *James O'Kelly Schism*, 27–28.

15. Ibid., 5–7.

16. Alfred Wesley Hurst, "The Theology of the Reverend James O'Kelly" (University of Chicago, Bachelor's of Divinity Thesis, 1930), 45–46; Kilgore, *James O'Kelly Schism*, 6–7.

17. Kilgore, *James O'Kelly Schism*, 10–12; Letter of James O'Kelly, April 1787, in Clark, *Journal and Letters of Francis Asbury*, 3:51–53.

18. Although the council's decisions were to be unanimous, no resolution was binding upon a district until the local conference had approved it. But as O'Kelly foresaw, what one district might approve, another might reject. See O'Kelly, *Author's Apology*, 17–19; Kilgore, *James O'Kelly Schism*, 12–13.

19. O'Kelly, *Author's Apology*, 17.

20. Clark, *Journal and Letters of Francis Asbury*, 1:620, entry dated January 12, 1790.

21. O'Kelly, *Author's Apology*, 22–23; Kilgore, *James O'Kelly Schism*, 15–17.

22. Tigert, *Constitutional History of American Episcopal Methodism*, 243–54; Andrews, *Methodists and Revolutionary America*, 202; MacClenney, *James O'Kelly*, 60–71. The General Conference with representatives from each regional conference, meeting every four years, became the central governing body.

23. O'Kelly, *Author's Apology*, 20.

24. Ibid., 55, 57; Nathan O. Hatch, "The Christian Movement and the Demand for a Theology of the People," *Journal of American History* 67 (1980): 555.

25. O'Kelly, *Author's Apology*, 42.

26. Ibid., 46.

27. Ibid., 48–51.

28. Some adherents retained the label of Republican Methodist. See MacClenney, *James O'Kelly*, 155–56.

29. Clark, *Journal and Letters of Francis Asbury*, 1:735, entry dated November 21, 1792.

30. Devereux Jarratt, quoted in Kilgore, *James O'Kelly Schism*, 34.

31. Clark, *Journal and Letters of Francis Asbury*, 2:12–13, entry dated April 23, 1794.

32. William Watters to Edward Dromgoole, May 16, 1795, in William Warren Sweet, *Religion on the American Frontier, 1783–1840*, Vol. 4, *The Methodists* (Chicago: University of Chicago Press, 1946), 147.

33. Clark, *Journal and Letters of Francis Asbury*, 2:105, entry dated November 23, 1796. See also entry dated November 25, 1796.

34. *Minutes of the Annual Conferences of the Methodist Episcopal Church for the Years 1773–1828*, vol. 1 (New York: T. Mason and G. Lane, 1840).

35. Sweet, *Virginia Methodism*, 131–34; MacClenney, *James O'Kelly*, 123–24; Kilgore, *James O'Kelly Schism*, 34; Andrews, *Methodists and Revolutionary America*, 202.

36. Clark, *Journal and Letters of Francis Asbury*, 2:163, entry dated July 1, 1798.

37. Ibid., 2:459, entry dated February 13, 1805.

38. MacClenney, *James O'Kelly*, 154.

39. Milo T. Morrill, *A History of the Christian Denomination in America, 1794–1911* (Dayton, OH: The Christian Publishing Association, 1912), 19–20.

40. John B. Boles, *The Great Revival, 1787–1805: The Origins of the Southern Evangelical Mind* (Lexington: University Press of Kentucky, 1972); Paul K. Conkin, *Cane Ridge: America's Pentecost* (Madison: University of Wisconsin Press, 1990); Ellen Eslinger, *Citizens of Zion: The Social Origins of Camp Meeting Revivalism* (Knoxville: University of Tennessee Press, 1999).

41. Morrill, *History of the Christian Denomination*, 126–34; Kilgore, *James O'Kelly Schism*, 35–38.

42. James O'Kelly, *An Address to the Christian Church under the Similitude of an Elect Lady and Her Children* (Richmond, VA: Jones and Dixon, n.d.), 19.

43. Kilgore, *James O'Kelly Schism*, 75–78.

44. See Hatch, *The Democratization of American Christianity*.

Suggested Readings

James O'Kelly's works are not very accessible. The most important is *The Author's Apology for Protesting against the Methodist Episcopal Government* (Richmond, VA: John Dixon for the author, 1798). This work is heavily consulted for most studies about O'Kelly. The classic biography, published in 1910, is Wilbur E. MacClenny's *The Life of Rev. James O'Kelly and the Early History of the Christian Church in the South* (Indianapolis, IN: Religious Book Service, 1950, reprint edition), but it is a very partisan treatment. Most of the other biographies likewise cast James O'Kelly as a pioneer of Christian liberty. More balanced is Charles Franklin Kilgore, *The James O'Kelly Schism in the Methodist Episcopal Church* (Mexico City: Casa Unida de Publicaciones, 1963). See also Milo T. Morrill, *A History of the Christian Denomination in America, 1794–1911* (Dayton, OH: The Christian Publishing Association, 1912).

The Methodist side of the schism is represented first by Nicholas Snethen, *A Reply to an Apology for Protesting against the Methodist Episcopal Government* (Philadelphia: Henry Tuckniss, 1800). Most early denominational histories also attack O'Kelly. See, for example, Abel Stevens, *History of the Methodist Episcopal Church*, 3 vols. (1867; reprint ed., New York: Hunt and Eaton, 1889); Edward J. Drinkhouse, *History of Methodist Reform*, 2 vols. (Baltimore: The Board of Publication of the Methodist Protestant Church, 1899); and John J. Tigert, *A Constitutional History of American Episcopal Methodism* (Nashville, TN: Publishing House of the M. E. Church, South, 1894).

Contemporary sources besides O'Kelly's works include the three volumes of *The Journal and Letters of Francis Asbury* (London: Epworth Press, and Nashville, TN: Abingdon Press, 1958), edited by Elmer T. Clark. See also Jesse Lee's *A Short History of the Methodists in the United States of America* (Baltimore, 1810; reprint, Rutland, VT: Academy Books, 1974); Thomas Ware, *Sketches of the Life and Travels of Rev. Thomas Ware* (New York: T. Mason and G. Lane for the Methodist Episcopal Church, 1839); Nathan Bangs, ed., *The Life of Freeborn Garrettson, Compiled from His Printed and Manuscript Journals and Other Authentic Documents* (New York: J. Emory and B. Waugh, 1832).

The best recent studies of American religion in the early national period include the following: Russell E. Richey, *Early American Methodism* (Bloomington: Indiana University Press, 1991); Nathan O. Hatch, *The Democratization of American Christianity* (New Haven, CT: Yale Universtiy Press, 1989); Christine Leigh Heyrman, *Southern Cross* (New York: Alfred A. Knopf, 1998); Paul K. Conkin, *American Originals, Homemade Varieties of Christianity* (Chapel Hill: University of North Carolina Press, 1997); Cynthia Lynn Lyerly, *Methodism and the Southern Mind, 1770–1810* (New York: Oxford University Press, 1998); John H. Wigger, *Taking Heaven by Storm: Methodists and the Popularization of American Christianity* (New York: Oxford University Press, 1998); Dee E. Andrews, *The Methodists and Revolutionary America, 1760–1800: The Shaping of an Evangelical Culture* (Princeton, NJ: Princeton University Press, 2000). See also, for the beginning of the Christian movement in Kentucky, John B. Boles, *The Great Revival, 1787–1805: The Origins of the Southern Evangelical Mind* (Lexington: University Press of Kentucky, 1972); Paul K. Conkin, *Cane Ridge: America's Pentecost* (Madison: University of Wisconsin Press, 1990); and Ellen Eslinger, *Citizens of Zion: The Social Origins of Camp Meeting Revivalism* (Knoxville: University of Tennessee Press, 1999).

5

Gabriel

Artisan, Slave, and American Revolutionary

Douglas R. Egerton

Slavery troubled many Americans. Initially the institution had existed in various parts of the colonies, both North and South. Increasingly, however, slavery had become more restricted to the South, particularly after the Revolutionary War. That fact caused those who saw the holding of one human being by another as evil, or at least un-American in the Land of the Free, to focus their efforts on that region. The South thus viewed itself as under attack. Regional anger intensified, and over the years the debate hardened.

Some southerners argued that to Christianize and "civilize" the once-African slaves, they had to be held in servitude. Others noted the existence of some form of slavery in biblical times and in the civilizations of ancient Greece and Rome. Still others, less forcibly, stressed the need to keep slavery for economic reasons. At some level in all these arguments lay the issue of race. Considering blacks inferior and dangerous if freed, their owners and other supporters of the system said that emancipation would destroy the South and bring untold disasters.

Critics of slavery stressed the moral high ground: slaves as humans with souls had been formed in the image of God, desired liberty, and deserved freedom. They pointed to evils within the system, such as violence by masters to slaves and sales that separated families.

Remaining almost absent from the national debate were those actually held in slavery. Proslavery and antislavery advocates both claimed to speak for them, but the voices of the slaves themselves were rarely heard. Many struck out at the system quietly, for significant obstacles stood in the way of most large-scale revolts. Slaves might "accidentally" sabotage tools, slow down in their work, or even run away. Still, a few sought to go beyond these tactics and challenge the institution in broader ways. One of those slaves was Gabriel, whose story exemplifies the contradictions of the system and illustrates how fiercely the fires of freedom could burn within an individual. His fight for liberty showed the nation the flaws in the proslavery argument and would be followed by other rumored or actual plots for insurrection. Yet, in the end, only a bloody civil war could finally break the chains of slavery.

Douglas R. Egerton received his Ph.D. in 1985 from Georgetown University and is currently professor of history at Le Moyne College in Syracuse, New York. His books include *Charles Fenton Mercer and the Trial of National Conservatism* (1989), *Gabriel's Rebellion: The Virginia Slave Conspiracies*

81

of 1800 & 1802 (1993), *He Shall Go Out Free: The Lives of Denmark Vesey* (1999), and *Rebels, Reformers, and Revolutionaries: Collected Essays and Second Thoughts* (2002). He currently is writing *A History of the Atlantic World, 1400–1888* (with Jane Landers and Donald R. Wright).

The art of biography is deceptively simple. Even when the subject proves a willing participant by leaving behind diaries, letters, and autobiographies, there is little guarantee that the biographer can accurately recover the past. Memories fade, documents get misplaced, and some diarists lie as readily in their journals as they do in person. The task, of course, becomes harder still when the subject belongs to that class of people scholars call the "historically inarticulate," that is, working people who lacked the time or ability to communicate with the present generation through the written word. Perhaps no better example exists of this unfortunate maxim than the short, unhappy life of the Virginia slave named Gabriel, who swung from the gibbet in 1800 for the crime of desiring liberty.

According to Thomas Henry Prosser, the young slave's owner at the time of his execution, Gabriel was born in 1776, the year in which another Virginian, Thomas Jefferson, pronounced a self-evident truth: that all men were created equal and were endowed with certain natural and inalienable rights, among which were "life, liberty, and the pursuit of happiness." Most likely, Gabriel was born just outside of Richmond on Brookfield plantation, the estate of Thomas Prosser Sr., a wealthy tobacco planter. The master of Brookfield owned fifty-three bondpersons, which made the estate large by Virginia standards; only three other Henrico County planters possessed more slaves.[1]

Among the families in the Brookfield slave quarters was a couple with three sons. The identity of the parents is lost to history, but the sons are not. Martin was by far the oldest, Solomon was the middle child, and the youngest was christened Gabriel, after the divine messenger. Beyond that simple outline, absolutely nothing is known of the family, including whether Gabriel's parents were Africans or enslaved Virginians. Perhaps nothing speaks more eloquently about the dehumanizing nature of early national slavery than the fact that one of the most influential Americans of the Revolutionary generation lacks a precise birthdate and a definite birthplace.[2]

In the popular imagination, Virginia dwellings all resemble the mansions of the Founding Fathers. Thomas Prosser's long, two-story frame house was admittedly no Monticello, but it boasted single-story wings on either side and spacious porches front and rear. Considerably less elegant was the small cabin in which Gabriel lived with his brothers and one or both of his parents. Most slave cabins were crude affairs constructed of rough-hewn boards and designed to be easily dismantled and moved. As a result, few had plank floors, and most used small holes in the walls for ventilation. The chimney was pasted together from mud and sticks. "As to the furniture of this rude dwelling," remembered one bondman, "it was procured by the slaves themselves." Straw-filled ticks under thin blankets provided the only warmth and comfort at night.[3]

Early on, however, Gabriel was chosen for a singular fate. Perhaps it was young Thomas Henry, also born in 1776, or perhaps it was his mother Ann Prosser (plantation mistresses occasionally watched over the slave children as their parents labored in the fields), or perhaps, although this is less likely, it was his father, but *somebody* at Brookfield taught young Gabriel how to read. If Ann Prosser was indeed his teacher, it was a foolhardy gesture; a bondman who could read and write was a bondman with access to information about the world at large. Scholars estimate that only about 5 percent of Chesapeake slaves in Gabriel's day were literate, so his literacy marked him as a most unusual child. His rudimentary education was an example of how those who wished to maintain slavery sometimes engaged in practices at odds with that wish.[4]

Around 1786, about the same time that Gabriel learned to read, he and his brother Solomon went into the plantation's forge for training as blacksmiths. Every estate of considerable size required a number of highly skilled laborers. Enslaved blacksmiths shod horses, forged simple tools, and sharpened the long scythes used for mowing wheat and grass. Most likely Gabriel's father was a smith. In Virginia the children of skilled slaves commonly inherited their parent's profession; daughters of house servants became the next generation of domestic slaves, and sons of artisans became artisans. Few slaves acquired property beyond the odd chair or quilt, but they could pass on to their offspring their most valued possession: the skill that kept them out of the tobacco fields. (The considerably older Martin, for unknown reasons, was taught neither a trade nor how to read. Possibly Martin had a different father, which would have made him only a half-brother to Gabriel and Solomon.)[5]

Work as a craft apprentice provided Gabriel with considerable status in the slave community—as did his ability to read and write. Certainly there could be little doubt that Gabriel was an atypical bondman. By the mid-1790s, as he neared the age of twenty, he stood "six feet two or three inches high," and the strength in his chest and arms betrayed nearly a decade in the forge. A long and "bony face, well made," was marred by the loss of his two front teeth and by "two or three scars on his head," the results, no doubt, of the aggressive young slave mixing it up with other young men in the quarters. His hair, like his complexion, was very dark, and he wore it cropped close to his head. (There is no truth to the pervasive myth that Gabriel allowed his locks to grow long in imitation of the Biblical Samson.) According to journalist James Thomson Callender, area whites regarded him as "a fellow of courage and intellect above his rank in life."[6]

During these years, Gabriel met a young bondwoman named Nanny and fell deeply in love. Probably Nanny was one or two years Gabriel's junior. Chesapeake slave women typically married young; most bore children and settled into permanent relationships by the age of twenty. Some masters recognized such unions, primarily for reasons of plantation stability and labor control, but the state of Virginia did not. Little is known about Nanny, including the identity of her owner. (Her name does not appear in the 1783 tax rolls of Thomas Prosser, so if she lived at Brookfield she was either purchased or born after that date.) Most likely she lived on a nearby farm or tobacco plantation. According to regional black oral tradition, Nanny bore Gabriel several children, and their descendants carried the surname of Randolph into the twentieth century.[7]

In the fall of 1798 change came to Gabriel's world with the death of Thomas Prosser. The old master died quietly at his estate on Sunday, October 7. The end was not unexpected; during the previous year Prosser had drafted a will. Through it, Thomas Henry, at the young age of twenty-two, became the lord of Brookfield and the master of approximately fifty men, women, and children.[8]

Eager to squeeze every ounce of profit out of his new estate, Thomas Henry Prosser evidently allowed some of his slaves to participate in a practice that was both dangerous and lucrative: hiring their time around Henrico and the nearby city of Richmond. Even the largest and most efficient plantations could not keep their bond artisans fully occupied year-round; therefore, many owners hired their craftsmen out to neighboring farmers and town dwellers. Even with all the work to be done at Brookfield, Gabriel and, to a lesser degree, Solomon spent more than a few days each month smithing in and around Richmond. Though no less a slave in the eyes of the law, Gabriel enjoyed a rough form of freedom. Indeed, his ties to his owner became so tenuous that numerous historians have incorrectly identified him as a free man.[9]

This relative freedom of movement between the countryside and the city was only one point at which urban bondage began to disintegrate. Even more dangerous was that specie—hard currency—fell into the pockets of enslaved craftsmen like Gabriel. On the plantations, master and slave formed a rather feudal bond. There the relationship between the two, despite the fact that bondpersons were engaged in coerced labor, was primarily social rather than economic (since no money changed hands). But the kind of self-hire permitted by owners that allowed slaves to shop about for temporary owners and retain a small share of the wages earned marked a relationship based largely upon market considerations. Admittedly most of Gabriel's hard-earned salary went to Prosser, but a portion of it did not. For a man raised to believe that the acquisition of any sort of property was impossible, cash became a new and potent symbol of liberty and power.[10]

On occasion, plantation masters hired their artisans out to white artisans in Richmond who found themselves long on orders and short on apprentices. This practice became especially common in the decades after the Revolution, when skilled whites who wished to avoid the sort of inexpensive competition that slave hires presented abandoned the South for Philadelphia. Undoubtedly a few of the craftsmen who hired bondmen like Gabriel reflected the attitudes of Henrico planters. According to the census of 1782 two area blacksmiths owned seven enslaved assistants. But other workmen were veterans of Virginia's short-lived abolitionist movement or had been touched by the evangelical revolt of the mideighteenth century. Particularly in small shops, unpretentious white craftsmen drew no line of demarcation between work and social intercourse. In this casual atmosphere black and white mechanics toiled side by side and enjoyed the stories and jokes that made the workday go more swiftly. They often developed ties that cut across racial lines. According to conventional wisdom, such forms of interracial labor solidarity were not supposed to occur in the early national Chesapeake. But quite often they did.[11]

Ultimately, Richmond-area artisans—bond or free, black or white—dealt directly with urban merchants; for slave craftsmen the power of the merchants could be devastating. Unscrupulous businessmen often underpaid or even openly cheated bond hires, for blacks could not take them to court or testify against them. In a system in which the failure to pay one's master a fixed sum could cost a slave the privilege of hiring out, even a single encounter with a dishonest businessman could doom a bondman to life in the countryside. Evidently, Gabriel found himself in this situation at least once. According to his friend Ben, another of Prosser's slaves, Gabriel came to see Richmond's "merchants," and not whites in general, as his chief antagonists. Caught between the financial demands of his master and the strange new power of merchant capital, Gabriel increasingly sought a way to pull both down at once.[12]

View of Richmond from the banks of the James River by Benjamin Henry Latrobe. *Courtesy of the Maryland Historical Society, Baltimore, Maryland*

Given Gabriel's desperate need to earn enough cash to keep his master content, it is not surprising that his notions of justice increasingly took on a decidedly urban flavor. The economic tone of the city was far removed from that of the sleepy Virginia countryside. Surrounded by an atmosphere of business enterprise—and driven by the need to stay solvent—the black artisan was hardly impervious to the claims of money and property. (Money could, after all, purchase his and Nanny's freedom.) It was natural that Gabriel was influenced by the bold words of the white workers he encountered in the forge and waterfront taverns. More than a few white radicals insisted that laboring men should be politically superior to those, like the merchants or planters, who squeezed profits from the sweat of those who worked with their hands. And so Gabriel came to dream not merely of freedom but also of an equally inestimable treasure: the right to his earnings—all of them.[13]

Above all, Gabriel was a Virginian. Raised amid the heady talk of liberty and natural rights and inspired by the words of the Richmond artisanal community, Gabriel began to ponder what the Revolutionary War legacy of his state meant to African Americans. Like the patriots of 1776 he desired freedom—both personal and economic. Like the white and black craftsmen among whom he labored, Gabriel desired to pull down "the merchants" and "possess ourselves of their property." As an artisan he was a radical, but as a slave artisan he was a revolutionary.[14]

Such utopian dreams emboldened Gabriel to challenge the white authority he had never accepted and no longer feared. In September 1799 he moved toward overt rebellion. Probably, Gabriel commonly engaged in the theft of food, for bondpeople found it necessary to supplement their high-starch diet with beef and pork. Slaves, of course, did not regard the raiding of a pen as theft. Stealing was defined as theft from other slaves, or Prosser's demand for the lion's share of Gabriel's earnings. But one particular time Gabriel was caught. Absalom Johnson, a former overseer who rented a portion of Nathaniel Wilkinson's neighboring plantation, came upon Gabriel, his brother Solomon, and Jupiter, a bondman of Wilkinson's, dragging a hog from his pen. Furious, Johnson began to berate the three men. Slaves learned early on how to don the mask of obedience, but Gabriel had moved far beyond that charade. He launched himself at the overseer's legs, and the two men fell in a thrashing tangle of limbs. Gabriel got the best of the fight. Johnson lost his pride and, rather more seriously, the better "part of his left Ear."[15]

Pig stealing was a minor crime. Attacking and biting a white man was quite another matter; it carried a capital penalty. On October 7, Gabriel was "set to the Bar [and] charged with Maiming Absalom Johnson." Under the 1692 statute that established slave courts of oyer and terminer, five justices of the peace tried him. There was no jury and no appeal, except to the governor. The public defender assigned by the court, Charles Copland, received five dollars for his services. Because evidence against Gabriel—the severed ear—was overwhelming, the justices wasted little time in finding him guilty. But Gabriel escaped the gallows, at least for that year, under a curious 1792 statute that allowed convicted bondmen the option of "benefit of clergy." If Gabriel could recite a verse from the Bible—as well he could, thanks to the religious faith of his parents—he would not hang but rather be publicly "burnt in the left hand [by] the Jailor." Should Gabriel again be convicted of a felony, the brand marked him as ineligible for a second reprieve.[16]

By the fall of 1799, Gabriel, now a branded criminal, stood on the edge of rebellion, and not merely the sort of resistance that represented the personal victory of stealing a hog or overcoming a white neighbor in a bloody fistfight. His court appearance and his brief incarceration in the Henrico jail proved the final blows in a long series of assaults on his natural rights. In a different world, Gabriel would have prospered. His quick intelligence, his imposing size, and his craft skills would all have marked him as a young man with fine prospects. But this was not a different world; Gabriel was a black man in Jeffersonian Virginia. One possibility was flight to the north. But that course would force him to abandon his wife and parents, and in any case the Fugitive Slave Act of 1793 existed to keep potential runaways like Gabriel in chains. The alternative was armed rebellion, and as the new century dawned, he began to formulate a plan.[17]

Gabriel explained his emerging scheme to Solomon and Ben. In Gabriel's plan black insurgents, including urban bondmen, would meet at Brookfield before marching on Richmond. Fighting in three groups, they would attack the capitol building, the magazine, and the state penitentiary, where arms were also stored. (Contrary to popular legend very few white Virginians owned their own rifles; rather, the state owned and supplied arms for local militia companies.) Having captured their objectives, Gabriel's forces hoped to fortify Richmond as best they could and await word that other cities had been taken or that slaves from other parts of the state were heading for Richmond. At that point, it was expected that embattled whites would "agree to their freedom" and allow the liberated slaves to assume their rightful place in society. "On the day when it was agreed to," Gabriel promised, he "would dine and drink with the merchants of the city."[18]

In retrospect it appears absurd that Gabriel truly believed that a handful of murdered whites and a few dozen hostages, including Governor James Monroe, might goad the Virginia elites into accepting liberty for blacks. But hindsight frequently obscures historical context. As a literate man, Gabriel well knew that states just to the north were slowly moving against unfree labor. In 1783, Pennsylvania became the first state to pass a law for gradual emancipation. New York finally followed suit in 1799—the year of Gabriel's arrest—and New Jersey was considering similar legislation. (It would finally adopt such a law in 1804.) More to the point the slave rebellion in the French colony of Saint Domingue showed Gabriel that freedom could be his, if only he was willing to fight for it.[19]

In the spring of 1800, during his frequent trips into town, the young blacksmith began quietly to spread word of his plan and to recruit followers. Gabriel acted cautiously; he first approached other slave hirelings, especially those who, unlike himself, lived away from their masters, an arrangement that further weakened white control and supervision. Not surprisingly, his method of recruitment, even his very language, was informed by his elite status as an enslaved artisan. Would they "join a free mason society," Gabriel and his chief lieutenants asked, "a society for fight[ing] the White people for their freedom?"[20]

Soon reports of the plot began to hum rapidly along the slave grapevine, through the back alleys, hidden taverns, warehouses, and docks of the port town. The mechanics Gabriel enlisted were not sworn to secrecy, yet most were careful not to reveal the plan to bondmen who had close ties to their owners or who spent most of their time laboring beside their masters on rural farms. At first the number of recruits was small, but freedom of movement and the ease of communication that bond hires enjoyed permitted them in turn to recruit others. One of the conspirators, William Young's Gilbert, routinely wrote "himself a Pass" so he could travel freely about the Richmond area.[21]

As recruits joined, word of the conspiracy began to spread beyond Henrico County. Black artisans used their freedom of movement to journey far outside the region. George Smith "hire[d] his time" from Ann Smith, his mistress, and traveled to neighboring towns, while Sam Byrd Jr. rented out his labor "for the greater part of the summer" so that he might have leisure to "engage a number of men in the adjacent counties and in Petersburg," a city twenty-five miles to the south. Byrd even journeyed "as far [northwest] as Charlottesville," the home of Vice President Jefferson, "to inlist men." It is significant that as the conspiracy grew, it remained the secret of like-minded bond artisans in Virginia urban areas.[22]

Communications among slaves in the different towns were not intended to be so precise that revolts in several places could begin at exactly the same time. Instead, Gabriel hoped that under the leadership of Sam's two free uncles, Jesse and Reuben Byrd, together with John Scott, an enslaved Petersburg craftsman, a "union of plan" among the towns could be arranged so that the other conspirators would know to rise after he and his Richmond followers had "commenced the insurrection."[23]

With many slaves and free blacks from Richmond to Petersburg aware of the plan, the message began to flow down the James River to Suffolk and Norfolk. Black boatmen who worked Virginia's inland waterways had long been the carriers of both illicit information and runaway slaves as well as the legal cargoes they ferried for Chesapeake merchants. Now several became involved as couriers. One of them, Jacob, the property of William Wilson, was a skipper for hire who regularly "passed between [Petersburg] and Norfolk." As with the Petersburg conspirators, the bondmen of the lower James were to gather on a yet to be appointed date near Norfolk and await word of the Richmond uprising. By the end of July, news of the revolt had spread to at least six Virginia towns; it was, as Governor Monroe later conceded, a secret known "in many and some distant parts of the State."[24]

Given the enormous might of Virginia's white majority, however, the successful recruitment of soldiers sufficient to hold Richmond ultimately depended upon Gabriel's ability to convince his nervous followers that the early fall of 1800 was the ideal moment to rise against their masters. The key was the coming election. Spending many of his days in town, Gabriel was hardly unaware that the republic was in the midst of a bitter and divisive presidential contest. Republican journalist James Thomson Callender had recently been imprisoned under the hated Sedition Act, and rumor had it that if Jefferson were victorious the Federalists would not relinquish power. The *Richmond Virginia Argus* even charged that area Republicans were stockpiling rifles. For slave hirelings who had their own grievances against the Federalist merchant class, the battles appeared to be theirs as well. "We have as much right to fight for our liberty as any men," insisted Jack Ditcher, a leading insurgent.[25]

By taking advantage of the political turmoil, Virginia's urban slaves might force the merchant elite to agree to black freedom—provided enough hostages were taken. Already surrounded by a hostile sea of Republicans who were reputed to be arming themselves, the tiny Federalist island of Richmond, unarmed and defenseless, would be unable to do anything save surrender. It was not merely that the conspiracy developed during a time of division among whites; it was also that artisan Gabriel, sharing the small-producer ideology of many urban Republicans, hoped to join in and exploit that division. Gabriel's error was not one of logic but rather of information. His limited urban vista led him to believe that the partisan struggle was between Republican artisans and Federalist merchants; Republican planters such as Jefferson and Monroe evidently played no part in his calculations, for he never identified them, or indeed whites in general, as his enemies.[26]

Even so, Gabriel well knew that his white artisan brethren might not support his cause unless forced to do so by sheer numbers of insurgents. To achieve such numbers he needed to reach out to the less politicized rural slaves. It was a dangerous gamble. On most farms the tie between master and slave was far closer than in the cities or on large plantations like Brookfield. Gabriel feared that one of the "outlandish" slaves might reveal the plot to his owner. But the urgent need for soldiers finally outweighed prudence. On August 10, following the funeral of a black child on the plantation of William Young, "Gabriel gave an invitation to some of the Negroes to drink grog down at the Spring." There he announced he planned to lead a revolution not simply for black freedom but also "for his Country."[27]

As one by one the slaves rose to their feet in support, Gabriel's lieutenants worked their way through the crowd "and enlisted a considerable number who signed a paper" with their names or their marks. Gabriel informed the gathering that he "fully expected the poor White people [to] join him, and that two Frenchmen had actually joined." The rebels, he shouted, could count on the aid of "every free negro and mulatto" as well as more than a few "of the most redoubtable democrats in the State." Before dispersing, the bondmen agreed that the night of the rising should be Saturday, August 30. Most Chesapeake slaves did no labor on Sunday, and it would not be unusual for area authorities to see blacks moving toward the city late on a Saturday evening.[28]

Just as all was in readiness, nature took a hand in the affair. "About Sunset," James Thomson Callender noticed from his cell window, "there came on the most terrible thunder Storm, accompanied with an enormous rain, that I ever witnessed in this State." Walls of water halted any movement about the countryside, and formerly shallow creeks washed away fragile wooden bridges and cut off communications between Brookfield and the city. Henrico whites noticed Richmond slaves "going [away] from the town" (although it was normal to see rural slaves flocking toward the city), but these slaves were unable to reach the assigned rendezvous point of Brook Bridge. In desperation, Gabriel and Jack Ditcher spread the word as best they could for their soldiers "to meet at the tobacco house of Mr. Prosser the ensuing night."[29]

What Gabriel did not know was that the plot had already been revealed. Two slaves named Pharoah and Tom, belonging to Prosser's neighbor Mosby Sheppard, informed their owner that Gabriel was to lead an uprising that very night. Pharoah, a recent recruit who had long resided on the Sheppard farm, perhaps saw the information as the safest path to his own freedom. Sheppard spread the alarm in his neighborhood and then galloped for town to inform Governor Monroe. At almost the same moment, a Petersburg slave informed his master, Benjamin Harrison, "that the slaves, free negroes & Mulattoes did intend to rise" and that "two white men," whom he named, "were concerned" in the plot.[30]

Virginia authorities were in a state of absolute terror. Richmond resembled a city besieged. Militia companies marched about the penitentiary and the capitol, and patrols swept the outskirts of the city and arrested any slave suspected of taking part in the conspiracy. Governor Monroe established a special board of inquiry composed of two magistrates, Miles Selden and Gervas Storrs, and the Henrico County court of oyer and terminer was convened "without delay." Attorney James Rind was assigned to represent those taken into custody for trial.[31]

By the time the Henrico militia reached Brookfield, the black general was nowhere to be found; with the exception of the unfortunate Solomon, the leadership cadre had vanished. How Gabriel and Ditcher escaped remains a mystery. Most likely, Gabriel moved south along the swampy Chickahominy River. When the young blacksmith next appeared, two weeks had elapsed and it was Sunday, September 14. Four miles below Richmond, Gabriel spied the three-masted schooner *Mary*, under the command of Captain Richardson Taylor. Either the rebel leader recognized one of the blacks on deck or he was simply desperate. Throwing aside the crude sword he had hammered from a wheat scythe, he swam out to meet the ship and clambered aboard.[32]

Although a former overseer, Taylor was a recent convert to Methodism. Perhaps his reading of John Wesley's *Thoughts upon Slavery* led him to understand that a world based upon racial categories was an ungodly one. But there is little doubt that the white skipper knew precisely who his curious guest was. Unfortunately for Gabriel, one of the bondmen aboard, Billy, who hired his time from his master Miles King, had heard of the $300 reward on Gabriel's head, enough money to purchase his own liberty. When the *Mary* reached Norfolk on September 23, Billy raced for the homes of constables Obediah Gunn and Robert Wilson. Trapped below deck, Gabriel "manifested the greatest firmness and composure, shewing not the least disposition to equivocate or screan himself from justice." The constables arrested Taylor for "intentionally aiding and assisting" in Gabriel's flight, and until the entire matter could be cleared up, they took Billy into custody as well. Perhaps nothing better illustrates the strange ambiguity of the Age of Revolution than the fact that Gabriel was spirited toward freedom by a white man and betrayed for silver by a fellow slave.[33]

For more than a week after his return to Richmond, Gabriel sat isolated in the penitentiary. Finally, on October 6, his trial began. According to young William Wirt, the future U.S. attorney general, the scene at the Henrico courthouse "was so crowded and tumultuous" that he could barely elbow his way inside. When questioned, Gabriel spoke "so low that he could not be heard at the distance of four feet." But young Ben Woolfolk, who turned his coat in exchange for his life—but not his liberty—testified that at every meeting it was Gabriel who took the lead in "the business" of revolution. To the audible sound of uncomfortable white patriots squirming in their seats, Woolfolk explained how Gabriel planned to carry their flag on the night of the rising. It bore the oddly familiar slogan: "death or Liberty."[34]

The trial lasted less than an hour. (Four other men were tried earlier that day.) "It is the unanimous Opinion of the Court," declared Miles Selden, "that the Negro man Slave Gabriel is Guilty of the Crime with which he stands accused and for the same that he be hanged by the neck untill he be dead." Since the court was condemning human property, it valued Gabriel at the impressive sum of $500—an inadvertent admission of his intellect and ability—payable to Thomas Henry Prosser. Gabriel then made his single request. He asked to have his sentence delayed for three days, so that he could hang on the same morning as George Smith, Sam Byrd Jr., and the other four slaves sentenced to swing on October 10.[35]

As the sun broke over the town, Gabriel had his hands tied behind him and was loaded into a tumbrel for transportation to the city gallows near Fifteenth and Broad Streets. A considerable crowd had gathered, but probably his wife was not among them. Indeed, it is likely that Gabriel had not seen Nanny since his flight from Brookfield. A myth later arose that as he mounted the steps, Gabriel "lost all firmness [and showed] nothing but abject fear," a legend for which there is no supporting documentation. There is every reason to believe that the young revolutionary died as he had lived his life, with quiet composure, before a horde of vengeful whites. The trapdoor fell open, and Gabriel, at long last, found freedom. "I do hereby certify," scribbled a pleased Mosby Sheppard, that Gabriel "was executed agreeably to the within Centance of the Court."[36]

Governor Monroe had long since lost all stomach for mass executions, if only because of the price of compensating so many masters for their confiscated property. Writing from Monticello, Jefferson suggested that the state assembly "pass a law for [the] exportation" of those who were not regarded as ringleaders by the courts. As a result, seventeen bondmen, including Jack Ditcher, who had surrendered on October 8, were sold to traders who carried them to Spanish New Orleans. Even so, by the time gravediggers laid down their shovels following the hanging of a young revolutionary in Petersburg on October 24, twenty-seven bondmen had paid with their lives for their desire to be free. That figure included William Wilson's Jacob, the black skipper, who allegedly hanged himself while in custody. Nanny, however, was left alone. Given the patriarchal culture of the time the justices may have assumed that Nanny was but a timid follower of a domineering husband and thus posed no danger following his death.[37]

The failure of Gabriel to liberate his followers led to even more restrictive laws after 1801. The "question is now a plain one," observed one Virginian. "Shall we abolish slavery, or shall we continue it?" But if the state assembly opted to keep "the ferocious monster" of slavery, a Fredericksburg newspaper editorialized, "we must keep him in chains." Within months, legislators enacted harsh new laws restricting the movement of slaves and free blacks. The city of Richmond established a sixty-eight-man public guard, an expensive force in an era of largely unpoliced cities. Each night at 9:00 PM, the guard rang the town bell, and any bondmen caught on the streets after that knell were herded into pens near the market square, where they were stripped and whipped with "as many stripes" as the guard officer "might see proper to inflict."[38]

Historians are inclined to depict the American Revolution as a radical affair, and perhaps with good reason. The disestablishment of the Anglican Church, the creation of the Bill of Rights, the election of key federal officials, and the move toward a more democratic franchise in most states were not merely progressive, but indeed radical developments. The events of Gabriel's brief life—as well as the failure of leading Virginia politicians to move decisively against unfree labor—are reminders that while the American Revolution freed the United States from British control, it did not truly institutionalize the ideals of the Declaration of Independence. The last words here on the alleged radicalism of the Revolution in the border South go to an unnamed soldier in Gabriel's army, who told the court that risking his life in the cause of liberty was a noble act. "I have nothing more to offer than what General Washington would have had to offer, had he been taken by the British and put to trial," the young bondman patiently explained. "I have adventured my life in endeavouring to obtain the liberty of my countrymen, and am a willing sacrifice in their cause." Upon hearing his declaration, white patriots promptly sentenced him to swing.[39]

Notes

1. Thomas Prosser, Henrico County Personal Property Tax, 1783, Library of Virginia, Richmond, Virginia (hereafter cited as LV).

2. On Gabriel's age see *Richmond Virginia Argus*, September 23, 1800. For the fact that Martin was far older than his two brothers, see the testimony of Prosser's Ben at trial of Prosser's Martin, September 12, 1800, Executive Papers, Negro Insurrection, LV.

3. Brookfield, Mutual Assurance Society Policies, Map, vol. 40, no. 1119, August 3, 1806; Josiah Henson, *Father Henson's Story* (Saddle River, NJ: Literature House, 1970), 18.

4. Deborah Grey White, *Ar'n't I a Woman? Female Slaves in the Plantation South* (New York: Norton, 1985), 53; *Norfolk Herald*, September 16, 1800; John C. Miller, *The Wolf by the Ears: Thomas Jefferson and Slavery* (New York: Free Press, 1977), 256–57.

5. Mary Beth Norton, Herbert Gutman, and Ira Berlin, "Afro-American Family," in Ira Berlin and Ronald Hoffman, eds., *Slavery and Freedom in the Age of the American Revolution* (Urbana: University of Illinois Press, 1986), 181–82; John B. Boles, *Black Southerners, 1619–1869* (Lexington: University Press of Kentucky, 1984), 145.

6. *Richmond Virginia Argus*, September 23, 1800; *Norfolk Herald*, September 16, 1800; James Callender to Thomas Jefferson, September 13, 1800, Jefferson Papers, Library of Congress (hereafter LC).

7. Testimony of Burton's Daniel at trial of Burton's Isaac, September 11, 1800, Executive Papers, Negro Insurrection, LV. In 1998, at the dedication of the "Gabriel's Rebellion Historical Marker," a lifetime resident of Henrico informed me that he attended a segregated high school in the late 1930s with two young men named Randolph, who claimed to be Gabriel's descendants.

8. *Richmond Virginia Gazette and General Advertiser*, October 9, 1798.

9. Among the works that describe Gabriel as a free black are Gary Nash, *Race and Revolution* (Madison, WI: Madison House, 1990), 79; Miller, *Wolf by the Ears*, 126; and Fawn Brodie, *Thomas Jefferson: An Intimate History* (New York: Norton, 1974), 342.

10. Eugene D. Genovese, *The World the Slaveholders Made: Two Essays in Interpretation* (New York: Pantheon, 1969), 16, 121, 126.

11. Raymond B. Pinchbeck, *The Virginia Negro Artisan and Tradesman* (Richmond, VA: William Byrd Press, 1926), 47; Mechal Sobel, *The World They Made Together: Black and White Values in Eighteenth-Century Virginia* (Princeton, NJ: Princeton University Press, 1987), 49–50; Ira Berlin, *Slaves without Masters: The Free Negro in the Antebellum South* (New York: Oxford University Press, 1974), 28.

12. Testimony of Prosser's Ben at trial of Gabriel, October 6, 1800, Executive Papers, Negro Insurrection, LV.

13. Clement Eaton, *The Growth of Southern Civilization, 1790–1860* (New York: Harper and Row, 1961), 270; Philip J. Schwarz, *Twice Condemned: Slaves and the Criminal Law of Virginia, 1705–1865* (Baton Rouge: Louisiana State University Press, 1988), 120.

14. Testimony of Prosser's Ben at trial of Gabriel, October 6, 1800, Executive Papers, Negro Insurrection, LV; Confession of Prosser's Solomon, September 15, 1800, Executive Letterbook, LV.

15. Alex Lichtenstein, " 'That Disposition to Theft, with Which They Have Been Branded': Moral Economy, Slave Management, and the Law," *Journal of Social History* 21 (1988): 413–40; Trial of Prosser's Gabriel, October 7, 1799, Henrico County Court Order Book, LV.

16. "An Act Concerning Slaves, Free Negroes, and Mulattoes," December 17, 1792, in Samuel Shepherd, ed., *The Statutes at Large of Virginia, 1792 to 1806*, 11 vols. (New York: AMS Press, 1970 reprint), 1:127.

17. James C. Ballagh, *A History of Slavery in Virginia* (Baltimore, MD: Johns Hopkins University Press, 1902), 92, claims that Gabriel did not have "an especial personal grievance to inspire him." Aside from his bondage and that of his family being a "personal grievance," certainly his public branding by a white jailer counted as a special form of humiliation.

18. Michael A. Bellesiles, *Arming America: The Origins of a National Gun Culture* (New York: Knopf, 2000), 246–48; Confession of Prosser's Solomon, September 15, 1800, Executive Letterbook, LV; Testimony of Prosser's Ben at trial of Gabriel, October 6, 1800, Executive Papers, Negro Insurrection, LV.

19. Gary B. Nash and Jean Soderlund, *Freedom by Degrees: Emancipation in Pennsylvania and Its Aftermath* (New York: Oxford University Press, 1991), 137–40; Graham R. Hodges, *Root and Branch: African Americans in New York and East Jersey, 1613–1863* (Chapel Hill: University of North Carolina Press, 1999), 168–71; Graham R. Hodges, *Slavery and Freedom in the Rural North: African Americans in Monmouth County, New Jersey, 1665–1865* (Madison, WI: Madison House, 1997), 134–37; Thomas O. Ott, *The Haitian Revolution, 1789–1804* (Knoxville: University of Tennessee Press, 1973), 120.

20. Testimony of Ben Woolfolk at trial of Sam Byrd Jr., September 27, 1800, Executive Papers, Negro Insurrection, LV; Testimony of Ben Woolfolk at trial of George Smith, September 19, 1800, ibid.

21. William Bernard to James Monroe, September 20, 1800, ibid.; Testimony of Ben Woolfolk at trial of Young's Gilbert, September 22, 1800, ibid.

22. Testimony of Ben Woolfolk at trial of George Smith, September 19, and at trial of Sam Byrd Jr., September 27, 1800, ibid.; Confession of Young's Gilbert, September 22, 1800, ibid.

23. Testimony of Prosser's Ben at trial of Gabriel, October 6, 1800, ibid.; James McClurg to James Monroe, no date, ibid.; *Fredericksburg Virginia Herald*, September 23, 1800.

24. *Richmond Virginia Argus*, October 10, 1800; *Norfolk Herald*, October 2, 1800; James Monroe to William Prentis, October 11, 1800, Preston Family Papers, LC.

25. *Fredericksburg Virginia Herald*, May 9, 1800; *Richmond Virginia Gazette*, January 25, 1799; Testimony of Prosser's Sam at trial of Jack Ditcher, October 29, 1800, Executive Papers, Negro Insurrection, LV.

26. This idea is based on, but varies from, that advanced by Eugene D. Genovese, *Roll, Jordan, Roll: The World the Slaves Made* (New York: Pantheon, 1974), 593.

27. *Richmond Virginia Argus*, October 3, 1800; Testimony of Price's John at trial of Young's Gilbert, September 22, 1800, Executive Papers, Negro Insurrection, LV.

28. Testimony of Price's John at trial of Young's Gilbert, September 22, 1800, Executive Papers, Negro Insurrection, LV; Confession of Ben Woolfolk, September 17, 1800, ibid.; *Fredericksburg Virginia Herald*, September 23, 1800.

29. James Thomson Callender to Thomas Jefferson, September 13, 1800, Jefferson Papers, LC; *Richmond Virginia Argus*, October 10, 1800; James Monroe to General Assembly, December 5, 1800, Letterbook, Executive Communications, LV.

30. Mosby Sheppard to James Monroe, August 30, 1800, in *Journal of the Senate of the Commonwealth of Virginia* (Richmond, VA: Thomas Nicolson, 1801), 26; Joseph Jones to James Monroe, September 9, 1800, Executive Papers, Negro Insurrection, LV; Household Papers, 1794–1812, Account Book, p. 39, Box 668, Mosby Sheppard Papers, Henrico County Human Services Office.

31. *Fredericksburg Virginia Herald*, September 23, 1800; *Norfolk Herald*, October 18, 1800.

32. Thomas Newton to James Monroe, September 24, 1800, Executive Papers, Negro Insurrection, LV; *Boston Gazette*, October 9, 1800; *New York Spectator*, October 4, 1800.

33. *Fredericksburg Virginia Herald*, October 3, 1800; *Norfolk Herald*, September 25, 1800; John Moss to James Monroe, September 28, 1800, Executive Papers, Negro Insurrection, LV; Thomas Newton to James Monroe, September 27, 1800, ibid.

34. William Wirt to Dabney Carr, October 6, 1800, Wirt Papers, Valentine Museum, Richmond, VA; Testimony of Ben Woolfolk at trial of Gabriel, October 6, 1800, Executive Papers, Negro Insurrection, LV.

35. Sentence of Prosser's Gabriel, October 6, 1800, Executive Papers, Negro Insurrection, LV; *Norfolk Herald*, October 11, 1800.

36. *Fredericksburg Virginia Herald*, October 14, 1800; Certification of death for Prosser's Gabriel, October 20, 1800, Auditor's Item 153, Box 2, LV. The claim that Gabriel died badly was made by Robert R. Howison, *A History of Virginia*, 2 vols. (Philadelphia: Carey and Hart, 1846), 2:392.

37. Thomas Jefferson to James Monroe, September 20, 1800, Jefferson Papers, LC. A discussion of the number of slaves hanged for complicity in Gabriel's plot may be found in Douglas R. Egerton, *Gabriel's Rebellion: The Virginia Slave Conspiracies of 1800 & 1802* (Chapel Hill: University of North Carolina Press, 1993), 186–88.

38. Donald R. Wright, *African Americans in the Early Republic, 1789–1831* (Arlington Heights, IL: Harlan Davidson, 1993), 97; *Fredericksburg Virginia Herald*, September 23, 1800; Marianne Buroff Sheldon, "Black-White Relations in Richmond, Virginia, 1782–1820," *Journal of Southern History* 45 (1979): 34–35.

39. Robert Sutcliff, *Travels through Some Parts of North America, in the Years 1804, 1805, and 1806* (Philadelphia: B. and T. Kite, 1812), 50.

Suggested Readings

The chief source for Gabriel's life and conspiracy are the papers collected at the Library of Virginia, Richmond, under the heading "Executive Papers, Negro Insurrection." A number of newspapers, many of them available on microfilm, also covered the collapse of the plot and the subsequent executions. Among the most thorough are the *Richmond Virginia Argus*, the *Fredericksburg Virginia Herald*, and the *Norfolk Herald*.

The two standard accounts of the affair are Douglas R. Egerton, *Gabriel's Rebellion: The Virginia Slave Conspiracies of 1800 & 1802* (Chapel Hill: University of North Carolina Press, 1993), which largely focuses on the event; and James Sidbury, *Ploughshares into Swords: Race, Rebellion, and Identity in Gabriel's Virginia, 1730–1810* (Cambridge, Eng.: Cambridge University Press, 1997), a broader examination of race relations in the region. Gerald W. Mullin's older study, *Flight and Rebellion: Slave Resistance in Eighteenth Century Virginia* (New York: Oxford University Press, 1972), contains an insightful chapter on the conspiracy. The pioneering account remains the section in Herbert Aptheker, *American Negro Slave Revolts*, 5th ed. (New York: International Publishers, 1983). Aptheker has done more than any other scholar to repudiate the insidious fiction of slave docility.

For the larger context of the times, one should consult Donald R. Wright, *African Americans in the Early Republic, 1789–1831* (Arlington Heights, IL: Harlan Davidson, 1993), and Sylvia R. Frey, *Water from the Rock: Black Resistance in a Revolutionary Age* (Princeton, NJ: Princeton University Press, 1991). Philip J. Schwarz, *Twice Condemned: Slaves and the Criminal Law of Virginia, 1705–1865* (Baton Rouge: Louisiana State University Press, 1988), contains the best discussion of Gabriel's 1799 brush with the law.

6

Mag Preston
Personal Honor in Southern Politics

Randolph Hollingsworth

The popular image of the southern woman before the Civil War generally reflects one shaped by motion pictures such as *Gone With the Wind*. While that film actually did feature a strong female character in the person of Scarlett O'Hara, more often the southern belle is portrayed as a different sort. Attended by slaves, the frivolous ladies of the mansion greet guests and maneuver their hoop skirts from room to room. Placed on a pedestal by male society and subjected to paternalistic control, they appear only as actresses on a limited stage, one dominated by men in the public sphere.

The reality of women's antebellum lives was, not unexpectedly, much more complex. The story of the black slave woman varies considerably from that of the white plantation mistress—who lived, however, in her own form of servitude. The account of a "poor white" female differs from that of a woman living on the frontier, where the scarcity of females might give her greater control and choice. In short, the women of the South had various life experiences and displayed both weaknesses and strengths. Yet, at the same time, they shared common experiences. No matter the class, race, or region, for example, the high death rate from childbirth, for both mother and child, caused many to dread the next pregnancy. Women's lives represented not only a struggle for survival but also for respect, for a livelihood, for power, and more. Randolph Hollingworth writes about one of the upperclass women of that era, one whose upbringing and subsequent life seemed to mirror—on the surface—many of the stereotypes. But as her story shows, the truth for her went beyond the usual image. Mag Preston fashioned a life of many parts.

Randolph Hollingsworth is an administrator for the Kentucky Virtual University, a state agency, and currently is working on the Adult Education Initiative mandated by the Kentucky legislature. In 1999 she received a Ph.D. from the University of Kentucky in American History; her dissertation was entitled, "She Used Her Power Lightly: A Political History of Margaret Wickliffe Preston of Kentucky." She recently wrote the introductory essay for a reprint of the 1930 edition of Alice Stone Blackwell's *Lucy Stone: Pioneer Woman Suffragist* (2001).

In the early nineteenth century the Romantic Era celebrated an image of the white woman: in the fine arts, she was a ballerina or a long-necked muse; in religion, she was the ever-suffering Madonna; and in popular culture, she was the icon of the "domestic sphere." The historian Barbara Welter studied antebellum religious treatises, advice literature, and fashion magazines such as *Godey's Lady's Book* and wrote about a "cult" that defined "true womanhood" by four cardinal virtues: domesticity, piety, submissiveness, and purity.[1] Southern white women in particular appeared more like butterflies or flowers than human beings— merely ornamental in the public realm. They seemed practically useless in the new world being created by mechanical-minded males of the Industrial Age.

Yet southern women were nothing of the sort; whether white or black, most of them labored on farms. They served as important economic producers as well as consumers in the new postrevolutionary age. At some point in their lives they might also have moved into the urban working class to serve as factory workers or domestic servants. Some opted for communal organizations (such as the Shakers or Catholic sisterhoods) and lived a life of simplicity and austerity. Others became activist intellectuals, such as Delia Webster, headmistress of the Lexington Female Academy in Kentucky, who lost her social standing after she helped fugitive slaves escape. Some functioned as professionals: nurses, teachers, writers, or women of the stage. Yet, despite overwhelming evidence to the contrary, the public still perceived southern women most often as the ubiquitous ballroom belles.

The image of the southern belle symbolized, then and now, the Old South of the 1820s–1850s. This romantic picture showed a society that preferred its women to be charming and flirtatious coquettes who never yielded their purity. In the years between puberty and marriage, most white women came closest to personal freedom, for during these years, they were expected to be clever enough for certain types of conversation and daring enough for some heated love-talk. Marriage meant moving from one paternal figure to the next, from the Colonel drinking his mint julep on the white-columned veranda to the slim, aristocratic young swain.[2] The literature of the day pictured the sixteen-year-old marriageable daughter of the southern plantation owner, doted on by her rich father, as exuberant, a little vain, and somewhat naive.

Few southern belles were like the literary ones. In actuality most were strong women of means who, before the Civil War, used the ballroom and the dining room as a forum for their wit and influence. Historian Mary P. Ryan emphasized women's "multiple points of entry into the public life" in the nineteenth century, and she proved that they were not simply restricted to "domestic spheres."[3] In real life, belles functioned politically in multiple ways alongside and sometimes despite men—either as great entertainers in their homes, as letterwriters, as powerful marriage brokers for their children, or as flamboyant widows free to spend their money in whatever political cause they wished. In 1838, Kentucky became the first state in the union in which women won a limited right to vote—if heads of households, they could vote in school board elections. This did not result, however, from any particular progressive movement for women's rights. As historian Elsa Barkley Brown asserted, "all women do not have the same gender."[4] Women's race, class, region, and sexual orientation all combine to shape their thinking and actions. Elite women in particular functioned from a power base not accessible to the majority of nineteenth-century females.[5]

For elite women, unlike for farm workers or the urban poor, the "public arena" did not mean a particular geographical location, such as a politician's podium or a street vendor's corner. Instead, their "public" formed wherever an exclusive antebellum American white elite gathered together, whether on a dueling ground, at a dinner table, or at a spa. Antebellum women's political acts might be found not in a public campaign, but rather in private arenas such as wills dispensing valuable properties, carefully contrived utterances in a parlor, or personal letters seeking patronage favors for their kin. These more hidden activities proved as important as the more visible records they left—of clubs and community service, of fundraising for schools, asylums, orphanages, or missionary work.

Antebellum white men played certain roles also, but ultimately had much more freedom of choice in such matters. They could easily exclude women not only from the rituals of honor but also from the important decision-making processes at the core of honorable male behaviors. Many southerners saw themselves as part of a noble race, now under assault by the mores of the Industrial Revolution. Their revered values and virtues were embodied in the southern woman as guardian of that unsullied, domestic sphere—the home.

Focusing on one southern woman's life and letters and exploring the reality of her "separate sphere" provide a test of the stereotype of the belle's nonintellectual, nonpolitical life. The experiences and words of this one wealthy antebellum Kentucky white woman, a female known only to a few of the inner circles of polite society, and a person merely on the edges of the national elite, give us an often overlooked perspective in political and military history. Many politically minded antebellum women, for many different reasons, did not express themselves in the same venues or in the same ways that their male counterparts did, although they served an important role in many different arenas as a "critical public"[6]—just as their male counterparts did. Most upper-class women in Kentucky represented and preserved "the innate and indigenous conservatism of Kentuckians."[7] They stood at the heart of southern politics and the mythology of the Old South. In fact, the refrain for Stephen Foster's sentimental song, "My Old Kentucky Home," comforted the white slaveowner's wife who is crying after the forced sale of enslaved Kentuckians.

Margaret Wickliffe Preston was the favorite and youngest daughter of Robert Wickliffe, the largest slaveowner in Kentucky. Both her biological mother and her stepmother, Margaretta Preston Howard and Mary Owen Todd Russell, were wealthy heiresses who, upon marriage, had handed to Wickliffe extensive land holdings and skilled slaves. A lawyer-politician of Fayette County, Kentucky, Wickliffe displayed manners so courtly and a bearing so impressive that he was popularly known as the Old Duke. As a member of an upper-class family, one deeply enmeshed in political and legal controversies, Mag Preston grew up keenly aware of her class, race, and gender roles in both formal and informal settings. She knew that her kin expected her to maintain successfully their station in an upper-class society that transcended state and even national boundaries.

Her formal education added to such expectations. She first attended two exclusive schools for Lexington girls—the Lafayette Female Academy and Shelby Female Academy—along with her younger friend and distant cousin, Mary Todd. While Mary Todd continued her schooling in Lexington with the French refugee, Charlotte Mentelle, and went on to become First Lady in 1860, Mag Preston went north to a private school in Philadelphia, Madame Sigoigne's.

But marriage soon beckoned. In 1840, at twenty-one, she married the up-and-coming young Whig, William Preston. A graduate of Yale University who had attended Harvard Law School, he had recently returned home to Louisville to practice law. As was not unusual in southern elite weddings, the marriage linked extended kin: her mother was a Preston descendent. Both William and Mag held in common relatives who included two governors of Virginia—James Patton Preston and James McDowell. The several cousins on the national scene counted the Washington socialite, Eliza McDowell (who married Senator Thomas

Hart Benton of Missouri), and John C. Breckinridge, vice president and presidential candidate just before the Civil War.

After marriage, Mag Preston's life experiences and decisions reflect a consistent effort to maintain her status through the personal power she brokered. In one clear example, her political power lay not in the electoral vote but in the shaping of an event that led to an electoral victory. Mag Preston functioned as an important political actor in the story of the duel between her brother, Robert Wickliffe Jr., and antislavery advocate Cassius M. Clay. An important letter by Mag Preston to her husband's brother-in-law, Albert Sidney Johnston, secretary of war of the Texas Republic (and later a Confederate general), affected the outcome of the honorable exchange.[8] Her efforts helped craft the stage on which her brother had chosen to duel, and Mag Preston assured that her extended family's honor would be maintained both during and after the contest.[9]

The story began in the spring of 1841, when "Cash" Clay campaigned against Bob Wickliffe, "the Young Duke," in a race to represent Fayette County in the Kentucky legislature.[10] In a public debate in late April, Wickliffe suggested that his opponent's own in-laws, the wealthy Warfields of Lexington, did not agree with Clay's brand of abolitionism, and Wickliffe reiterated his more famous father's claim that Clay was simply an ignorant dupe of northern agitators. The volatile Clay took exception to the mention of his wife and her family as "inadmissible" and challenged Wickliffe.[11] Two weeks before the duel was to take place, a distressed Mag Preston wrote to Johnston, then visiting his relatives in Louisville: "I write my Dear Brother to implore you to come to Lexington immediately upon the receipt of this—I have found my family in a state of the deepest anxiety and affliction—Robert has accepted a challenge from Cassius Clay and has left town to escape the civil authorities."[12]

Her husband William Preston had just begun his law practice and had taken the introductory steps of a successful political career. But his personal honor—and, by extension, Mag's—would be at stake if the duel were to go bad. In addition, political groups in Kentucky had taken up social reform and had spoken out against dueling as a form of intemperance and evidence of aristocratic corruption. Preston's friend, Dr. John Lutz, refused to attend since it would jeopardize his professorship at nearby Transylvania University. "I have to depend on the college for a support and I am afraid that becoming connected with that affair, it might injure me greatly."[13] Nevertheless, dueling remained of great political and social import to the prominent families of Kentucky and across the South. A belle who was once courted by Bob Wickliffe, Louisa Bullitt, had watched the unfolding of the event with considerable interest: "Great apprehensions are had as to the result, both are excellent shots and it must be fatal either to one or both parties. Mrs. Clay I hear is in total ignorance of the affair. The Wickliffes are in great distress. Mrs. Preston and all his [Wickliffe's] family arrived a few days since."[14]

Mag Preston very likely knew that her brother had borrowed her husband's "small repeating pistol" in order "to be prepared & not to be bullied" during his candidacy for the legislature.[15] She was certainly aware that her brother's adversary was not averse to using backwoods tactics such as knifing, eye gouging, or ear biting. The historian Elliot J. Gorn posited that for backwoodsmen, scars were "badges of honor" since they showed that men had withstood pain.[16] However, for the southern elites, physical scarification (whip welts, missing eye or finger—or worse yet, nose) was public evidence of inferior status.[17] Mag Preston knew that if her brother stayed in Lexington, he or any advocate of his, such as her own husband, might be drawn into a dishonorable fistfight. Nor did she want either her brother or husband to be left with visible scars. Cash Clay was renowned for his physical violence, and she knew that any male ritual to "save face" was not just a metaphor. She assured Albert Sidney Johnston of her "unbounded confidence" in his "courage and discretion" and asked if he would function as her brother's "friend and adviser." She wrote to him, she said, "without consulting anyone," but she knew that her family would agree with her plea and feel gratitude for his presence as her brother's second.[18]

In other words, she was asking him to give her family the "gift" of his weighty influence in a ritual of exchange between political foes. Historian Kenneth Greenberg wrote that southern men of honor constantly competed against each other in games of chance, and that a duel simply represented the most extreme form of a gamble. Wickliffe—her brother—would succeed in the gamble if he displayed superior marksmanship, manly valor, and cool demeanor under fire. Additionally his choice of seconds and of a negotiator whose version of the events afterwards would be acceptable to all was crucial. Mag thus worked, quietly, to make certain the family's honor remained intact.

Wickliffe and Clay met at a farm called Locust Grove near Louisville; Col. William R. McKee was Clay's second, as Mag hoped, and Johnston was Wickliffe's. According to Johnston's later statement of events, the first shot "was exchanged which proved ineffectual." Clay still insisted that his honor had not been restored and demanded further satisfaction for the insults he claimed he had received from Wickliffe during the public debate. He demanded another round "which was promptly accorded." While the seconds carefully reloaded the pistols, they also negotiated whether or not the "point of honor was satisfied." During this verbal exchange, they discovered that Clay was not satisfied on the "point, namely the manner in which R. Wickliffe JR had alluded to Mr. Clay's wife in public debate."[19] Subsequently, Wickliffe wrote a long explanation that he had not known that the perceived insult to Mary Jane Warfield Clay was the point of honor, since Clay had "not specified any particular ground for the challenge," and that had he known, he would never have exchanged shots with Clay but would have apologized immediately for introducing a lady's name in public debate. Bob Wickliffe had assumed that the honor of his father was at stake, and he was ready to die for the reputation of the Old Duke—just as his older brother Charles had done in 1829.[20] The men finally retreated from the field, though no verbal reconciliation between the two satisfactorily reestablished their honor. As Clay wrote about it forty-five years later, "We left the ground enemies, as we came."[21]

The aftermath of the duel was as important as the exchange of shots on the field of honor. Those present had to record events and all participants had to agree on the written record in order for the trial by ordeal to be complete and honor restored. Wickliffe wrote to Preston and assured him that he had symbolically defeated Clay and his political backers. By inference, Clay had lost the challenge, both of the duel and of the political campaign, since he had backed out of the duel: "Even the bullies and blacklegs no longer speak of him as the 'Little Black Bull with hair on his back three inches long.' "[22]

In June, when he wrote a triumphant letter to Johnston telling him that the statement of events had been signed, he related "the best thing that has ever been said of the difficulty between Clay & myself." He wrote that during a large gathering, the details of the duel were being discussed and a "lady with great naiveté" spoke out: "La! Isn't it strange that Mr. Clay did not think of his wife until after the first shot? I think he ought according to every rule of gallantry to have fought *first* for his wife and *then* for himself. Now suppose Mr. Wickliffe had shot Mr. Clay, why then *Mrs.* Clay's honor would have been unavenged!"[23] Clay was thus exposed, and the duel continued in the sense that a woman implied that Clay was a trickster, a sly manipulator, a man without honor.

This lady's public comment had unmasked Cash Clay, in Bob Wickliffe's view, and he was exultant.

Clay's version of events published in 1886 was very different from the "Statement" he signed in 1841 right after the duel. He admitted in 1841 that Wickliffe did not know of his particular offense against Clay, that is, his reference to "my wife's name in a speech," until after the first shot was exchanged. In his memoirs, he left the reader thinking that he fought the duel in order to protect the honor of his wife's name. More likely, Clay was angry at any snide reference to the marital differences widely known but rarely voiced. As in today's political maneuvering, a man's sexual relations provided ample images for a public unmasking. In his memoirs, Clay wrote that he thought highly of the Wickliffe-Preston families and that Bob was "a gallant fellow." Clay regretted that he "ever did so foolish a thing."[24]

Not coincidentally, Wickliffe won the election; Mag Preston masterfully orchestrated the cast of characters in the duel and perhaps it was she who had landed the final blow with the clever quip at the assembly. The Wickliffe-Clay duel involved not just the exchange of bullets but also the verbal record that Johnston constructed. And Johnston would not have been there without Mag Preston's letter. The public scrutiny of this ordeal also included women's words after the duel. Her elite world valued this sort of maneuvering by women, and Mag Preston's actions in the Clay-Wickliffe duel emphasized the role of class and kinship networks in antebellum politics.

Like the more famous Mary Todd Lincoln, Mag Preston had grown up in a household where local, state, and national politics conjoined to fuel everyday conversations. Her father, the Old Duke of Fayette County, served as a powerful local agent for the Democratic Party and had been an avid opponent of Henry Clay since the 1820s. Conversely, Mag Preston's stepmother, Mary Owen Todd Russell Wickliffe, contributed to the cause of the African colonization of former slaves, as did the Wickliffes' neighbor, Whig leader Henry Clay. Early on, Mag Preston became keenly aware of the intricacies of the political debates of the day. Her interest did not cease when she married.

In 1844, Kentucky Democrats celebrated the narrow win in the presidential election by the pro-Texas Democrat, James Polk, over Clay. In Louisville, Mag Preston rejoiced in the streets along with other Democrats, and she wrote to her father in Lexington that she had won $700 in her successful bet on the outcome of the election. "The roaring of cannon and the shouts of the democrats now sounding in my ear excites me so agreeably that I cannot contain myself in the house—I wish I were near you to choke you with kisses and congratulations, to see your face brighten with joy."[25]

Mixed emotions soon resulted, however, for President John Tyler interpreted Polk's win as a mandate for the annexation of Texas and moved to escalate the simmering hostilities against Mexico. Kentuckians, especially the Prestons' extended kin who had speculated in Texas landholdings, readied to fight for Texan independence. In May 1846 the governor urged Kentuckians to organize militias, and Mag's husband raised money from Louisville businessmen, volunteered for service, and was appointed as lieutenant colonel of the Fourth Regiment, Kentucky Volunteer Infantry.[26] Because William Preston had not attended military school, he was given the less noble task of getting supplies through to the Mexican front. Nevertheless, in that society a show of militarism was as important to his masculinity and class status as was his success as a lawyer and politician.

As usual, Mag and the children went to live with the Old Duke in Lexington for the summer to escape the malarial diseases of the river city, but this time she stayed there while her husband prepared to depart for Mexico. However, he did not leave until eighteen months later. That separation caused Mag to scold Preston for neglecting her and giving rise to gossip. She warned him that their peers noticed his lack of attention: "Do come down for I have not had an opportunity of exhibiting you this summer in Lexington and it is reported from your long absence the last time that you were down, that there is a coolness between us."[27]

Yet once William Preston left for Mexico in November 1847, Mag Preston wrote him sentimental letters. The language she used reflected her era's conventions of spiritualized marital love. At the same time, she expressed her need to be physically near her husband: "It is raining in torrents, I am in my room alone, and when I think of the distance that separates us, the uncertainty of when we are to meet, I feel as if my heart would break; but it has taught me one lesson dear Will, that all the happiness I have enjoyed I have derived from you and the world is dark to me without you."[28] In another letter she admitted that her jealous nature made her fear that she loved him more than he loved her. She regretted her earlier behavior as a flirt: "It has been my study since, as before marriage to make you feel that I did not care for you, and I have always endeavoured to *wound*, rather than flatter your vanity." Whenever she doubted his love for her, she "call[ed] forth the ambitious dreams of my childhood" to console her, but then she remembered that "my first and only wish has been, and is still, to be, the all absorbing feeling of your nature, as you have been of mine."[29]

Her barely masked expressions of sexual desire intermingled with her fear of possible adultery: "Pa says, Don't be uneasy my child; your husband is too far away from you to think of you, and there are a great many dark Senoritas to aid him in forgetting you."[30] She reminded him of his marriage vows and told him that he would have to swear his fidelity on her Bible when he got home: "I hope you will make good use of [the Bible] I gave you and remember all the vows you will have to take upon it, when you return; for I tell you now, when my heart yearns to see you, that I would rather never see you, though you are dearer to me than life; than believe that you would betray all the love I have felt for you." This love entailed not just her affection but also her unflagging faith in his behavior as a gentleman: "Do not think I doubt you, God knows I do not, that I fully confide in your affection and in your honor— and I pray to Him most fervently that He will restore you to me and to your children."

In these early love letters she conjured up images of a Victorian domestic scene. She warned her husband that her "reason will not bear the trial I have to endure; all I ask is tranquility—the days pass slowly and when evening comes, when I used to welcome you home, my spirits sink."[31] Seen in isolation, this part of her letter conjures up the stereotypical middle-class wife waiting at home by the fire until the husband returned from his job in the chaotic and immoral world of law and finance. However, Mag Preston meant Glendower, her father's house, as "home," and her husband's regular absence from "home" before he left for Mexico was not due to a regular job, but to his legal, political, and military activities in Louisville, an eight-hour train ride away.

In the same letter in which she summoned the idyllic images of "home" versus the public sphere, she spoke of her slave hires, her husband's bank notes, and her own politics. She voiced her despair by claiming that although an enthusiastic Democrat, she "would see Mr. Clay President, if it would bring you home." Love, honor, and politics all came in conflict within her. Just as the British deified their heroes of the Napoleonic Wars, the Americans, Mag Preston knew, would garner heroes from the fight against Mexican tyranny. Her husband's political future rested on his military conduct in this important test of American nationalism. She was willing to give all this up, however, when she asserted, "I find when I am most in love, I am the least ambitious."[32]

If Mag Preston ever really stopped being ambitious, it was not for long. By January 1848 her letters expressed an anxious optimism for her husband's well-timed and carefully orchestrated gamble with the American military venture into Mexico. "I feel that all I have on Earth, is cast upon this die, and it causes a sickening excitement in my heart— If you are fortunate and distinguish yourself, the future seems all too bright—If the reverse; I have nothing farther to hope for in life." She told him that she spent her time teaching the children and "looking to a future," one in which she expected his participation in the war to reap for them "the reputation of an able and efficient officer, and perhaps with some military glory to bequeath to your children."[33]

After four months, Mag Preston began writing to her husband of her fears that the reason she did not hear from him regularly was that he had fallen sick or because guerrillas had killed him. She confessed that since he had left, she had had bad dreams every night, "some of them I have no doubt would amuse you exceedingly." She dreamed "frequently" of the scene of his return when "you did not seem as glad to see me, as I expected you would be." Other times, she dreamed of arguments with him: "I have been in the most indignant passions with you, that you did not reply unhesitatingly to all my questions" about his fidelity. Finally, "last night I was infuriated at your telling me that I did not look pretty."[34] Two weeks later she referred to her continued bad dreams and said they were making her "superstitious."

She increasingly regarded her dreams as supernatural predictions. She warned him that "unless you have kept my memory sacred and pure, I never wish to see you again—If you have not stood the test, for God [*sic*] sake never return—Go rather to the farthest extremity of the Globe; for the Earth is not wide enough to separate you, as far from me as I desire you should be, if your constancy has not been equal to mine." Her jealousy led her to admit "the very apprehension makes my hatred for you at times as rancorous, as my love is deep and devoted at others."[35] She admitted that her sister Mary easily teased her with hints of his infidelities with Spanish women: "She often tries to excite my jealousy and might succeed but for the *Oaths* that my valuable letters [from Preston] contain."[36] By April she wrote to him that she no longer had those bad dreams, "not one, since I received your last two letters—Continue in all you write me to assure me of your constancy, it affords me more consolation and happiness than everything else on earth beside."[37]

The historian Bertram Wyatt-Brown suggested that the marriages between loving, equal partners in the nineteenth-century South were the exception since "honor, not conscience, shame, not guilt" formed the basis of southern culture.[38] The marriage between Mag Preston and William Preston was no exception. As time passed she made fewer statements of sentimental love in her letters, and the reasons for her hatred and frustration became increasingly complex. Early letters to her Mexican hero exposed the root of these feelings: she feared his dishonor if he lost his bet—if the army sent him home "Disgraced and Degraded— Great God—Death, anything, but that."[39] She held the strong conviction that association with the regular army was immoral: "As to your getting a Colonelcy in the regular army, I oppose it with my whole heart—There has been, and will always be a profligacy and dissoluteness in the army that from my earliest childhood has given me a disgust to Army Officers."[40] She needed to be sure that he had preserved his "honor inviolate" so that he could return "with a pure conscience and we may again be happy."[41] Their marriage was "an honourable estate,"[42] which for her depended on his taking, and retaking, an oath of fidelity. Most important, her calculated appeal to his honor reinforced the framework of their marriage, an important piece to her power base.

Upon his return from Mexico in 1848, with reputation enhanced and honor intact, William Preston moved swiftly into the morass of antebellum party politics. Although he had seen no real battle action, Preston became an acknowledged hero of Kentucky and gained admirers for his outspoken challenge to the Know-Nothing Party in the Kentucky legislature. He won election to the U.S. House of Representatives, and in 1854 the largest Freemason lodge of nineteenth-century Kentucky (No. 281) organized in Louisville and named itself after him.

Mag Preston had made her husband promise to keep a journal of his exploits in Mexico, a document that would eventually be beautifully bound in leather.[43] It is likely that she placed that book into the hands of the right men (such as General Winfield Scott) and women (such as Varina Davis) who then would remember to further his career (as they did) in the 1850s and 1860s. Preston's greatest successes were yet to come. President James Buchanan appointed him to the top diplomatic post to Spain in 1858, and the Preston family left the United States to live among European aristocracy. The two elder daughters made their debut in Madrid, and newspapers and personal letters attested to Mag Preston's social success in her ministerial residence. Later, during the Civil War, now-Confederate General Preston was appointed to serve as ambassador to Mexico and was given the task of attempting to earn international recognition for the Confederate States of America. His failure coincided with the death of the Confederacy, and he generally faded from political life.

His wife continued on, however, as a leader in her own right, as a great ballroom belle and marriage broker for her children, staying at all the fashionable spas and attending the best parties in New York, Washington, Chicago, Cincinnati, Louisville, St. Louis, and New Orleans. She focused on the refurbishing and renovation of her father's mansion, Glendower, in Lexington so that she could entertain the society among whom her daughters would eventually take their own leadership roles. Mag coached her son to socialize with the Roosevelts and Astors of New York, and the great thoroughbred farms of the Bluegrass evolved into national showcases. Mag Preston speculated in the booming petroleum business; her husband had gambled on real estate projects and coal mining.

Mag Preston and her children not only outlived General Preston, but they also exceeded his sociopolitical rank. She did not have to rely on her husband's status to make her own children's future secure. Her wider kin networks served as important channels of economic and political power, and women played a large role in key decision making. Mag Preston's experiences and tactics show that she functioned as an important and influential politico both in the extended family and among a national elite. For Margaret Wickliffe Preston, her "public life" was not only in her house but might also be at a Virginia spa or a European court, and honor played as important a role for her as for her husband. Honorable behavior conveyed community membership; conversely, the upper-class community determined its boundaries by observing and castigating those who did not exhibit honorable behavior. In this rarified world, Mag Preston functioned within the cultural boundaries of southern honor, and as a consequence she exerted great influence, both personally and indirectly through her extended kin. Her life experiences, like those of so many of her sex in that society, defied stereotypes. Southern women's varied experiences show how hidden political history included both men and women in the early nineteenth century.

Notes

1. Barbara Welter, "The Cult of True Womanhood, 1820–1860," *American Quarterly* 18 (1966): 151–74.

2 Bertram Wyatt-Brown, *Southern Honor: Ethics and Behavior in the Old South* (New York: Oxford University Press, 1982), 22, 126, 195, 204, 221, 227.

3. Mary P. Ryan, *Women in Public: Between Banners and Ballots, 1825–1880* (Baltimore, MD: Johns Hopkins University Press, 1990), 4.

4. Elsa Barkley Brown, " 'What Has Happened Here': The Politics of Difference in Women's History and Feminist Politics," *Feminist Studies* 18 (1992): 295–312.

5. See George E. Marcus, " 'Elite' as a Concept, Theory, and Research Tradition," in *Elites: Ethnographic Issues*, George E. Marcus, ed. (Albuquerque: University of New Mexico Press, 1983), 20.

6. Nancy Isenberg, *Sex and Citizenship in Antebellum America* (Chapel Hill: University of North Carolina Press, 1998), 206n.

7. Hambleton Tapp and James C. Klotter, *Kentucky: Decades of Discord, 1865–1900* (Frankfort: Kentucky Historical Society, 1977), 4–5. "Conservative thought, with some exceptions, had more or less prevailed in Kentucky since the beginning of statehood in 1792."

8. See Charles P. Roland, *Albert Sidney Johnston* (Austin: University of Texas Press, 1964), 107–8.

9. See Kenneth Greenberg, *Honor and Slavery* (Princeton, NJ: Princeton University Press, 1996), 74. "The central purpose of a duel was not to kill, but to be threatened with death . . . . Each man shot a bullet and gave his adversary a chance to demonstrate that he did not fear death; honor was more important than life."

10. See Robert Wickliffe Jr., "Election book" and his draft of "Speech to the Whig Young Men of U.S. in Baltimore, May 4–5, 1841," in Box 40, Wickliffe-Preston Family Papers, University of Kentucky Special Collections and Archives, Lexington (hereafter referred to as W-PFP).

11. Cassius Marcellus Clay, *The Life of Cassius Marcellus Clay* (New York: Negro Universities Press, 1969; orig. pub. 1886), 80.

12. Mag Preston to Albert Sidney Johnston, April 30 [1841], Johnston Papers, Barret Collection, Tulane University, New Orleans.

13. John Lutz to William Preston, May 3, 1841, Box 44, W-PFP.

14. See "Daughter" to Miss Susan C. Green, Bullitt Family Papers, University of Kentucky, Special Collections and Archives. See also Bob Wickliffe's plea to William Preston to help him reply to a love letter from Louisa (October 16, 1838, Box 43, W-PFP).

15. R. Wickliffe Jr. to "Preston," March 24, 1841, Box 40, W-PFP.

16. Elliott J. Gorn, " 'Gouge and Bite, Pull Hair and Scratch': The Social Significance of Fighting in the Southern Backcountry," *American Historical Review* 90 (1985): 28, 42.

17. Greenberg, *Honor and Slavery*, 15, 53–59.

18. Mag Preston to Albert Sidney Johnston, April 30 [1841], Johnston Papers, Tulane.

19. Document without heading, beginning "The following are the circumstances as they occurred at the meeting between C. M. Clay Esq. & R. Wickliffe Jr. Esq. on the 13th May 1841" and signed "A. Sidney Johnston," Johnston Papers, Tulane. See also Robert Wickliffe Jr. to William Preston, May 27, 1841, Box 40, W-PFP.

20. Robert Wickliffe Jr. to William Preston, May 27, 1841, Box 40, W-PFP. See J. Winston Coleman Jr., *The Trotter-Wickliffe Duel: An Affair of Honor in Fayette County, Kentucky, October 9th, 1829* (Frankfort, KY: Roberts Print. Co., 1950).

21. Clay, *Life*, 81.

22. Robert Wickliffe Jr. to William Preston, May 27, 1841, Box 40, W-PFP.

23. Robert Wickliffe Jr. to A. Sidney Johnston, June 4, 1841, Johnston Papers, Tulane.

24. Clay, *Life*, 81.

25. Mag Preston to Robert Wickliffe Sr., November 13, 1844, Box 44, W-PFP.

26. Charles S. Harper to William Preston, February 18, 1839, Box 43, W-PFP. See also Preston's letter to Robert Wickliffe Sr., May 23, 1846, Box 45, W-PFP.

27. Mag Preston to William Preston, August 22, 1847, Box 45, W-PFP.

28. Ibid., November 13, 1847.

29. Ibid., March 30, 1848.

30. Ibid., February 22, 1848.

31. Ibid.

32. Ibid., November 13, 1847. See also ibid., December 13, 1847 ("When you left me, I was miserable and thought for several weeks that my life was so wretched without you—that there was nothing left to interest me"); or January 30, 1848 ("When I think of seeing you, it seems to me it will be *rapture overwhelming*"); or March 30, 1848 ("I do not ask fame, wealth, power, all seem insignificant to me, when I *feel* that you love me").

33. Ibid., January 16, 1848.

34. Ibid., February 28, 1848.

35. Ibid., March 11, 1848.

36. Ibid., April 9, 1848.

37. Ibid., April 16, 1848.

38. Wyatt-Brown, *Southern Honor*, 22.

39. Mag Preston to William Preston, February 28, 1848, Box 45, W-PFP. She was relating her sympathy for Lizzie Robinson, whose husband was court-martialed by Preston for cowardice and dishonesty and returned to Lexington in disgrace.

40. Ibid., May 13, 1848.

41. Ibid.

42. *The Book of Common Prayer . . . According to the Use of the Protestant Episcopal Church in the United States of America* (New York: James Pott & Co., 1907), 277. This edition's version of the marriage ceremony had been in use since the U.S. Episcopal Church began in 1790.

43. A copy of William Preston's *Journal in Mexico: Dating from November 1, 1847, to May 25, 1848* (Paris: Lecram-Servant, 192[?]) is in the University of Kentucky, Special Collections and Archives.

Suggested Readings

For antebellum literature that depends on the stereotypical southern belle, see works by the popular writer, John Pendleton Kennedy. Kennedy crafted this icon into his character Bel Tracy in *Swallow Barn*, published in 1832. Harriet Beecher Stowe's *Uncle Tom's Cabin or, Life Among the Lowly* published in 1852 had both the butterfly-belle (Little Eva) and the lazy hypochondriac of the belle-gone-bad (her mother, Marie St. Clare).

On women's history, two great historians should be praised: Ann Firor Scott and Gerda Lerner. Scott's landmark study, *The Southern Lady*, undertook a key goal: to bring southern women into the discourse of legitimate historical study of the post-World War II era. Gerda Lerner insisted throughout her series of essays in *Why History Matters* that we must ask ourselves questions that can be answered only when we include both men's and women's activities and ideas. Joan Cashin's *Family Venture: Men and Women on the Southern Frontier* (New York: Oxford University Press, 1991) succeeds in this task admirably. For more on southern women, see Jane Turner Censer's *North Carolina Planters and Their Children, 1800–1860* (Baton Rouge: Louisiana State University Press, 1984); Suzanne Lebsock's *Free Women of Petersburg: Status and Culture in a Southern Town, 1784–1860* (New York: W. W. Norton & Co., 1984); Elizabeth Fox-Genovese's *Within the Plantation Household: Black and White Women of the Old South* (Chapel Hill: University of North Carolina Press, 1988); Catherine Clinton's *Tara Revisited: Women, War, and the Plantation Legend* (New York: Abbeville Press, 1995); and Margaret Ripley Wolfe's *Daughters of Canaan: A Saga of Southern Women* (Lexington: University Press of Kentucky, 1995). These books have excellent bibliographies. A useful essay is by Virginia Kent Anderson Leslie, "A Myth of the Southern Lady: Antebellum Proslavery Rhetoric and the Proper Place of Woman," in *Southern Women*, edited by Caroline Matheny Dillman (New York: Hemisphere Publishing Corporation, 1988).

For mythologized versions of the Wickliffe-Clay duel (*sans* females and pro-Clay), see Roberta Baughman Carlée, *The Last Gladiator: Cassius M. Clay* (Berea, KY: Kentucke Imprints, 1979), 35; also see H. Edward Richardson, *Cassius Marcellus Clay: Firebrand of Freedom* (Lexington: University Press of Kentucky, 1976), 34–35. For a more recent interpretation, see Stanley Harrold, "Violence and Nonviolence in Kentucky Abolitionism," *Journal of Southern History* 55 (1991): 15–38. For a psycho-ethnological thesis on the southern Scots-Irish genetic tendencies, see Richard E. Nisbett and Dov Cohen, *Culture of Honor: The Psychology of Violence in the South* (Boulder, CO: Westview Press, 1996). Other important resources for understanding the rituals and rules of plantation society from 1790 to 1860 are: Daniel Blake Smith, *Inside the Great House: Planter Family Life in Eighteenth-Century Chesapeake Society* (Ithaca, NY: Cornell University Press, 1980); Steven M. Stowe, *Intimacy and Power in the Old South* (Baltimore, MD: Johns Hopkins University Press, 1987); Brenda E. Stevenson, *Life in Black and White: Family and Community in the Slave South* (New York: Oxford University Press, 1996); and J. William Harris, *Plain Folk and Gentry in a Slave Society: White Liberty and Black Slavery in Augusta's Hinterlands* (Middletown, CT: Wesleyan University Press, 1985).

For information on antebellum Kentucky's black population and slavery, see Marion B. Lucas, *A History of Blacks in Kentucky*, vol. 1 (Frankfort: Kentucky Historical Society, 1992); Alice Allison Dunnigan, *The Fascinating Story of Black Kentuckians: Their Heritage and Traditions* (Washington, DC: Association for the Study of Afro-American Life and History, 1982); and John B.

Boles, *Black Southerners, 1619–1869* (Lexington: University Press of Kentucky, 1983).

For a survey of William Preston's political and military career, see Peter J. Sehlinger, "William Preston, Kentucky's Diplomat of Lost Causes," in *Kentucky Profiles: Biographical Essays in Honor of Holman Hamilton*, ed. James C. Klotter and Peter J. Sehlinger (Frankfort: Kentucky Historical Society, 1982), 73–98. For a history of the political consequences of the Mexican War, see Otis A. Singletary, *The Mexican War* (Chicago: University of Chicago Press, 1960); and Dean B. Mahin, *Olive Branch and Sword: The United States and Mexico, 1845–1848* (Jefferson, NC: McFarland & Co., 1997). For more on the public expectations of male Kentuckians in the Mexican war, see Damon R. Eubank, "Kentucky in the Mexican War: Public Responses, 1846–1848" (Ph.D. dissertation, Mississippi State University, 1989); and idem, "A Time of Enthusiasm: The Response of Kentucky to the Call for Troops in the Mexican War," *Register of the Kentucky History Society* 90 (1992): 323–44.

7

Frederick Law Olmsted
A Connecticut Yankee in King Cotton's Court

John C. Inscoe

Perceptions and understandings of a region emerge not only from within but also from the observations of those from outside a place. Over the years, many have recorded their views of the South, for both national and international audiences. Some offered sympathetic studies, others more critical ones, but only a few gained recognition for their balanced and nuanced views.

One of those people was landscape architect Frederick Law Olmsted, best known as the designer of New York's Central Park. But southern historians remember him also as a person whose travel accounts covered almost the entire region—the seacoast, piedmont, and mountain South, the plantation and poor white South, the eastern regions and the western frontier, the black South and the white one. His writings offer many observations valuable to those searching for specific aspects of the antebellum period. They have endured.

In an era without radio or television, where poor or expensive transportation facilities made travel difficult, people often formed their opinions about a place from what they read. Travelers to a region could thus play an important role, as Olmsted did, in shaping perceptions, and perceptions could then grow into reality in the minds of readers. John C. Inscoe here looks at the man, his motives, his works, and why he wrote them, in order to understand a key source in southern history.

John C. Inscoe is professor of history at the University of Georgia in Athens. He is the author of *Mountain Masters: Slavery and the Sectional Crisis in Western North Carolina* (1989), the coauthor of *The Heart of Confederate Appalachia: Western North Carolina's Civil War* (2000), and the editor of *Appalachians and Race: The Mountain South from Slavery to Segregation* (2001).

Antebellum Americans outside the South came to understand slavery as it existed below the Mason-Dixon Line in a variety of ways and from a variety of sources. Fugitive slave narratives were among the most authentic and most compelling of these sources, if only because they conveyed so intimately and with such immediacy the personal traumas of those who had triumphed over the oppression—physical and psychological

117

—they endured as bondsmen and women. As speakers and as writers (often in collaboration with abolitionist sponsors and colleagues), these former slaves told and retold their stories to audiences and readerships that grew more interested and more incensed as the antislavery movement intensified.

Equally effective was a much rarer form of first-hand testimony: that by a few whites who had lived on southern plantations and were troubled by what they observed of the lives and labor of their families' slaves. The most prominent of these were women, such as British actress Fanny Kemble, who spent only ten months on her new husband's rice and cotton plantations on the Georgia coast, and Sarah and Angelina Grimké, who were born and raised on a South Carolina plantation before moving north to become leaders in both the abolitionist and women's suffrage movements. Levi Coffin, a North Carolinian from a nonslaveholding family, moved to Ohio where he participated in the Underground Railroad movement. He wrote vividly about the traumas of the slave trade as he had observed it in childhood.

Most other northern abolitionists witnessed the horrors of the "peculiar institution" only from the peripheries. William Lloyd Garrison's only ventures below the Mason-Dixon Line were trips to Baltimore; Benjamin Lundy lived for several years in Wheeling, Virginia (later West Virginia); and Harriet Beecher Stowe made only one trip into Kentucky, seeing slavery primarily from the vantage point of her home across the Ohio River in Cincinnati, the northern entry point for many escaped slaves. All of these individuals wrote vividly about the cruel treatment of slaves by their masters, of families split at slave markets and auctions, and of coffles of chained men and women as traders moved them south.[1]

Northern travelers who made more extensive forays into the South often contributed significant documentation of slavery as they saw it. Some went into the region for the express purpose of recording their observations of the "peculiar institution" for a northern readership. Others, in the South for different reasons, were so shocked or troubled by what they saw that the experience itself made them converts to abolitionism and inspired them to articulate their reactions in print. "No man can visit the South for the first time without having his views of slavery, whatever they may be, to some extent modified," wrote Charles Grandison Parsons in his book *Inside View of Slavery*, which he published in 1855 upon his return from a tour of the region.[2] A decade and a half earlier abolitionist Theodore Dwight Weld, Angelina Grimké's husband, had recognized the power of such firsthand observation in mobilizing antislavery sentiment among northern readers and compiled a remarkable body of both inside and outside observations into a volume he called *American Slavery As It Is*, with an only slightly exaggerated subtitle, *Testimony of a Thousand Witnesses*.[3] Foreign visitors to the United States—including the German Karl Bernhard; Frederika Bremer, a Swede; and numerous Englishmen and women, such as Sir Charles Lyell, George Featherstonaugh, Harriet Martineau, and James Silk Buckingham—often included extensive commentary on the South as part of lengthy travel narratives aimed at enlightening European readers on American life, North and South.[4]

Of all these varied voices—oral and written, fictional and nonfictional, in newspapers, pamphlets, journals, and books—no observer of antebellum southern life wrote more thoroughly or more systematically about the region than did Frederick Law Olmsted. Over a period of about fourteen months from 1852 through 1854, Olmsted made two tours of the South. He traveled from Virginia to Georgia to Texas and back, from Atlantic seaboard to western frontier, from lowlands to highlands, from major cities to large sugar, rice, and cotton plantations, from remote farms to small towns. That range of travels provided him with as vast a firsthand view of the workings of the southern economy and society as any journalist achieved prior to the Civil War. Literary critic Edmund Wilson, in summing up Olmsted's achievement, wrote that "he tenaciously and patiently and lucidly made his way through the whole South, undiscouraged by churlish natives, almost impassable roads or the cold inns and uncomfortable cabins in which he spent most of his nights. He talked to everybody and he sized up everything, and he wrote it all down."[5] In so doing, he provided not only his contemporaries but also, perhaps more important, historians of slavery and the Old South with one of the richest, most carefully observed, and most voluminously documented contemporary accounts we have of southern life in all its various manifestations. No single primary source has been more widely cited and quoted by scholars of the antebellum South than have Olmsted's writings on the subject.

Curiously, despite his significant journalistic contributions before the Civil War and their later historical value, Olmsted is far better known for later achievements in very different enterprises. He soon followed his southern tours and the published accounts with the first and most significant of his many landscape designs—the creation of New York City's Central Park. That project was interrupted by the Civil War, which took him to Washington, DC, to organize and direct the U.S. Sanitary

Frederick Law Olmsted. *Library of Congress*

Commission. Midway through the war he moved to California, where he supervised mining enterprises and mobilized the first forest preservation efforts in the West. His postwar career covered a remarkable array of major projects in landscape design and urban planning, including Boston's Back Bay, the U.S. Capitol grounds, numerous college campuses such as Stanford and the University of California at Berkeley, and George Vanderbilt's opulent Biltmore estate in the North Carolina mountains, through which Olmsted had traveled more than forty years earlier. Olmsted's design of Chicago's Columbian Exposition in 1893 was one of his last major efforts, though he lived until 1903.

Before launching that career for which he is most remembered, Olmsted made his mark as a travel writer. Born in Hartford, Connecticut, in 1822, the product of a comfortable New England upbringing and a Yale education, Olmsted seemed to have been imbued with a strong sense of wanderlust. He dropped out of college in 1840 to sail as a common seaman on a voyage to China and the South Pacific that lasted nearly four years. With his brother John Hull Olmsted and John Hull's former roommate at Yale, Charles Loring Brace, Frederick made an extensive tour of Europe and the British Isles in 1850. Upon his return he wrote vivid descriptions of their trip and his observations of British farm life and practices, which he compiled and published in 1852 as a well-received book entitled *Walks and Talks of an American Farmer in England.*

Yet from the time of his return from Europe, Olmsted found himself, like many of his fellow Americans, increasingly concerned over escalating sectional tensions. In coming to terms with the territorial gains of the Mexican War and other gnawing matters regarding slavery's status and federal policy toward it, Congress had contrived a makeshift and ultimately fragile series of legislative maneuvers that came to be known as the Compromise of 1850. Although most of its terms were considered gains by the free-soil interests seeking to ban slavery in the new lands acquired from Mexico, northerners vehemently opposed the Compromise's one major concession to slaveholding interests—new, more rigid legislation by Congress to enable masters to retrieve escaped slaves and to penalize those who sheltered them and sought to bar their return to their owners. This Fugitive Slave Act flew directly in the face of those most involved in antislavery activity and, more than any previous development, mobilized abolitionists and won new recruits to their cause. Within a year of its passage, Harriet Beecher Stowe had channeled her anger over the act into a fictional condemnation of the slaveholding South. Appearing in book form in 1852 (after newspaper serialization), *Uncle Tom's Cabin* launched the most widespread and emotion-laden wave of sentiment against slavery yet throughout much of nonsouthern America and abroad.

It was at that point that Frederick Law Olmsted found himself ready to make his own contribution to this new level of frenzied propagandizing. But unlike most other northerners who wrote about the evils of slavery as they observed it, Olmsted was no abolitionist. While he did oppose the new Fugitive Slave Act, he harbored ambivalent sympathies for those it sought to return to bondage and those from whom they had fled. The Constitution was, for Olmsted, the ultimate authority with regard to slavery and he insisted that nothing in it gave the federal government any power to interfere with one's ownership of others, or with state statutes protecting that right. "The law of God in our hearts binds us in fidelity to the *principles* of the Constitution," he insisted, principles he felt were not to be found in either abolitionism or in slavery.[6]

It was this reluctance to succumb to the impassioned arguments of abolitionist friends, and his willingness to find fault with advocates of both sides of the debate over slavery, that led the closest of those friends, Charles Brace, to mention Olmsted's name to Henry Raymond. Raymond, the editor of a newly established newspaper, the *New York Daily-Times* (later to become the *New York Times*), was looking for a writer to send into the South to provide readers with unbiased analysis of the conditions currently generating so much debate and political upheaval. Olmsted's moderate views gave him the credibility of an objective journalist and thus made him an ideal candidate for the assignment that Raymond offered him late in 1852. Olmsted himself agreed that he was the ideal correspondent to cover so volatile a subject. "I am not a red-hot Abolitionist like Charley [Brace] but am a moderate Free Soiler," he said. "On the whole, I guess I represent pretty fairly the average sentiment of good thinking men on our side."[7]

Olmsted saw even more opportunity in his mission than did Raymond. From this trip and the journalistic reports it generated, he planned to produce "a valuable book of observations on the Southern Agriculture & general economy as affected by Slavery: the condition of the slaves—prospects—tendencies—& reliable understanding of the sentiments and hopes & fears of sensible planters & gentlemen that I should meet." Ultimately he believed that he could use facts to overcome "the deluge of spoony fancy pictures now at its height" (an obvious reference to *Uncle Tom's Cabin*) and thus calm the collective emotional fervor that he saw fueled by abolitionist propaganda with little basis in actuality.[8]

Olmsted also made it clear from the outset that whatever benefit of the doubt he might give to slaveholders—stuck as they were with an inefficient and antiquated labor force not of their own making—he would hold them accountable for how they treated the blacks over whom they ruled. In the first report in his series "The South," which appeared in the *Daily-Times* on February 6, 1853, Olmsted (who wrote anonymously, using only the term "Yeoman" as a byline) informed his readers that "I shall endeavor to ascertain the general disposition and purposes of our Southern fellow-citizens with regard to Slavery, and shall look for any indications of a changing character, advance or otherwise, in civilization, religion and intelligence, of the African race under the influence of the circumstances as it exists at the South."[9]

With his mission defined, Olmsted headed south in December 1852. Traveling by train, stagecoach, and steamship, he covered considerable ground before his return to New York early in April 1853. His route took him down the Atlantic seaboard: from Washington, DC, he moved through Virginia and the Carolinas to Savannah, where he arrived in late January 1853. He rapidly crossed Georgia to Columbus, and then into Alabama where he spent two weeks moving between Montgomery and Mobile. From Mobile he traveled to New Orleans, and spent nearly a month exploring the city and other parts of Louisiana. By mid-March he was on a steamboat moving up the Mississippi River, with stops at Vicksburg and Memphis before returning north.[10] That four-month trek served as the basis not only for a full year's worth of weekly reports in the *Daily-Times*, but the first of three book-length narratives, *Journey in the Seaboard Slave States*, a 700-page volume published in 1856 in both New York and London.

From the outset, Olmsted's determination to take in all facets of southern life and labor was apparent, as his first dispatches from Virginia demonstrated. In them, he provided first impressions of race relations as seen from his railroad car: "I am struck by the close co-habitation and association of black and white—negro women carrying black and white babies together in their arms; black and white children playing together (not going to school together); black and white faces are constantly thrust together out of the doors, to see the train go by"; a detailed description of a "Negro funeral" he observed on the outskirts of Richmond, at which he was "deeply influenced by the unaffected feeling, in connection with the simplicity, natural rude truthfulness, and absence of all attempt at formal decorum in the crowd"; and an analysis of the plight of free blacks, in which he quoted a local historian who called them "the most vicious and corrupting of the varied materials making up our social system."[11]

In those same early days of his tour in Virginia, Olmsted observed and described slavery in a variety of venues. He visited a coal mining operation manned by both hired slaves and white workers, English and Welsh; a tobacco plantation, where the owner told him that despite its widely acknowledged ruinous effects on the soil, "if he was well-paid for it, he did not know why he should not wear out his land"; and the

Great Dismal Swamp, where runaway slaves often sought permanent refuge and even raised families, inspiring Olmsted to comment: "What a life it must be: born outlaws, educated self-stealers; trained from infancy to be constantly in dread of the approach of a white man as a thing more fearful than wild-cats or serpents, or even starvation."[12]

The narrative pattern established in his opening Virginia dispatches continued throughout both his trips. Olmsted deemed no encounter, interview, or observation unworthy of his attention or of several pages of commentary. Although the original intent of his mission was to focus on agriculture, Olmsted spent relatively little time on plantations. He carried only a handful of letters of introduction to planters and failed to make contact with several of them. Perhaps it was because of these missed opportunities that Olmsted's experiences and writings became so multifaceted, with as much attention devoted to cities, small towns, small farms, and even remote wilderness areas as to the vast cash crop enterprises that epitomized southern life for so many outsiders.

Despite the seeming randomness—and indiscriminate inclusiveness—of this Connecticut Yankee's coverage of what he saw, observations related to slavery dominated his reports, and certain themes emerged early and were sustained throughout. Olmsted sought to maintain the objectivity that he and Raymond had touted in introducing his series; he was especially careful to avoid harsh criticism of slaveholders' treatment of their black property. But while he eschewed the moral high ground that he so abhorred in abolitionist rhetoric, he readily found much to fault about slavery and about slaves. Most notably, he stressed the economic inefficiency of black bondage and its stifling of both agricultural diversity and industrial development throughout the region.

"The negroes are a degraded people," he wrote, "degraded not merely by position, but actually immoral, low-lived; without healthy ambition; but little influenced by high moral considerations, and in regard to labor, not at all affected by regard for duty." He observed a "capitalist" in Petersburg, Virginia, supervising a construction project. In noting how slowly slaves were carrying bricks and mortar to waiting masons, a northern man standing with Olmsted commented on what seemed to be their intentional indolence. In response, "the builder started to reprove them, but after moving a step, turned back and said: 'It would only make them move more slowly still when I am not looking at them, if I hurry them now.' " And in his most telling comment, the builder reasoned, "What motive have they to do better? It's no concern of theirs how long the masons wait. I am sure, if I was in their place, I shouldn't move as fast as they do."[13]

Far more than his fellow commentators on the South, Olmsted chronicled the considerable variety of nonplantation enterprises that used slave labor—coal mines, salt mines, ironworks, logging camps, turpentine operations, railroad construction, fisheries, tobacco factories, brickyards, sawmills, and tanneries. In describing these operations as well as the more familiar agricultural enterprises, Olmsted stressed not only the relative inefficiency of slaves' efforts but also the fact that their presence shut out opportunities for gainful employment for white laborers. Some of it was by choice: "No white man," Olmsted found, "would ever do certain kinds of work (such as taking care of cattle, or getting water or wood to be used in the house), and if you should ask a white man you had hired to do such things, he would get mad and tell you he wasn't a nigger." The same was true of women: "Poor white girls never hired out to do servants' work, but they would come and help another white woman about her sewing or quilting, and take wages for it."[14]

Olmsted also stressed the limitations slavery imposed on a more diversified agricultural output, which would have freed planters of their dependency on—and exploitation by—northern middlemen who controlled the cotton and tobacco markets with which they had to deal. In seeking to instruct a Carolina planter on the imbalance in regional market exchanges, Olmsted told him that "I have raised hay, potatoes, and cabbages, on my farm in New York, that found a market in Richmond, but here you have capital soil for such crops; how is it you don't supply your own market?" The planter replied that he "should be laughed at if I bothered with such small crops." Olmsted scoffed at these short-sighted farmers, noting that "they leave such little crops to the niggers and yankees, and then grumble because all the profits of their business go to build 'Fifth-avenue palaces' and 'down-east school houses.' "[15]

Olmsted's reports from his first trip—forty-eight in all—appeared on a nearly weekly basis in the *Daily-Times*, most of them published after his return to New York in April and continuing through February 1854. They were widely read and discussed well beyond a local readership. Perhaps to Olmsted's satisfaction, his so-called objectivity drew criticisms both from proslavery advocates and from abolitionists. Henry Raymond was enthusiastic about Olmsted's dispatches, declaring them "decidedly the best reports that have ever been made" about the South, and reveled in the controversy they generated.[16] He urged his correspondent to return to the South, and Olmsted was eager to do so. But he proposed a somewhat different plan to make this second trip more of a western tour than another southern one, moving through Texas and on to California, thus providing his readers with reports on the two states whose status in the Union had spurred the nation's current sectional tension.

Raymond agreed, and in November 1853, seven months after his return home, Olmsted set out again. He was accompanied by his brother John Hull Olmsted, who was attracted by the potential benefits of the southwestern climate for the tuberculosis from which he suffered. Moving quickly by train and steamboat to New Orleans by way of Cincinnati and Nashville, they headed west along the Red and the Sabine Rivers into Texas. Once beyond the traditional plantation society of east Texas, Frederick and John found themselves in a very different world. They discovered San Antonio's mix of Mexicans, Indians, and Americans who made the Spanish mission city a vibrant microcosm of the Lone Star State's multicultural frontier society, and were intrigued enough to abandon any plans to move on to the West Coast. The brothers spent five months touring Texas's cities, towns, rugged mountains, broad plains, and rapidly developing Gulf Coast. Much of that time they were "roughing it," traveling on horseback, camping in a tent, and accompanied by a pack mule.

Finally, in late May, they turned east again. In New Orleans, John left his brother to return home, and Frederick proceeded on his own for another two months through different parts of the same states through which he had moved on the first trip. This time he explored their less settled "backcountry" regions—northern Mississippi and Alabama, and the Appalachian areas of Georgia, Tennessee, North Carolina, and Virginia. Only at the end of July 1854 did he depart the South through Richmond, just as he had first come into it over a year and half earlier. From this second trip, more than twice the length of the first in both time and distance, Olmsted produced far fewer newspaper reports, though he documented all he saw, and did so just as thoroughly as he had for his first trip. He and John Hull accumulated enough material, in fact, to produce a 500-page volume on their Texas travels alone, entitled *A Journey through Texas: Or a Saddle-Trip on the Southwestern Frontier*, published in 1857, and a two-volume account of Frederick's remaining two months of that trip, made alone, *A Journey in the Back Country*, which appeared in 1860. John Hull, who compiled and edited the Texas volume, died of tuberculosis just before its publication, at the age of thirty-two.

Olmsted and his brother, John Hull, camping in Texas in 1854. From Olmsted, *A Journey through Texas*, frontispiece.

While there was much about Texas that appealed to both Olmsteds, the discovery of its German settlements most intrigued Frederick and inspired some of his most ardent proselytizing on the benefits of a free-soil society. German immigrants had moved into central Texas in large numbers in the 1840s and had already created thriving, well-established communities there by the time the Olmsteds visited them. They first encountered Germans in San Antonio and through them discovered the smaller nearby towns of Neu Braunfels and Sisterdale, in which they spent considerable time. Frederick was fascinated by the first concentration of self-conscious nonslaveholders he had come across in the South, and was quick to credit their prosperity and cultural development to the absence of black property. "Our journey through Eastern Texas was disagreeable in the extreme—an unpleasant country and a wretched people—bad supplies and bad weather," he complained of the plantation region of the state. "With Western Texas, however, we have been greatly pleased. The country has a great deal of natural beauty and we have fallen among a German population very agreeable to meet; free-thinking, cultivated brave men."[17]

He described the artisans, merchants, and farmers throughout the German settlements as "men accustomed to hard labor with their own hands, for the support of themselves and their families." He praised their intelligence, enterprise, and work habits as well as "their rational regard for liberty," and claimed that "there are no capitalists among the Germans, but they will inevitably gain wealth much more rapidly than the Anglo-Americans." Nor was it likely that they would ever "fall into those indolent and inefficient habits which so generally characterize Anglo-American settlers," especially those with slaves.[18]

One of Olmsted's biographers called his account of his Texas travels "a morality play that contrasts the highly idealized, educated, and cultivated Free-Soil German settlers of West Texas with a grim portrait of unrelieved coarseness and ignorance among the slaveholders, rich and poor, of East Texas."[19] So enamored was the *Times* correspondent with the former that he renewed his interest in the Free Soil movement in the Northeast, which encouraged colonization by nonslaveholding immigrants and New England farmers to prevent further encroachment of contested territories by slaveholding interests. Olmsted particularly welcomed the prospect that Texas itself would be divided into further states, reflecting the free-soil commitment of Germans and Mexicans along its southern and western frontiers, and wrote extensively about the benefits of the fragmentation of the largest southern state.

Central to Olmsted's view of the detrimental effects of slavery was the cultural and social stagnation it imposed on white southerners. Slavery robbed the region's yeomen of any Calvinistic work ethic or of any incentive for self-improvement, material or otherwise. But what made Olmsted's commentary most original was that his findings about poor whites—"unambitious, indolent, degraded and illiterate . . . a dead peasantry so far as they affect the industrial position of the South"—were almost equally applicable to the ruling class. The primary reason, he maintained, was "the degradation of all labor which is affected by Slavery." As a disillusioned foreign mechanic who had moved back to New York after a brief stint in the South told Olmsted, "Why, you see, Sir, no man will work along side of a nigger, if he can help it. It's too much like as if he was a slave himself."[20]

Olmsted found such attitudes and their ruinous effects throughout the South and commented on them frequently. But it was his encounter with the Texas Germans that provided him with the most viable support for these claims—stark contrasts that he would continue to see as he moved eastward through the "backcountry" of the central and upper South, where he found a far smaller slave populace than he had seen elsewhere. As he had in New Braunfels and Sisterdale in Texas, Olmsted found exceptions to the deplorable conditions of the plantation South along another of its peripheries—the Southern Appalachians.

As he moved into the hill country of northern Alabama early in the summer of 1854, Olmsted reported: "Today I am passing through a valley of thin, sandy soil, thickly populated by poor farmers. Negroes are rare, but occasionally neat, new houses, with other improvements, show the increasing prosperity of the district." At the same time, he noted, "The people are more social than those of the lower country, falling readily into friendly conversation with a traveler. They are very ignorant; the agriculture wretched and the work hard."[21] Olmsted expanded on this ambivalent portrait of a people both poverty stricken and contented in their nonplanter environment as he moved north and east into the Great Smoky and Blue Ridge Mountains of Tennessee, North Carolina, and Virginia. He noted a different temperament among those with whom he talked. "Compared with the slaveholders," he wrote about southern highlanders, "these people are more cheerful, more amiable, more sociable, and more liberal. Compared with the non-slaveholders of the slaveholding districts, they are also more hopeful, more ambitious, more intelligent, more provident, and more comfortable."[22]

Olmsted documented the degenerative effects of slavery on both the character and well-being of slave owners in this predominantly nonslaveholding region. One northern Alabamian offered him some advice as to the accommodations he should seek as he moved into the mountains. "The richer a man is . . . and the more niggers he's got, the poorer he seems to live. If you want to fare well in this country you stop to poor folks' housen; they try to enjoy what they've got, while they ken, but these yer big planters they don't car for nothin' but to save."[23]

The point was confirmed as Olmsted moved into East Tennessee and contrasted the accommodations of his highland hosts on two consecutive nights there. One was the residence of a slaveholder; the other was not. Though similar in size and furnishings—"both houses were of the best class common in the region"—and though the slaveholder was the wealthier of the two, Olmsted claimed that he lived in much less comfort at his house. It was dirty, disorderly, and in need of repair; he and his wife were "very morose or sadly silent"; the household's white women were "very negligent and sluttish in their attire," and the food was badly cooked and badly served by their slaves. By contrast, Olmsted's next host, a nonslaveholder, lived in much neater, well-ordered, and comfortable quarters. The women were clean and well dressed, and everyone was "cheerful and kind." The food served was abundant and wholesome (the first good food Olmsted claimed to have had since Natchez, Mississippi, months earlier), and all work was carried on far more smoothly and conscientiously.[24]

Although such convenient contrasts may strain credibility, the southern highlands, like the Texas frontier, provided Olmsted with revealing variations to his theory that the negative effects of a slaveholding society extended well beyond its black victims. Yet he maintained that, for all his sharp critiques of the "peculiar institution," he did not advocate its elimination. "The subjection of the negroes of the South to the mastership of the whites," he wrote, "I still consider justifiable and necessary, and I fully share the general ill-will of the people of the North toward any suggestion of their interfering politically to accomplish an immediate abolition of slavery." "For us to cry out for Abolition," he insisted, would be "impracticable, fanatical, mischievous and unjust."[25]

On the other hand, Olmsted recognized that slavery's end was an eventuality that must be acknowledged and for which slaves must be trained. Hardly a moralist, Olmsted reasoned that freeing slaves with no preparation for their postemancipation welfare would accomplish little in terms of overcoming the evils—to do so would be "no more immediately practicable than that abrogation of hospitals, penitentiaries, and boarding schools."[26] It was the responsibility of all masters to prepare those in their care for the challenges of freedom, just as a father raises his children for the independence of adulthood. "The negroes come to us from barbarism as from a cradle," he wrote, "with a confused, half-developed mind, with strong and simple appetites and impulses, but whimsical and unreliable," all limitations they could overcome under the tutelage and care of paternalistic white guardians. But it was not merely those charges to whom owners had responsibility. "The improvement and elevation of the negro," he pointed out, was a duty owed to the nation at large, in order to assure "the honor, safety and future prosperity of the country whose institutions we unite to govern and protect."[27]

In perhaps his greatest deviation from abolitionist arguments, Olmsted downplayed widespread instances of owners' cruelty or mistreatment of their human property. "The people of the South . . . are as kind to their slaves as any people could be imagined to be." He was quick to credit their "kindness" to their own self-interest and good business sense. Slaves were adequately fed, clothed, and housed if only because to deny such basic care and sustenance would jeopardize their effectiveness as workers or their resale value. And, as with so many white southern defenders of their labor system, Olmsted turned to comparative perspectives to make his case. He insisted that slaves were "generally abundantly provided with coarse food—more so than the agricultural laborers of any part of Europe." He acknowledged that whipping was common on plantations, but in terms of discipline, he wrote, "I think the condition of the negroes is just about what that of the seamen has formerly been in our Navy, and still is in the English service." Olmsted documented several instances of extreme violence, including the deaths of several slaves, but even that, he insisted, had to be seen in a broader context: "Very few overseers punish their slaves . . . so wantonly, brutally, passionately, or cruelly as I have seen a clergyman in New England punish boys entrusted to him for education." In short, Olmsted reasoned that any man with a large group of dependents subject to his full authority, whether "negroes or sailors, or peasants or children," would most likely resort to "the use of the lash or other humiliating punishments."[28]

As one biographer has noted, "No abler, friendlier, or less self-righteous observer ever traveled the South prior to the Civil War."[29] And yet Frederick Law Olmsted remained as ambivalent about the southerners and their way of life at the end of his travels as he had been at the beginning. He insisted that there were "peculiar virtues in the South, too little known or considered, the setting forth of which would do good." But he also made it clear that there was much of which he disapproved. In the very next sentence he wrote: "I will not conceal for a moment that I was disappointed in the actual condition of the people of the South, citizen and slave; that the more thoroughly and the longer I was acquainted with that which is ordinary and general, the greater was my disappointment."[30]

By the time Olmsted's impressions were in print and circulating widely, in both newspaper and book form, objective analysis of the South among northerners was becoming increasingly rare. The fact that his writings were less inflammatory or emotional than most assessments of slavery by the mid-1850s meant that they were probably less influential in changing readers' minds or mobilizing strong opinions on either side of the issue. Nevertheless, no contemporary of his provided those interested in the South and its "peculiar institution" with a greater sense of how many ways masters and slaves and slaveholders and nonslaveholders interacted with each other and the wide range of social, economic, and geographic situations in which they did so.[31]

Even before much of his commentary appeared in print, Olmsted himself had already moved on to a very different career—he was named superintendent of Central Park in 1857—that would gain him far more lasting prominence and acclaim during his lifetime. And yet a number of contemporaries recognized the long-term implications of his southern chronicles. Harvard scholar Charles Eliot Norton declared with great prescience that "they have permanent value, and will be chief material for our social history whenever it is written." Norton's colleague, poet James Russell Lowell, agreed. He informed Olmsted that "I have learned more about the South from your books than from all others put together, and I valued them the more that an American who can be patient and accurate is so rare a phenomenon."[32] Time has validated both of these assessments, and historians remain very much in the debt of this Connecticut Yankee, whose voluminous observations still inform our own understanding of slavery and the antebellum South during the final decade of both.

Notes

1. James L. Huston, "The Experiential Basis of the Northern Antislavery Impulse," *Journal of Southern History* 56 (1990): 609–40.

2. Charles Grandison Parsons, *Inside View of Slavery: Or a Tour among the Planters* (Boston: J. P. Jewett and Co., 1855), 53, quoted in Huston, "The Experiential Basis of the Northern Antislavery Impulse," 626.

3. Theodore Dwight Weld, *American Slavery As It Is: Testimony of a Thousand Witnesses* (New York: American Anti-Slavery Society, 1839).

4. Karl Bernhard, Duke of Saxe-Weimar Eisennach, *Travels through North America during the Years 1825 and 1826*, 2 vols. (Philadelphia: Carey, Lea and Carey, 1828); Frederika Bremer, *The Homes of the New World: Impressions of America* (New York: Harper and Bros., 1853); Sir Charles Lyell, *A Second Visit to the United States of North America*, 2 vols. (New York: Harper & Bros., 1849); George W. Featherstonaugh, *Excursion through the Slave States, from Washington on the Potomac to the Frontier of Mexico* (New York: Harper & Bros., 1844); Harriet Martineau, *Society in America*, 2 vols. (London: Saunders and Otley, 1837); and James Silk Buckingham, *The Slave States of America*, 2 vols. (London: Fisher & Co., 1842). For a sampling of their writings and those of many other commentators on southern slavery, see Willie Lee Rose, ed., *A Documentary History of Slavery in North America* (New York: Oxford University Press, 1976).

5. Edmund Wilson, *Patriotic Gore: Studies in the Literature of the American Civil War* (New York: Farrar, Straus, and Giroux, 1962), 221.

6. Quoted in "Introduction" to Charles E. Beveridge and Charles Capen McLaughlin, eds., *The Papers of Frederick Law Olmsted*, vol. 2, *Slavery and the South, 1852–1857* (Baltimore: Johns Hopkins University Press, 1981), 5 (hereafter cited as *Papers of Olmsted*, 2).

7. Frederick Law Olmsted (FLO) to Frederick Kingsbury, October 17, 1852, in ibid., 82.

8. Ibid.

9. "The South," No. 1, *New York Daily-Times*, February 16, 1853, in ibid., 86.

10. For annotated itineraries of Olmsted's two trips through the South, see Appendix II of *Papers of Olmsted*, 2:467–82. See also the maps of his trips, on pp. 112, 272, 296, and 308.

11. Frederick Law Olmsted, *Journey in the Seaboard Slave States, with Remarks on Their Economy* (New York: Dix and Edwards, 1856), 17, 25, 125. Over 300 of this volume's 700 pages are devoted to Virginia, although it was one of eight states through which Olmsted traveled on this "journey."

12. Ibid., 90, 159–60.

13. Ibid., 209–10.

14. Ibid., 82–83.

15. Quoted in Witold Rybczynski, *A Clearing in the Distance: Frederick Law Olmsted and America in the Nineteenth Century* (New York: Scribner, 1999), 114.

16. Ibid., 124; Laura Wood Roper, *FLO: A Biography of Frederick Law Olmsted* (Baltimore: Johns Hopkins University Press, 1973), 90–92.

17. Omsted to Anne Charlotte Lynch, March 12, 1854, in *Papers of Olmsted*, 2:271–72.

18. "A Tour of the Southwest," No. 12, *New York Daily-Times*, June 3, 1854, in *Papers of Olmsted*, 2:305–6.

19. Melvin Kalfus, *Frederick Law Olmsted: The Passion of a Public Artist* (New York: New York University Press, 1990), 166.

20. "The South," No. 47, *New York Daily-Times*, January 26, 1854, in *Papers of Olmsted*, 2:252–53.

21. Frederick Law Olmsted, *A Journey in the Back Country, In the Winter of 1853–54*, 2 vols. (New York: Mason Brothers, 1860), 1:245–46.

22. Ibid., 293.

23. Ibid., 234–35.

24. Ibid., 268–70.

25. Ibid., vi; "The South," No. 27, *New York Daily-Times*, June 30, 1853, in *Papers of Olmsted*, 2:180.

26. Olmsted, *Journey in the Back Country*, 1:iv–v.

27. "The South," Nos. 27 and 28, *New York Daily-Times*, June 30 and July 8, 1853, *Papers of Olmstead*, 2:180, 186.

28. "The South," No. 47, *New York Daily-Times*, January 26, 1854, *Papers of Olmsted*, 2:248–49. This particular column consisted of Olmsted's "general conclusions" about the condition of slaves as he had observed them over the course of the first of his two trips south.

29. David Freeman Hawke, "Editor's Introduction" to *The Cotton Kingdom: A Selection* (Indianapolis, IN: Bobbs-Merrill Co., 1971), x.

30. Olmsted, *Journey in the Back Country*, 1:v.

31. Fascination with the South by no means ended in the antebellum era, and commentary by outside observers of the South continues to fuel a publishing tradition that has extended from Reconstruction—J. T. Trowbridge, *The Desolated South, 1865–66: A Picture of the Battlefields and of the Devastated Confederacy* (New York: Duell, Sloan and Pearce, 1866); Sidney Andrews, *The South Since the War, as Shown by Fourteen Weeks of Travel and Observation in Georgia and the Carolinas* (Boston: Ticknor and Fields, 1866); and Edward King, *The Great South*, 2 vols. (Hartford, CT: American Publishers, 1874, 1875)—to recent works, including: V. S. Naipaul, *A Turn in the South* (New York: Knopf, 1989); Tony Horowitz, *Confederates in the Attic: Dispatches from the Unfinished Civil War* (New York: Pantheon, 1998); and Thomas C. Dent, *Southern Journey: A Return to the Civil Rights Movement* (New York: William Morrow, 1997). For an extended analysis of northern writings on the post-Civil War South, see Nina Silber, *The Romance of Reunion: Northerners and the South, 1865–1900* (Chapel Hill: University of North Carolina Press, 1993).

32. Both quotes from Wilson, *Patriotic Gore*, 220–21.

Suggested Readings

There are several biographies of Olmsted, most of which emphasize his later careers, particularly that of landscape architect and designer. These include Laura Wood Roper, *FLO: A Biography of Frederick Law Olmsted* (Baltimore: Johns Hopkins University Press, 1973); John Emerson Todd, *Frederick Law Olmsted* (Boston: Twayne Publishers, 1982); Melvin Kalfus, *Frederick Law*

Olmsted: The Passion of a Public Artist (New York: New York University Press, 1990); and Witold Rybczynski, *A Clearing in the Distance: Frederick Law Olmsted and America in the Nineteenth Century* (New York: Scribner's, 1999). Most of these works devote only a single chapter to Olmsted's antebellum travels in the South, although Rybczynski provides insightful coverage in the twenty pages he devotes to this phase of Olmsted's career.

An essay collection that gives more weight to this aspect of his career is *Olmsted South: Old South Critic/New South Planner*, ed. Dana F. White and Victor A. Kramer (Westport, CT: Greenwood Press, 1979). For an essay on the latter part of Olmsted's second trip, his tour through the southern highlands, see John C. Inscoe, "Olmsted in Appalachia: A Connecticut Yankee Encounters Slavery and Racism in the Southern Highlands, 1854," *Slavery & Abolition* 9 (1988): 171–82.

All four of the volumes Olmsted himself wrote about his southern travels—*A Journey in the Seaboard Slave States* (1856); *A Journey through Texas* (1857); *A Journey in the Back Country* (1860); and a two-volume compilation of all three, *The Cotton Kingdom* (1860)—are available in several editions. The most useful single volume on Olmsted's travel writings on the South is in Volume 2 of the five-volume *Papers of Frederick Law Olmsted*, ed. Charles E. Beveridge and Charles Capen McLaughlin (Baltimore: Johns Hopkins University Press, 1981). This volume, entitled *Slavery and the South, 1852–1857*, includes private correspondence from Olmsted written between 1854 and 1857, and articles from his series, "The South," as they first appeared in the *New York Daily-Times* in 1853 and 1854. A brief compilation of the reports in book form appears as *The Cotton Kingdom: A Selection* (Indianapolis: Bobbs-Merrill Co., 1971).

There is a considerable literature on antebellum travel writing that puts Olmsted's trips and the reports they generated into a broader literary and political context. A solid, but dated, bibliographic work is the three-volume *Travels in the Old South*, ed. Thomas D. Clark (Norman: University of Oklahoma Press, 1959), especially Volume 3: *The Antebellum South, 1825–1860: Cotton, Slavery, and Conflict*. Particularly applicable to the issues dealt with here is James L. Huston, "The Experiential Basis of the Northern Antislavery Impulse," *Journal of Southern History* 56 (1990): 609–40. Edmund Wilson included Olmsted in his collective portrait of writers of the Civil War era, *Patriotic Gore: Studies in the Literature of the American Civil War* (New York: Farrar, Straus, and Giroux, 1962).

8

George Washington Harris
The Fool from the Hills

John Mayfield

The antebellum South included many contradictory images. One featured a proper, pious, almost Puritan-like plantation society, governed by strict rules of decorum, honor, and justice. On the other hand, another focused on a raw, backwoods frontier South of rough fights, bawdy jokes, and few limits on behavior. Both images contained elements of fact and fiction.

Southern literature before the Civil War often reflected those two regional worlds. One group of authors offered traditional themes in their work. William Gilmore Simms, John Pendleton Kennedy, Paul Hamilton Hayne, and Henry Timrod represented those who used historical romances or plantation novels to tell a story in an ideal, genteel, and sentimental tone. But other writers presented the speech and resentments of a very disparate people. The words of Davy Crockett and Augustus Baldwin Longstreet exhibited the earthy temper of the southern yeoman class, but none did so better than George Washington Harris. His Sut Lovingood tales featured racy anecdotes, sharp imagery, folk dialect, and strong satire. They skewered most of the institutions of the Old South at one time or another and well represented the humor of the common folk.

John Mayfield is professor of history and department chair at Samford University in Birmingham, Alabama. He is a former member of the editorial board of the *Journal of the Early Republic*. Professor Mayfield is the author of *Rehearsal for Republicanism: Free Soil and the Politics of Antislavery* (1980); and *The New Nation, 1800–1845* (1982). He is writing a book about southern humor.

L et us consider Fools and their uses. Fools hold a special place in every culture's history, and they come in all kinds of guises. In the medieval and Renaissance eras, Fools, court jesters, served an official function. They were virtually the only persons allowed to lampoon a king to his face. Kings kept them around, in fact, to keep a grip on

This essay originally appeared in Michael A. Morrison, ed., *The Human Tradition in Antebellum America* (Wilmington, DE: Scholarly Resources, 2000), 229–43.

137

reality. Fools pop up at carnivals, at Mardi Gras, and at circuses. Since the age of print, they have become fixtures in literature, and now they have moved into film. A Fool laughs at society, and, importantly, he laughs at the laugher, so that no one walks away feeling superior or unchanged. Fools keep us from taking ourselves too seriously, and that helps us keep going. They live in the borderlands between life and art; they break down the barriers between what is proper and what is absurd.

Americans, however, are often uncomfortable with Fools. Perhaps it is a manifestation of our business culture or our inclination to take ourselves too seriously. We were, after all, the "City on the Hill" all the way back to the colonial era—out to show the world how it is done right—and we are incorrigible reformers. The British are much better at accepting things as they are than Americans, who still hope to improve everything. For that reason, English humor tends to farce while Americans excel at irony. Only occasionally do we let a true Fool take the stage.

Then there is Sut Lovingood, a southerner of no fixed address or occupation. He is virtually unknown outside a few circles, yet he may be the original and best American Fool of all. An east Tennessee businessman, George Washington Harris, created Sut in a series of yarns written chiefly during the 1850s and 1860s.[1] Sut describes himself as a "nat'ral born durn'd fool," without "nara a soul, nuffin but a whisky proof gizzard," with "the longes' par ove laigs ever hung tu eny cackus." His sole purpose in life is getting drunk, getting girls, and getting "intu more durn'd misfortnit skeery scrapes, than enybody, an' then run outen them faster, by golly, nor enybody" (172). When challenged to justify himself, his answer is direct and simple: "Yu go tu *hell*, mistofer; yu bothers me" (232).

Sut Lovingood exists for the practical joke. Anything—rich, poor, male, female, animal, human, old, young—is fair game. So, we have Sut slipping two live lizards up a circuit preacher's pants leg just to watch him scream. "Brethren, brethren . . . the Hell-sarpints *hes got me!*" he hollers, and strips and runs naked through the mostly female crowd (56). Or we have Sut breaking up Mrs. Yardley's quilting bee, for no reason beyond sheer maliciousness, by tying a clothesline row of quilts to a horse's saddlehorn, then splintering a fence rail over the poor animal " 'bout nine inches ahead ove the root ove his tail' " (143). The horse manages to knock down just about everything in sight, including Mrs. Yardley, who dies either from being run over or from the shock of losing a nine-diamond quilt, depending on who tells the story. Sometimes we find Sut at the receiving end, as when he lusts a little too openly after Sicily Burns ("Sich a buzzim! Jis' think ove two snow balls wif a strawberry stuck but-ainded intu bof on em" [75]). Sicily, no virgin she, slips him raw baking soda as a "love potion." As the gas comes frothing out of Sut's "mouf, eyes, noes, an' years" he thinks, "*Kotch agin, by the great golly!* . . . same famerly dispersishun to make a durn'd fool ove myse'f . . . ef thar's half a chance. Durn dad evermore, amen!" (81).

How do we explain a creature such as this? Sut Lovingood is not from the business culture; he is outside modern sensibilities. He comes from a world of physical—not psychological—pain and deprivation, and he responds accordingly with violent and uncompromising energy. Maybe, we hope, he is the voice of the forgotten poor. In the preface to his yarns, for example, Harris lets Sut explain that he will be happy if he can give a laugh to "eny poor misfortinit devil hu's heart is onder a millstone, hu's ragged children are hungry, an' no bread in the dresser, hu is down in the mud, an' the lucky ones a'trippin him every time he struggils tu his all fours, hu has fed the famishin an' is now hungry hisself, hu misfortins foller fas' an' foller faster, hu is so foot-sore an' weak that he wishes he were at the ferry" (ix). Ultimately, though, this explanation does not work, at least not in any traditional way. Poor people come in for his pranks just as surely as rich ones. There is no irony to his life, no expectations. He knows he's worthless and so lives entirely for the moment. He was born a Fool from a Fool. He will die that way, probably from a clean shot to the heart from some young woman's husband.

Still, Sut is not alone in American humor. He has his peers among the bear-eaters and ripsnorters of Davy Crockett's time and in the rough humor of the frontier West, where physical cruelty and practical joking were the norm. A Fool exactly like Sut, however, could only come from the South—the prosperous and poor, proud and humiliated antebellum South that has been the genesis of so many of our national dreams and nightmares. He could not have originated in the North or Midwest. The dry business culture there simply could not sustain a creation such as Sut. Moreover, he could only have been created by a particular type of southerner, one who was fiercely devoted to his region—even to the point of supporting secession without stint or reservation—and who knew the South's customs, proprieties, and expectations to the letter. Only one who knows what is not foolish can create a perfect Fool.

George Washington Harris created the Lovingood stories in a series of newspaper and magazine sketches that began in the 1840s and culminated in a book, *Sut Lovingood: Yarns*, published in 1867. Were it not for the yarns, history would have passed him by, and it almost did. He was born in western Pennsylvania in 1814. Little is known of his parents, except that George was named after his father and that his mother had been married once before and had a son, Samuel Bell, who was Harris's half-brother. Samuel Bell moved to the small town of Knoxville, Tennessee, a few years after Harris was born and brought the young boy with him shortly thereafter. No one knows what happened to George's parents; they may have gone to Tennessee or they may have died.[2]

Harris spent his early years learning skills and developing ambition. Samuel Bell was a trained metalworker who specialized in first-rate small arms, such as pistols, knives, and swords. He taught Harris the trade in a shop in Knoxville, and Harris kept one hand in the profession for most of his life. But George Washington Harris seems to have been a mobile, restless youth who was not entirely happy with the limitations of his half-brother's style of life. He was a small man, reputedly quick and agile, who briefly rode jockey in local quarter races. Like most young men, he was eager to set out on his own. The opportunity came when he was only nineteen. A company took him on as captain of a steamboat making the run from the port of Knoxville along the Tennessee River to the Ohio, and Harris stayed in the job for five years. In 1838 he helped transport Cherokees out of the Tennessee Valley and on to the Trail of Tears to their new homes in Oklahoma. He was apparently good at his job, maintained discipline, and took care of his equipment.

What would have been a lifetime dream for many young men was, for Harris, the first of many jobs. In 1835 he married the daughter of the inspector of the Port of Knoxville (who also owned the local racetrack) and began a family. Whether he grew tired of life on the river or whether his family and father-in-law pressured him to settle down is not known. Whatever the motive, in 1839 he took out a loan, bought a substantial farm near the Great Smoky Mountains, and settled into apparent respectability. He listed his occupation as "manufacturer and trader"—which meant that he probably farmed some, traded some, and made or fixed things. He had a nice house, carpets, books, china, a bay mare, and three slaves, plus a wife and three children. By any measure he had moved, young, into what would later be called the Victorian middle class. He had also contracted that most middle-class of burdens, a large debt. He could not maintain it. By 1843 the farm and house and carpets and at least one of the slaves were gone, and Harris took his family back to Knoxville.

There he opened a metal shop, like his half-brother, and began to settle down in earnest. The shop was large and could handle both delicate jobs and heavy machinework, but the venture did not last. By the end of the decade, Harris had signed on as superintendent of a glass factory (more likely a large shop), while he continued to do some silversmithing on the side. He apparently needed to work two jobs, for Harris still tried to maintain a large household, including two slaves and a washerwoman. If there was any consistency to his career thus far, it seems to be in his capacity for hard work and constant debt in the pursuit of the image of prosperity. During the 1850s, Harris went through an astonishing number of job changes for someone of his age and respectability. He was a steamboat captain again in 1854 and a mine surveyor the next year. The year after that he borrowed money to start a sawmill, which failed, then became for a short time a postmaster, then a railroad conductor. During the Civil War, he moved around, living for a while in northern Alabama and then Georgia. After the war he went back to Tennessee to work for the railroads again. He was still in that line when he died in 1869.

Sometime in the 1840s this fairly unremarkable man, who had had only a year-and-a-half of schooling in his life, began to write. He may have done some newspaper work for the Democratic *Knoxville Argus* in the mid-1840s, but his first attributable stories were for a national magazine, the *Spirit of the Times*, published out of New York by William T. Porter. Porter catered to sporting men from the northern and southern gentry, and his magazine recorded horse racing, fox hunting, and other pursuits of the leisure class. It also fielded some of the best and most original humor of the times, with a preference for southern tales about coon hunts, wrasslin' matches, quaint folkways, and generally weird backwoods characters. Most of the major humorists of the Old Southwest published stories in the *Spirit* at one time or the other, and most followed the formula of having a genteel narrator introduce a colorful character who then entertained the company with a story in dialect. The *Spirit* was a natural place for Harris to start, and his first stories read pretty much like the rest of the magazine's submissions: folksy characters out making fools of themselves for the rich folk to snort at.

Except even these stories suggest something different, something really anarchic, at work. His first story of any worth, "The Knob Hill Dance," is in most respects an ordinary tale of a hillbilly hoedown. For sexual references and sheer irreverence, however, it pushed the limits for its time. Girls come to the dance "pourin out of the woods like pissants out of an old log when tother end's afire" wearing everything from homespun to calico—but not silk. Any girl who wore silk would "go home in her petticote-tale *sartin*, for the homespun would tare it off of hir quicker nor winkin, and if the sunflowers dident help the homespuns, they woudn't do the silk eny good." Translation: What the dancing did not wear out, the bushes would. Everybody drinks, dances, eats, rolls on the bed, and the whole thing ends in a glorious brawl. The narrator describes walking home with his girl, and a "rite peart *four-leged* nag she is. She was *weak* in *two* of hir legs, but t'other two—oh, my stars and possum dogs! they make a man swaller tobacker jist to look at 'em, and feel sorter like a June bug was crawlin up his trowses and the waistband too tite for it to get out."[3] He wants to marry her, or so he says. Porter's magazine was one of the few, perhaps the only, outlet for innuendos such as these, but on at least one occasion during these early years even Porter had to reject one of Harris's stories as too salty.

Harris's output was erratic until 1854, when he discovered Sut Lovingood. The original was probably Sut Miller, a local from somewhere around Ducktown, Tennessee (Harris was working there as a mine inspector). Harris added "Lovingood"—sexual reference no doubt intentional—and put him in the saloon of Pat Nash (also a real person), talking to a gentlemanly narrator named, wouldn't you know, "George." The first story, published in the *Spirit* and revised later for Sut Lovingood's *Yarns*, was a knockout: "Sut Lovingood's Daddy, Acting Horse."

It is unlike any other story of its time. Sut rides up to Pat Nash's saloon on the spindliest horse ever born and begins right away to explain that this nag is "next to the best hoss what ever shelled nubbins or toted jugs," his lamented Tickytail, who is now dead. "Yu see, he froze stiff; no, not that adzactly, but starv'd fust, an' froze arterards" (20). From that unlikely introduction, Sut jumps cleanly into an explanation of how Tickytail's death prompted Dad to act hoss. The whole family— sixteen kids plus a "prospect"—has lazed through the winter, "hopin sum stray hoss mout cum along." It never happened, so Dad lies awake one night "a-snortin, an' rollin, an' blowin, an' shufflin, an' scratchin' hisself, an' a-whisperin at Mam a heap—an' at breckfus' I foun' out what hit ment" (22). Dad will pull the plow himself, act hoss.

He is pretty good at it, maybe too good. Dad gets Sut and Mam to fashion him a harness from pawpaw bark and a bridle from an umbrella brace, and he runs around on all fours practicing snorting and kicking up his heels and trying to bite someone. Mam "step'd back a littil an' were standin wif her arms cross'd a-restin' 'em on her stumick, an' his heel taps cum wifin a inch ove her nose. Sez she: 'Yu plays hoss better nur yu dus husban'.' He jes run backards on all fours an' kick'd at her agin, an'—an' pawd the groun wif his fis" (23). So Sut leads him off to the field, and they do get into it nicely. Dad snorts and pulls, Sut begins dreaming of the corn crop they will get in (and the whiskey it will produce), and then Dad charges straight into "a ball ho'nets nes' ni ontu es big es a hoss's hed, an' the hole tribe kiver'd 'im es quick es yu culd kiver a sick pup wif a saddil blanket" (24). Dad tears off like, well, a scared horse through bushes and then seven panels of fence. He loses the harness, his clothes, everything except the bridle and "ni ontu a yard ove plow line sailin behine, wif a tir'd-out ho'net ridin on the pint ove hit" (25). When he gets to the bluff overlooking the river, he jumps in. While he bobs up and down trying to get free of the hornets, Sut begins mocking him. "Switch 'em wif yure tail, dad. . . . I'll hev yer feed in the troft, redy; yu won't need eny curyin tu-nite will yu?" (26, 27). Dad cusses him back so bad that Sut leaves for the mines for a few days. "Yere's luck tu the durned old fool," he toasts, "an' to the ho'nets too" (28).

That broke the mold. Never mind that Harris's comic imagery and use of language was far ahead of anyone else writing in the field; those are subjects in themselves. He had created a comic masterpiece from a most un-southern, un-Victorian, un-middle-class subject—a father's total humiliation. If he could do that, he could savage every other sacred cow (or horse) in the culture, and he did. The rest of the yarns, published in bits and pieces over the next dozen years and then carefully, painstakingly revised into a book, went after preachers, virgins, marriage, sentimentality, the home and hearth, anything that came within Sut's reach.

Therein lies the incongruity. How could tales this anarchic, this crude, this foolish, come from the pen of an ordinary, debt-ridden small-businessman and devoted family man from what should have been one of the most socially conservative parts of the country? One would expect him to come up with the kind of overblown heroics and sticky romantic goo that made for quick contracts and high-volume sales. Instead, he created a Fool. It all seems incongruous, but perhaps only such a man could have written such tales.

Despite the constant debt and the frequent career moves, Harris was firmly rooted in the culture and politics of a particular place—east Tennessee. It was a place where several of the South's subcultures came together. There were mountain folk and river folk, and Harris had met them on his travels. There were townsmen and businessmen passing through, and Harris had dealt with those, too. There were slaveholders, not the cotton snobs from south Alabama or Mississippi, but slaveholders nonetheless with a claim to all that implied in the complex social relations of the South. There were the rich and the frightfully poor, and Harris saw them. His whole environment, in fact, was a mosaic of often contradictory ideals.

So was Harris. Consider, for example, his religious convictions. Harris was a solid, traditional Presbyterian. For years the First Presbyterian Church of Knoxville had a Harris family pew, and one of Harris's sons was named for the pastor there. Harris's devotion to his church was no mere social formality. Friends called him a "blue Presbyterian," which meant simply that he took his church seriously, did not work on Sunday, and raised a strict household. The religious culture around him was a good deal more diverse. East Tennesseans worshipped through established churches, circuit preachers, evangelical and holiness groups, revivals, tent meetings, and virtually anything else that prayed or sang. Some parts of the church-going population stayed strictly to themselves; others moved in and out of these religious expressions as the spirit—and opportunity—moved them. Still other parts preferred to have nothing to do with the whole scene, considered preachers frauds and hymn-singing noise, and saved Sunday mornings for the hangover. Harris pretty certainly was familiar with all these practices and shades of opinion; as a riverboat captain and railroad man, he must have seen it all. At the core, however, he was a proper man.

He was also a southern fire-eater. Harris began and ended life a staunch southern Democrat. He supported James Buchanan in 1856, wrote a rather bad political satire about the Republican and Know Nothing candidates, and got rewarded with the postmaster job. That same year, Harris was elected a city alderman. More important, in 1856, Harris went to Savannah for the Southern Commercial Convention—a loose cover for the crazier secessionists of the time. In 1859 he went to Nashville for the Democratic state convention and got appointed to the state central committee. His politics became more and more extreme. After Lincoln's election the following year, Harris wrote three vicious parodies of the new president, comparing him to a dried-out frog nailed to a board. This sort of thing was more popular in west Tennessee, where secessionists held a majority, than in unionist east Tennessee, so Harris left Knoxville. After the war, Harris wrote more nasty satires—this time on Grant, abolitionists, and radical Republicans. These satires were not his best work.

The convergence of Harris's middle-class propriety and his rabid, arrogant sectionalism is suggestive. In real life, Harris was a fairly ordinary, proper townsman with a business to run, a family to raise, and a house to maintain. His record of successes, failures, ventures, and losses was not radically different from his peers in towns all over the country, South and North, or indeed over western Europe and England. Like it or not, Harris was a member of the urban middle class and partook of its Protestant ethics.

What Harris fancied himself to be may have been something different. His failed attempt at living the life of a country squire during the late 1830s and 1840s is intriguing, because it is at that point in his careers where he acquired both debt and slaves. Given the cost of slaves, even young ones, the two were intimately connected. Moreover, he kept slaves—as many as he could—even after his move to the city made servants a luxury he could not afford. The possession of slaves more than anything else defined status in the antebellum South. It was the entry card to the elite, the connecting link to the planter class. Like members of this planter class, Harris dabbled in horse racing, delighted in telling stories and generally being sociable, and fancied himself a rising politician. With a twist of luck here or there, Harris might have moved in the same circles as the great slave-owning class. With or without that twist of luck, he certainly knew what that class expected of its members. At the same time, he knew from daily experience what was expected of a Presbyterian businessman in a small southern town.

Harris, then, lived in the borderland between two worlds, two sets of values, two elaborate codes of behavior. On the one hand was the work ethic of the urban middle class, driven by respectability, self-discipline, commercial diversification, and success. On the other was the southern beau ideal—the leisured world of the gentleman planter with his slaves, horses, great and usually costly generosity, and touchy sense of honor. At points, these worlds crossed over, to be sure. The southerner's racism cut across occupations and class lines, and both the townsman and the planter were businessmen living off the profits of their enterprises. Moreover, it is arguable that the planter's real life was not leisured and hardly ideal. But as ideals, as something to strive for, the two styles were powerful—and essentially antagonistic. They could not coexist indefinitely. The Civil War destroyed the planter's hegemony, and in that sense the townsman won and created the New South. Before that happened, however, life was a good deal complicated for someone like Harris. Who should he be?

Alone among the great southern humorists, Harris rose up from nothingness, worked for a living at whatever came his way, and suffered the consequences of his mistakes directly, with no family safety net to cushion the blow. He also wrote when time was running out. The Lovingood yarns first appeared as newspaper and magazine articles during the 1850s, and Harris probably revised his material during the war years. These were precisely the years when the planters' dependence on slavery ripened into secession, when their sense of personal honor became translated into a sense of regional honor, when their cocky indifference to death and their penchant for violence got field-tested in humiliation and war. Harris, with his fire-eating secessionism and rabid hatred of Republicans and reformers, was right there with them, in spirit if not status.

Harris was a small businessman, however, and he came from a unionist part of this South, where the dominance of the planter and his style was just weak enough to let reality creep in. This was the area that produced Andrew Johnson. The slaveholding "aristocracy" was not popular among these nonslaveholders, who during the war refused to fight in the Confederacy and sometimes sent draft agents home across a horse. Still, slaveholders, even here, wielded great power. Harris was neither a fully independent townsman nor a slaveholder; he tried to be both, and he tried to do it in a particular place where the tensions between progressive South and planter South were acute, even deadly.

The range of pretensions and hypocrisies open to Sut's/Harris's mocking rage was sizable. Consider the properly Protestant side of Harris's South, the one that would surge through the New South like a collective atonement after the Civil War and turn Baptists into businessmen and Methodists into rich businessmen and crowd the whisky-drinking Episcopalians onto the golf courses and leave them there. Here Sut's favorite target was the self-sanctifying, meddlesome, predatory preacher. It is not that Parson Bullins, who gets the lizards up his pants leg, is a bad man. He is just an irritating windbag with an eye for women who has humiliated Sut by catching him in the bushes with a girl and then tattling to the girl's mother. So Sut goes to the service, full of repentance and lizards, to hear the parson work the women into a fever with the fear of Hell-serpents. "Tole 'em how they'd quile [coil] intu thar buzzims, an' how they *wud* crawl down onder thar frock-strings . . . up thar laigs, an' travil *onder* thar garters, no odds how tight they tied 'em, an' when the two armys ove Hell-sarpents met, then—That las' remark *fotch 'em.*" (53).

At this point the women are screaming, the preacher is waving his hands, and the lizards start their own travels up *his* garters. It is particularly satisfying to Sut that this preacher, who has seduced half the girls in the county, literally gets exposed. "Passuns ginerly hev a pow'ful strong holt on wimen," says Sut, "but, hoss, I tell yu thar airn't meny ove em kin run start nakid over an' thru a crowd ove three hundred wimen an' not injure thar karacters *sum*" (58). In other tales, Sut extended the same treatment to lawyers and sheriffs—anyone who pretended to be a pillar of the community.

The pretensions of the slaveholding class presented more of a challenge, yet Sut was up to the job. It may be difficult for modern readers to understand just how ingrained the idea of honor was to southerners. One's honor was a subtle, powerful combination of family name and social class, all expressed through an elaborate code of etiquette that made language, gesture, and appearance matters of life and death. To call someone a name, tweak his nose, or leer at his lady would bring instant and violent response. Above all, honor was about being manly. A gentleman had manners and poise; a common man was rough and plain. Each defended his honor among those of his social status. Gentlemen dueled and gave gifts; common men fought and bought each other drinks. Slaves were literally not men in this strutting culture, because they had no way to defend their honor and no gifts to give. A manly man did not fear death and would rather die—in a fight, in a duel, in a war—than be humiliated. Humiliation, in fact, separated men from notmen. Those who endured humiliation (and that included failed businessmen and people who work the retail trade, which is a daily exercise in fielding insults and snubs) may have qualified as Christian saints. They would not have made it as men in the Old South.[4]

Humiliation is central to the Lovingood tales. Sut does not just violate every rule; more to the point, he takes himself outside the rules. He humiliates himself but makes himself the central, most energetic and important part of the story. In that sense he negated the whole code of southern manhood. "I'm no count, no how. Jis' look at me! Did yu ever see sich a sampil ove a human afore? I feels like I' be glad *tu be* dead, only I'se feard ove the dyin. I don't keer for herearter, for hits onpossibil for me to hev ara soul. Who ever seed a soul in jis' sich a rack heap ove bones an' rags as this? I'se nuffin' but sum newfangil'd sort ove beas'. . . . a sorter cross atween a crazy ole monkey an' a durn'd, wore-out hominy mill. I is one ove dad's explites at makin cussed fool invenshuns. . . . I blames him fur all ove hit, allers a-tryin tu be king fool" (106–107).

In that one paragraph, Sut rejected most of what was essential to a southerner's manhood. He admits to being ugly, poor, afraid of dying, of dubious lineage and parenthood, indifferent to God and duty, and vengeful of his father. What is worse, he is actually proud of it.

The list goes on. Where true southern men were generous and off-hand about taking on a friend's debts, Sut simply steals. Where no man would stand for being called a liar, Sut announces to the world that he is a great liar, one of the best in creation. Where bearing and deportment were concerned, and no man could stand to be "unmasked" as fearful or even human, Sut unmasks himself, literally and physically (in one sketch he tries on a starched shirt, can't stand it, and ends up jumping buck naked from a sleeping loft). His kind of "duel" is to kick a dandified stranger in the rump and then run 119 yards between shots when the fop unexpectedly pulls a two-barrel derringer on him. Nothing in the code of southern honor fits Sut.

When it came to women, Sut violated every rule and mocked every ideal set forward by both Presbyterians *and* planters. The whole culture had made ice queens of women and put them on pedestals. Sut looked up the skirt. In "Rare Ripe Garden Seed" a man marries, then leaves for Atlanta after helping his young bride put in a garden of "rare," fast-growing seeds bought off a Yankee peddler. When he comes back, four and a half months after the wedding, she presents him with a newborn baby girl. He can count at least to nine on his fingers and is beginning to express some doubts, but his mother-in-law takes him in hand. It was eating the produce of the rare garden seed that made Mary develop so fast, she explains. "This is what cums of hit, an' four months an' a half am rar ripe time fur babys, adzackly," she says. "Tu be sure, hit lacks a day ur two, but Margarit Jane wer allers a pow'ful interprizin' gal, an' a yearly [early] rizer" (236). The real father, incidentally, is the local sheriff, whom Sut and the husband humiliate in a later tale.

More explicitly, Sut rated unwed women like horses. Young girls were fine, and old maids could be tamed, but widows were best. "Hits widders, by golly, what am the rale sensibil, steady-goin, never-skeerin, never-kickin, willin, sperrited, smoof pacers. They cum clost up tu the hoss-block, standin still wif thar purty silky years playin, an' the naik-veins a-throbbin, and waits fur the word, which ove course yu gives, arter yu finds yer feet well in the stirrup, an' away they moves like a cradil on cushioned rockers, ur a spring buggy runnin in damp san'. A tetch of the bridil an' they knows yu wants em to turn, an' they does hit es willin es ef the idea wer thar own" (141).

It is misogynist cant, but at least it is sincere cant. It utterly lacks the patronizing tone nineteenth-century men used to describe women, and one has to choose which attitude is worse. Sut's at least has a certain simple directness. "Men," he announces, "wer made a-purpus jis' tu eat, drink, an' fur stayin awake in the yearly part ove the nites: an' wimen wer made tu cook the vittils, mix the sperits, an' help the men du the stayin awake" (88). A woman who stepped outside that role, who wanted to take command and not simply cater to men, was greatly to be feared. "They aint human; theyse an ekal mixtry ove stud hoss, black snake, goose, peacock britches and d———d raskil. They wants tu be a man; an ef they cant, they fixes up thar case by bein devils."[5] This comes from a writer who was devotedly married to one woman for thirty-two years, until her death, and whose second wife was reputedly every bit as bright, intelligent, and assertive as he was. Harris was ever the devoted family man.

And that brings us back to Dad. Dad, of course, is the fool's Fool, the creator of Fools, the original of Fools. He is the antithesis of a southern patriarch and the whole manly social order built thereon. Lineage—breeding, if you will—was so vital to the South's social order that marriages were made on it, unlikely names came from it (for example, St. George Tucker), and whole genealogies were constructed around it. It is said that one never asks a true southerner who someone is when all you want is the name. Who you are goes back generations and out to fifth cousins. But Sut's dad is just Hoss, and when he dies, Sut and his Mam borrow a shingle cart for a hearse, ride the body around the field a few times, then drop it into a convenient crack in the ground, rather like dumping waste. Later that night, Mam says, " 'oughtent we to a scratch'd in a littel dirt on him, say?' 'No need, mam,' sed Sall [Sut's sister], 'hits loose yeath, an' will soon cave in enuff.' 'But, I want to plant a 'simmon sprout at his head,' sed mam, 'on account ove the puckery taste he has left in my mouth.' "[6]

Harris wrote that particular story after the Civil War, and arguably it is his final comment on the collapse of the Old South. Probably not. The story is entirely appropriate to the Fool that Harris had constructed before the war intervened and exploded the myth of southern superiority. Nothing that Sut Lovingood ever did was intended to support or even to reform the established order of the American South. He was anarchic, chaotic, irreverent, and true to his sense of self. He was a Fool. This may be what Faulkner meant when asked why he liked Sut. "He had no illusions about himself, did the best he could; at certain times he was a coward and knew it and wasn't ashamed; he never blamed his misfortunes on anyone and never cursed God for them."[7] It was probably George Washington Harris's best epitaph.

Notes

1. George Washington Harris, *Sut Lovingood: Yarns Spun by a "Nat'ral Born Durn'd Fool," Warped and Wove for Public Wear* (New York: Dick and Fitzgerald, 1867). Except where noted, all quotes from the tales are taken from this original edition.

2. The best biography of Harris is Milton Rickels's fine book (which also explores the notion of Sut as Fool, although from a different perspective). Milton Rickels, *George Washington Harris* (New York: Twayne Publishers, 1965).

3. George Washington Harris, *High Times and Hard Times: Sketches and Tales*, ed. M. Thomas Inge (Nashville, TN: Vanderbilt University Press, 1967), 47, 52.

4. The literature on southern honor is large and growing. Two places to start are Bertram Wyatt-Brown, *Southern Honor: Ethics and Behavior in the Old South* (New York: Oxford University Press, 1982); and Kenneth S. Greenberg, *Honor & Slavery: Lies, Duels, Noses, Masks, Dressing as a Woman, Gifts, Strangers, Humanitarianism, Death, Slave Rebellions, The Pro-Slavery Argument, Baseball, Hunting, and Gambling in the Old South* (Princeton, NJ: Princeton University Press, 1996).

5. "Sut Lovingood's Chest Story," in Inge, *High Times and Hard Times*, 120.

6. "Well, Dad's Dead," ibid., 211.

7. Quoted in Rickels, *Harris*, 95.

Suggested Readings

Blair, Walter. *Native American Humor*. 1937. Reprint, San Francisco: Chandler Publishing Co., 1960.

Cohen, Hennig, and William B. Dillingham, eds. *Humor of the Old Southwest*. 1964. Reprint, Athens: University of Georgia Press, 1994.

Day, Donald. "The Life of George Washington Harris." *Tennessee Historical Quarterly* 6 (1947): 3–38.

Greenberg, Kenneth S. *Honor & Slavery: Lies, Duels, Noses, Masks, Dressing as a Woman, Gifts, Strangers, Humanitarianism, Death, Slave Rebellions, The Pro-Slavery Argument, Baseball, Hunting, and Gambling in the Old South*. Princeton, NJ: Princeton University Press, 1996.

Harris, George Washington. *Sut Lovingood: Yarns Spun by a "Nat'ral Born Durn'd Fool," Warped and Wove for Public Wear*. New York: Dick and Fitzgerald, 1867.

———. *High Times and Hard Times: Sketches and Tales*. Edited by M. Thomas Inge. Nashville, TN: Vanderbilt University Press, 1967.

———. *Sut Lovingood's Yarns*. Edited by M. Thomas Inge. New Haven, CT: College and University Press, 1966.

Kuhlmann, Susan. *Knave, Fool, and Genius: The Confidence Man as He Appears in Nineteenth-Century American Fiction.* Chapel Hill: University of North Carolina Press, 1973.

Lynn, Kenneth S. *Mark Twain and Southwestern Humor.* 1959. Reprint, Westport, CT: Greenwood Press, 1972.

Mayfield, John. "The Theater of Public Esteem: Ethics and Values in Longstreet's *Georgia Scenes.*" *Georgia Historical Quarterly* 75 (1991): 566–86.

McClary, Ben Harris, ed. *The Lovingood Papers.* Knoxville: University of Tennessee Press, 1964.

Meine, Franklin J., ed. *Tall Tales of the Southwest: An Anthology of Southern and Southwestern Humor, 1830–1860.* New York: Knopf, 1930.

Rickels, Milton. *George Washington Harris.* New York: Twayne Publishers, 1965.

Shields, Johanna Nicol. "A Sadder Simon Suggs: Freedom and Slavery in the Humor of Johnson Hooper." *Journal of Southern History* 56 (1990): 641–64.

Wyatt-Brown, Bertram. *Southern Honor: Ethics and Behavior in the Old South.* New York: Oxford University Press, 1982.

Yates, Norris W. *William T. Porter and the Spirit of the Times: A Study of the Big Bear School of Humor.* 1957. Reprint, New York: Ayer Company Publishers, 1977.

9

Sam Houston
Unionism and the Secession Crisis in Texas

Randolph B. Campbell

Sam Houston seemed a man of many contradictions. He gained some fame as an Indian fighter, but later lived among the Cherokee and married into the tribe. He showed his military prowess in the decisive Battle of San Jacinto in the Texas Revolution, yet struggled constantly with a drinking problem. His personal life featured a disastrous first marriage and included his attack on an Ohio congressman, yet he served as president of the Republic of Texas and then as senator and governor of the State of Texas. Then in 1861 this man who had faced so many challenges had to meet one of the greatest of his life. As the South faced the issue of union or disunion, how would he go?

In the secession crisis following the election of Abraham Lincoln, eventually eleven states declared their intention to form a new nation, the Confederate States of America. Yet that process did not occur without debate or with absolute certainty. In the Lower South the decision came easier, although, as William Freehling points out, secessionists did not gain huge majorities: 56 percent of key votes in Georgia, 54 percent in Alabama and Louisiana. But the Upper South states divided even more. Some—Missouri, Kentucky, Maryland, and Delaware—never left the Union although they were slave states. Others rejected secession at first and joined only after the attack on Fort Sumter, and even then with varying degrees of support for the action. In a special convention, Virginia's secession act passed 88–55; Arkansas's popular vote on the matter brought only a 5,700 majority out of over 43,000 votes cast; Tennessee went that route later, by a 2-to-1 margin. North Carolina, the last to leave the Union, had initially turned down the call for a secession convention in February 1861 but joined the Confederacy following Virginia's secession.

Within this confederation of states, a sizeable minority of citizens had not supported secession. One of them was Sam Houston, Texas hero. His course shows how men of principle tried to avoid splitting the Union and how they sought to escape the death and destruction war would bring. At the same time, the actions of those opposing him illustrate the strength of the secessionist sentiment amid the rising tide of war. Fighting secession would be Houston's last battle.

Randolph B. Campbell is the author of *Sam Houston and the American Southwest* (1993); *An Empire for Slavery: The Peculiar Institution in Texas,*

1821–1865 (1989); and other books and articles on nineteenth-century Texas.
He is Regents Professor of History at the University of North Texas in Denton.

Sam Houston crossed the Red River into Texas for the first time on December 2, 1832, bearing a passport that described him as "General Sam Houston, a Citizen of the UNITED STATES, thirty-eight years of age, six feet, two inches in stature, brown hair, and light complexion."[1] His official purpose in entering Texas was to meet as a representative of the U.S. government with the Comanches, the fearsome lords of the Texas plains, and negotiate their acceptance of tribes from the Southeast who were being moved across the Mississippi. It was likely that the new arrivals such as the Cherokees and Creeks would sooner or later press into the hunting grounds of the Comanches, and the United States hoped to avoid trouble.

Sam Houston did not come to Texas, however, simply as a diplomat to the Comanches. He was also, like so many men who came to Texas in that age, looking for a new beginning. His life to that point had been marked by spectacular successes and even more spectacular failures. For all that he or anyone else knew, his greatest achievements were behind him—and he was not even forty.

Above all, Sam Houston seemed to be a man of extremes—extreme independence, extreme courage, and an extreme weakness for alcohol. Born in Virginia in 1793, he moved with his family to East Tennessee in 1807. He did not like farm work much, so when he was sixteen his family asked him to clerk in a store that they owned in town. He reacted by running away from home and living with the Cherokee Indians for nearly three years. No one ever told Sam Houston what to do or what to think.

Houston also had tremendous courage, a characteristic that became evident when he joined the regular army during the War of 1812 and fought under the command of General Andrew Jackson against the Creek Indians in Alabama. At the decisive Battle of Horseshoe Bend in March 1814, Lieutenant Houston took an arrow in the thigh as he led the first assault on the Creeks' breastwork of logs. He forced another soldier to pull the arrow out and then, disobeying Jackson's orders to stay out of the battle, led another attack on the Indians' final defensive position. This time two rifle balls hit him in the shoulder. The wounds were so severe that doctors did not believe that he would survive the night. Houston proved them wrong, but a full recovery took several years.

Samuel Houston in 1851 by the Meade Brothers (Charles Richard Meade and William Henry Meade). *Courtesy of the Museum of Fine Arts, Houston; Museum purchase with funds provided by Vinson & Elkins L.L.P. in honor of the Firm's seventy-fifth anniversary*

Unfortunately, to go with his independence and courage, Houston also had an extreme weakness for alcohol. When he was still a teenager he was arrested and fined for getting drunk on militia muster day and "riotously" and "wantonly" beating a drum outside the courthouse window

while the Blount County (Tennessee) court was in session. Later, when
he lived with the Cherokees again in what is now Oklahoma, he gave in
so completely to what he called the "flowing bowl" that the Indians
nicknamed him "Big Drunk."[2]

It is not surprising that his public career before he went to Texas
was also marked by extremes. After the War of 1812, Houston remained
in the army for several years but resigned in 1818, moved to Nashville,
Tennessee, and became a lawyer. He soon entered politics as a supporter
of Andrew Jackson, served two terms in Congress, and became governor in 1827. The next year, Jackson won the presidency, and Houston's
future seemed to have no limits. He planned to run for reelection as
governor in 1829, and some said that eventually he would be president.
Early in 1829, however, disaster struck. Houston, who was thirty-five,
married twenty-year-old Eliza Allen in January, and in April she left
him and went home to her family. Neither Houston nor his wife ever
told what had happened or why she left. More than likely she did not
love him but was pressured by her family into what they regarded as a
promising match. He discovered her true feelings and at least momen-
tarily lost his temper; she left him and rejected his efforts to win her
back. Rumors and gossip then ran wild. Houston, humiliated and feeling that he had lost the support of the people of Tennessee, resigned as
governor and went into what amounted to exile by going to live for the
second time with the Cherokees. He remained with them for more than
three years—a period that was in most respects the low point of his life.

By 1829 the band of Cherokees with whom Houston had lived as a
teenager had moved from Tennessee to the eastern region of what is
now Oklahoma, and he joined them there. He ran a trading post, married by tribal custom a Cherokee woman named Tiana Rogers, drank
too much on a regular basis, and made several trips back East. His behavior was often erratic; the most notorious example occurred in April
1832 when he attacked a congressman from Ohio named William
Stanbery on Pennsylvania Avenue in Washington. Stanbery had accused
Houston of fraud in seeking government contracts, and Houston
knocked him down and beat him thoroughly with a hickory cane. Arrested and tried for contempt by the House of Representatives, he defended himself brilliantly, winning cheers from the audience and
receiving only a meaningless reprimand from the "jury" of congressmen. President Andrew Jackson, who had never really lost faith in Houston, decided that he would be a good man to undertake a mission to the
Comanches in Texas.

Therefore, when Sam Houston went to Texas in December 1832, he had the record of a man of extremes, a man with a weakness for alcohol, who either ran away from his problems or rushed into action without stopping to consider the odds or probable consequences. After he arrived in Texas, Houston fortunately took a very different approach. Once he crossed the Red River and attained positions of great responsibility—commander in chief of Texan forces during the Revolution in 1836, president of the Republic of Texas from 1836 to 1838 and again from 1841 to 1844, U.S. senator from 1846 to 1859, and finally, governor of Texas from 1859 to 1861—caution and practicality became the keys to Sam Houston's career. He looked at the hard realities of every situation and carefully calculated the probable results of every decision. This approach led him to be right far more often than he was wrong, and it largely explains the success that he had as a leader in Texas until the fight over secession in 1861.

It is ironic that Houston's practical approach brought him into constant conflict with men who were extremists of the sort that he appeared to be when he had first come to Texas. They wrongly equated his caution and practicality with cowardice and a failure to uphold the interests of Texas and the South. To them, Sam Houston was a disgrace rather than a hero.

Houston's use of good sense and careful calculation once he attained positions of leadership and responsibility in Texas is perfectly illustrated by his role in the secession crisis of 1860–1861. He opposed secession with more courage and determination than any other individual of his rank in the entire South. And when Texas joined the Confederate States of America, he gave up the governorship rather than participate in what he regarded as a reckless, if not doomed, course of action.

Sam Houston always revered the Union, partly because his hero, Andrew Jackson, was a Unionist. On numerous occasions, Houston quoted Jackson's famous response in 1830 to John C. Calhoun's theory of nullification: "Our Federal Union, it must be preserved." Also, in part, Houston's unionism resulted from a simple belief, much like Abraham Lincoln's, that the United States was a good thing in the world that had to be preserved. Houston's unionism, however, also had a practical side. For one thing, he knew that the Republic of Texas probably had been saved from destruction by annexation in 1845. Although it had survived nearly a decade as an independent nation, it had neither the financial stability nor military strength to maintain that position indefinitely. Moreover he was convinced that the South and southern interests, including slavery, would be more secure in the Union than outside it. The Constitution of the United States, he constantly reminded Texans, protected the states' domestic institutions, such as slavery. If southerners rejected that protection and tried to leave the United States, he said, the North would never permit secession without fighting. Then, he argued, the North would prove stronger than the South, and slavery would be lost. Thus, Sam Houston's unionism was rooted in practical considerations as well as in hero worship and a deep faith in the nation.

Clearly, Houston's unionism did not mean that he opposed slavery. He grew up with the South's "peculiar institution" and owned slaves nearly all his life. He did not see slavery as a critical moral issue and had little patience for radicals who demanded immediate abolition. Viewed from a moral standpoint, his position did him little credit. On the other hand he just as consistently opposed proslavery enthusiasts and regarded their insistence on slavery's "rights," such as the "right" to expand into new territory, as an unreasonable threat to the peace and security of the Union.

Houston made his unionism absolutely clear within a year of his entry into the U.S. Senate in early 1846. The occasion was a speech in February 1847 in which he commented on the Wilmot Proviso, a proposal by Congressman David Wilmot of Pennsylvania that had angered many southerners by calling for prohibiting slavery in any territory that might be taken in the Mexican War. He began with some comments on slavery—calling it a "calamity under which the nation labored"—but at the same time arguing that it was an issue that had to be handled without extremism on either side. Above all, he said, it should not call forth talk of disunion. Then he launched into an impassioned defense of the Union that was reported in the *Congressional Globe* in these words:

> Disunion here? He could not bear the word. Let not the name of Texas, his home, the last to be incorporated into the Union, ever be blasphemed by the word "disunion." Let not the Union be severed. The boon we possess is too rich, too mighty, and too grand—the sum of human happiness we enjoy is too great, the amount of liberty is too precious! This question was not raised for our good. Why, was not the North dependent upon the South? And was not the South dependent on the North? Would it not be to each a suicidal act? and to both destruction? Disunion! It was a monster; and if he could, he would seize upon its mane, drag it forth, and inspect its scales, and if it had a penetrable spot, he would strike it to the vitals.[3]

The sectional tensions that began to mount with the Wilmot Proviso reached a new level of intensity during the Crisis of 1850—a sectional dispute arising primarily over the question of what to do about slavery in the territory just acquired from Mexico. Henry Clay proposed a compromise, and Houston supported the idea. Speaking before a packed Senate chamber in February 1850, he criticized fanaticism in both the North and the South and asked those present "whose piety will permit them" to pray for the Union. He even anticipated Abraham Lincoln's famed biblical reference of 1858, saying: "For a nation divided against itself cannot stand. I wish, if this Union must be dissolved, that its ruins may be the monument of my grave, and the graves of my family. I wish no epitaph to be written to tell that I survive the ruin of this glorious Union."[4]

By this time, prosouthern Texans had grown dissatisfied with their senator's stand on sectional issues. Former governor James Pinckney Henderson called the speech supporting compromise "the *damndest* outrage yet committed upon Texas." The condemnation would soon grow much stronger, but for the moment Houston emerged victorious. The Compromise of 1850 passed, sectional tensions eased, and Houston enhanced his national reputation. "Old Sam," wrote Texas Congressman David Kaufman, "is on rapidly rising ground."[5]

The spirit of compromise with its accompanying easing of tension between the North and South lasted nearly four years. Then in early 1854 the Kansas-Nebraska Act repealed the Missouri Compromise and opened anew the question of slavery in the Louisiana Purchase north of the line 36°30', an issue that had been settled since 1820. Alone among southern Democrats, Sam Houston opposed the act. He made a two-day speech against it in February 1854, pointing out that the Missouri Compromise, as a practical matter, protected the South—the minority section—more than the North. Repeal it, he warned, and the free-soil majority will overwhelm the slaveholding interest. He spoke again in the early morning hours of March 4 as the Senate prepared to vote. "*Maintain the Missouri Compromise!*" he said. "*Stir not up Agitation!* Give us peace!"[6] But the act passed.

Houston's vote drew the wrath of prosoutherners in Texas as never before. Even some of his old friends turned their heads and would not speak when he returned home in the spring of 1854. He tried to tell Texans that repeal of the Missouri Compromise line by the Kansas-Nebraska Act would upset the North and invite retaliation. This act, he prophesied, would result by 1860 in the election of a free-soil president. Secession and war would follow, he said, and the South would be overpowered by the stronger North and "go down in the unequal contest, in a sea of blood and smoking ruin."[7] This kind of cautious talk was not what most Texans wanted to hear or were likely to heed. The more they attacked Houston, however, the more fixed he became in his unionism. "My enemies," he told a crowd at San Jacinto in July 1855, "may fester in the putrescence of their own malignity. They cannot hurt or disturb me."[8]

Houston's six-year Senate term was not to end until 1859, but in 1855 the Texas legislature passed a resolution by a vote of 77 to 3 expressing its disapproval of his vote against the Kansas-Nebraska Act. Several newspapers called for his resignation, and the Democratic State Convention in January 1856 also passed a resolution condemning his vote. It seemed that Sam Houston's unionism had cost him any hope of reelection to the Senate, but he continued to condemn extremism, defend the Union, and hope that he could convince the voters to see things his way. In the spring of 1857 he decided to seek direct vindication from the people of Texas by running for the office of governor, although he had nearly two years left in his Senate term. "The people want excitement," he wrote Texas's other senator, Thomas J. Rusk, "and I had as well give it as anyone."[9] He was true to his word—campaigning across the state during the summer of 1857 in a crimson buggy furnished as a promotion by a plow salesman—and made at least sixty speeches in about sixty days. He defended the Union and attacked his extremist critics as only Sam Houston could. He called Louis T. Wigfall, the South Carolina-born ultrasoutherner from East Texas, "wiggletail" and termed John Marshall, editor of the Austin *Texas State Gazette*, a vegetarian whose "blood would freeze a frog." He was at too much of a disadvantage, however, and lost the election in August to Hardin R. Runnels, the regular Democratic candidate and a disciple of Calhoun, by a vote of 32,552 to 28,678. This defeat hurt his pride and added to his fears about the future, but on the surface he accepted the will of the voters with equanimity. He wrote his friend Ashbel Smith: "The fuss is over, and the sun yet shines as ever. What next?"[10]

What was next was a second campaign for governor against Runnels during the summer of 1859 following the close of his Senate term in the spring of that year. He did not actively seek a chance to campaign for the office, but his friends and admirers in Texas—and there were many in spite of (or in a few cases because of) the stands that he had taken—urged him to run, and he finally agreed. No doubt he welcomed the opportunity for vindication, which by 1859 was a fairly good possibility for several reasons. First, Runnels had not been a very successful governor, especially in matters of frontier defense. Many who had voted for him in 1857 would not return to the polls at all two years later. Second, the prosouthern extremists in Texas had gone a little too far for many when, as they renominated Runnels, they also urged reopening the African slave trade. Third, the fuss over the Kansas-Nebraska Act had receded into the past a little, allowing Houston's tremendous personal popularity to reassert itself. New arrivals in the state, and there were many, tended to support "Old Sam Jacinto."

Houston made no concessions on his unionism in order to win votes in 1859. The letter that he wrote announcing his candidacy said: "The Constitution and the Union embrace the principles by which I shall be governed if elected. They comprehend all the old Jacksonian National Democracy I ever professed, or officially practiced." In contrast to 1857, he made only one speech during the entire campaign, but in that he returned to his attack on the Kansas-Nebraska Act, pointing out that leading southerners now recognized that it was a "delusion and deception from the beginning."[11]

On August 1, 1859, Houston defeated Runnels by a vote of 33,375 to 27,500, roughly reversing Runnels's margin in 1857. It was a satisfying victory to Houston, but a little more than one year later, it placed him at the center of the contest over secession in Texas. Undoubtedly he did not want trouble, but southern extremists saw his election as a threat. The *Charleston Mercury* called him a "traitor who ought to fall never to rise again," and the defeated Runnels privately condemned the new governor's "Demagogical Union saving doctrines."[12]

Some considered Houston a potential Democratic presidential nominee in 1860. In January of that year a group of Galveston Democrats wrote to him to ask if his name could be put into consideration at the Democratic National Convention in Charleston. Houston refused because, he said, "sectional agitators" have replaced "national men" in control of the Democratic Party. This view was borne out at the Charleston convention when delegates from the Deep South walked out rather than accept a platform endorsing Stephen A. Douglas's Popular Sovereignty policy. The Democrats tried again in Baltimore in June, but there was another walkout, and the party split. Those who remained—the Northern Democrats—nominated Stephen A. Douglas. The Southern Democrats met at Richmond and nominated John C. Breckinridge. Houston's refusal to seek the nomination was wise. He had no chance with his old party.

Houston's only real hope for the presidential nomination in 1860 was as the candidate of the new Constitutional Union Party, which held a convention in Baltimore in early May. Texas Unionists placed his name before the convention, and on the first ballot he received the second largest number of votes, 57 to John Bell's 68 1/2. However, Bell was nominated on the second ballot.

One week later, Houston issued a public letter denying that he had authorized the use of his name in the Constitutional Union Party convention and saying that he would be a candidate only if "the people" wanted him to be. In late May he announced that as a result of a meeting at San Jacinto on April 21 where he had been urged to run, he had "consented to let my name go before the country as the People's Candidate for the Presidency."[13] This seems out of character for the usually practical and realistic Houston. How could a "People's Candidate" who had no support from a convention or any sort of party organization hope to succeed? There is no good evidence as to exactly what hopes he had in taking such a position. He soon recognized that he was only confusing the issue for unionist Texans and withdrew his name.

As the election neared—and the possibility of a victory by the Republican candidate, Abraham Lincoln, exacerbated sectional tensions—Houston began a speech-making campaign aimed at blocking extreme reactions on the part of Texans. Lincoln's election, he told an audience in Austin on September 22, would give "no excuse for dissolving the Union. The Union is worth more than Mr. Lincoln. . . . If Mr. Lincoln administers the Government in accordance with the Constitution, our rights must be preserved. If he does not, the Constitution has provided a remedy." Houston closed by damning what he called the "whipsters and Demagogues" who sought to mislead the people, and he urged Texans to avert the "calamitous curse of disunion."[14] His Thanksgiving Day Proclamation, issued on October 27, asked Texans to pray that God would "shield us still in the time of peril, that we may be preserved a United People, free, independent, and prosperous."[15]

Houston's pleas and prayers would not be answered. On November 6, 1860, Abraham Lincoln, the "Black Republican" whom Texans feared and hated so much, won the presidency. The governor spent Election Day in Austin and the next day, although not yet certain that Lincoln had won, confided his worst fears in a letter to Sam Houston Jr. "The price of liberty is blood," he wrote, "and if an attempt is made to destroy our Union, or violate the Constitution, there will be blood shed to maintain them. The Demons of anarchy must be put down and destroyed. The miserable Demagogues & Traitors of the land, must be silenced, and set at naught."[16] Houston was preparing mentally for his last battle.

Sam Houston fought secession in much the same way that he had fought the San Jacinto Campaign against General Santa Anna's Mexican army in 1836. That is, he delayed, retreated when necessary, and hoped that the passage of time would provide him with an opportunity to oppose disunion effectively. Secessionist leaders demanded the calling of a convention to consider disunion, but only the state legislature could call such a convention. The legislature, however, was not scheduled to meet until the next year, and only the governor could call it into special session. Houston refused. "So long as the Constitution is maintained by 'Federal authority,' " he wrote on November 20 to a group of Texans who asked his opinion on the crisis, "and Texas is not made the victim of 'federal wrong' I am for the Union as it is." "Passion is rash," he reminded them; "wisdom considers well her way."[17]

Texas secession leaders, however, refused to be deterred by Houston's delaying tactics. In early December they issued a call for the election of a convention to meet in Austin on January 28, 1861. The governor responded by calling the state legislature into special session on January 21, one week before the scheduled convention. Some among both his supporters and his opponents interpreted this as surrender, but anyone who knew Sam Houston could recognize it as another strategic retreat. He hoped that the legislative session could be used to head off the convention. That hope received another blow, however, when South Carolina seceded from the Union on December 20, 1860, providing new impetus for Texas disunionists.

As 1861 opened, and his cause grew steadily weaker, Houston began work on yet another fallback intended to protect Texas from destruction in civil war. He would yield to secession, he announced, if the people of Texas voted for it, but he wanted the state then to remain independent rather than to join a southern confederacy. Texas should, he told an audience in Waco in words very similar to those that he wrote to J. M. Calhoun, a commissioner sent by Alabama to Texas, unfurl "once again her Lone Star Banner and [maintain] her position among the independent nations of the earth."[18]

When the legislature met on January 21, Houston begged it to reject the convention scheduled to meet one week later and to give the people of Texas a chance to speak in a "legitimate manner." In concluding, he urged the legislature to reject those who wanted to "plunge madly into revolution." I have "not yet lost hope," he said, "that our rights can be maintained in the Union, and that it may yet be perpetuated."[19] The Hero of San Jacinto was retreating slowly and creating every delay that he could think of in the process.

The legislature largely ignored Houston. It decided that the convention scheduled to meet on the 28th represented the people of Texas, but it did decree that any action taken by the convention had to be ratified in a popular referendum. The convention assembled and on February 1 adopted an ordinance of secession by a vote of 166 to 8. Houston attended on the day of the vote because he wanted to show that he continued to trust in the people of Texas, and on February 9 he issued a proclamation calling for a statewide referendum on disunion to be held on the 23d. "I still believe that secession will bring ruin and civil war," he wrote in a public letter of February 20. "Yet if the people will it, I can bear it with them."[20]

On February 23, Texans endorsed disunion by an overwhelming 3-to-1 margin. Houston then had only one defensive position left—to have Texas maintain its independence rather than join the Confederacy. On March 5, however, the secession convention adopted an ordinance joining Texas with the new southern government. Houston challenged this directly, saying that the convention had exceeded its powers and that his state would never be annexed to another nation without the knowledge and consent of its people. The convention responded by requiring all state officials to take an oath of loyalty to the Confederacy and ordering the governor to appear at the capitol for that purpose at noon on March 16. After dinner with his family on the 15th, Houston read from the family Bible and retired to an upstairs bedroom where he paced for some time before coming down and saying to his wife: "Margaret, I will never do it."[21] He then spent the rest of the night writing an address to the people of Texas, explaining his refusal. Houston went to the capitol at noon on the appointed day, March 16, 1861, but while the secretary of the convention called his name three times, he sat in the basement whittling on a piece of pine wood. Two days later the convention declared the governor's office vacant and elevated Lieutenant Governor Edward Clark to Houston's position.

Houston remained calm and practical even in defeat. He rejected all suggestions that he use armed force to hold the governorship on the grounds that such an effort would bring the calamity of civil war to Texas before it began anywhere else. One offer of help came from a group of his friends on March 19 as he packed to leave Austin. He reacted in horror, however, at the thought of anyone "willing to deluge the capital of Texas with the blood of Texans, merely to keep one poor old man in a position for a few days longer, in a position that belongs to the people."[22] Twice within the next month—the exact dates are unknown—President Lincoln offered Houston military assistance if he would attempt to restore Texas to the Union. "Had I been disposed to involve Texas in Civil War," he wrote later in 1861, "I had it in my power, for I was tendered the aid of seventy thousand men [doubtless an exaggerated number] and means to sustain myself in Texas by adhering to the Union; but this I rejected."[23]

The Houston family left Austin on March 20 and headed for their home at Cedar Point on Galveston Bay. En route the deposed governor stopped at Brenham and spoke to a crowd at the courthouse, telling his listeners that demagogues had succeeded in "stilling the voice of reason" in Texas. As a result, he said, "The soil of our beloved South will drink deep the precious blood of our sons and brethren."[24] Texans who were busily celebrating secession did not want to hear warnings about the consequences of their action, and Houston's willingness to make such a statement in public was one more testimonial to his courage. The former governor was in Galveston on April 12 when the firing on Fort Sumter began the Civil War. The guns at Sumter, he told a crowd at Independence about a month later, have drowned the "voice of hope" and forced all men to choose. "The time has come when a man's section is his country," he concluded. "I stand by mine."[25]

Houston's role in the secession crisis may be interpreted in a variety of ways. Secessionists called him a "submissionist" who wanted to betray the South. This is understandable from their point of view, but in reality Houston was a southerner who loved the South. Some Unionists, especially outside Texas, called him a coward and a weak leader. That charge is not quite as understandable, especially in light of the overwhelming strength and determination of the secessionists. Houston always favored strategic retreat when faced with overwhelming opposition. It generally served him well and made sense in this case too—unless one thinks that he should have accepted Lincoln's offer and plunged Texas into civil war before fighting began anywhere else. (It would be well to remember also when evaluating this option that Houston was an old man with a young family. He had married Margaret Lea, a woman twenty-six years younger than he, in 1840. On March 2, 1861, he turned sixty-eight, but he had a family of eight children under the age of twenty, the last one born only the year before. Should a man of his years have been expected to leave his wife and family to lead an army into civil war?)

Finally, Houston's role in the crisis can be interpreted largely in terms of his faith in democracy. He had done everything that he could for more than ten years to convince the voters of Texas to uphold the Union. At times, most recently in the gubernatorial election of 1859, it seemed that he had been vindicated. When the crisis arose in 1860–1861, he was perfectly consistent in demanding a referendum, saying that he would accept only the authority of the people. The voters chose secession, and he seemingly accepted their decision. If the people willed it, he would bear it. However, the voters had not spoken on joining the Confederacy—so there he drew the line.

Some might say that Houston's support for the Confederacy once the war came calls into question the sincerity of his unionism over the years and his opposition to secession in 1860–1861. But this is hardly a fair criticism. It is true that he could have continued to support the United States, at least to the point of becoming an exile from Texas. But that seems too much to expect of a sixty-eight-year-old Democrat whose whole life depended on the South and Texas. He had taken every reasonable step to prevent disunion and Texas's entry into the Confederacy; but in the final analysis he could only respect the authority of the voters of his state, stand with his state and section, and hope for the best.

Even at that, Houston thought cautiously and defensively where Texas was concerned. He attempted to persuade his namesake son not to volunteer to serve outside the state. "It is every man's duty to defend his Country," he wrote Sam Jr., "and I wish my offspring to do so at the proper time and in the proper way. We are not wanted or needed out of Texas, and we may soon be wanted and needed in Texas. Until then, my son, be content."[26] The boy, however, with a disregard for parental wishes that his father should have recognized as a family tradition, joined the first volunteer unit raised in the area. Sam Sr. then had to live through an agonizing six months in 1862 when his son's name appeared on the list of Confederate dead and missing at the battle of Shiloh, which was fought in April. Houston did not know that the boy, who had been badly wounded and then imprisoned at Camp Douglas in Illinois, had survived until he appeared at home in October, haggard and on crutches but alive.

Sam Houston did not live to see the accuracy of his prophesy that the South, entering an unequal contest, would go down in smoke and blood. He left the Galveston area in October 1862 when Federal forces occupied the city for several months and moved to Huntsville, where he lived quietly until his death from pneumonia on July 29, 1863. According to family tradition, he spoke for the last time to his wife as she read the Bible at his bedside on the 26th: "Texas . . . Texas . . . Margaret." His state and his section had rejected his advice of caution and practicality in dealing with the issue of secession, and most Texans and southerners—except the slaves who were freed by the war—would pay a terrible price for their decision.

Notes

1. Sam Houston, *The Writings of Sam Houston*, ed. Amelia W. Williams and Eugene C. Barker, 8 vols. (Austin: University of Texas Press, 1938–1943), 4:11. Houston, whose birthday was March 2, 1793, was actually thirty-nine years of age when he first entered Texas.

2. Randolph B. Campbell, *Sam Houston and the American Southwest*, 2d ed. (New York: Longman, 2002), 5, 34.

3. *Congressional Globe*, 29th Cong., 2d sess., 459–60.

4. Houston, *Writings*, 5:144.

5. Llerena Friend, *Sam Houston: The Great Designer* (Austin: University of Texas Press, 1954), 203 (Henderson quotation), 213 (Kaufman quotation).

6. Houston, *Writings*, 5:522.

7. *Austin Texas State Gazette*, May 6, 1854.

8. Houston, *Writings*, 6:191.

9. Ibid., 6:444.

10. Ibid., 6:447.

11. Ibid., 7:339–40 (first quotation); 7:348 (second quotation).

12. Friend, *Sam Houston*, 326.

13. Houston, *Writings*, 8:66.

14. Ibid., 8:151, 156–57, 160.

15. Ibid., 8:173.

16. Ibid., 8:184–85.

17. Ibid., 8:194, 197.

18. Ibid., 8:228; Friend, *Sam Houston*, 334.

19. Houston, *Writings*, 8:247–51.

20. Ibid., 8:264.

21. Quoted in Friend, *Sam Houston*, 338.

22. Houston, *Writings*, 8:293.

23. Ibid., 8:312.

24. Ibid., 8:299.

25. Ibid., 8:302.

26. Ibid., 8:306.

Suggested Readings

The basic compilation of Houston's letters, speeches, and messages is Amelia W. Williams and Eugene C. Barker, eds., *The Writings of Sam Houston, 1813–1863*, 8 vols. (Austin: University of Texas Press, 1938–1943). A new, extremely valuable collection of previously unpublished letters is Madge Thornall Roberts, ed., *The Personal Correspondence of Sam Houston*, 4 vols. (Denton: University of North Texas Press, 1996–2001). Most of these letters were exchanged between Sam and Margaret Lea Houston.

Houston has attracted dozens of biographers. The most successful literary biography is Marquis James, *The Raven: A Biography of Sam Houston* (Indianapolis, IN: Bobbs-Merrill Co., 1929), which won a Pulitzer Prize. Llerena B. Friend, *Sam Houston: The Great Designer* (Austin: University of Texas Press, 1954), is the most scholarly biography, but it pays little attention to Houston's early years. A study that offers complete coverage of Houston's life and balanced interpretations of all the controversies in which he was involved is Marion K. Wisehart, *Sam Houston: American Giant* (Washington, DC: Robert B. Luce, 1962). Marshall De Bruhl, *Sword of San Jacinto: A Life of Sam Houston* (New York: Random House, 1993), is a highly readable account that appeared in conjunction with the 200th anniversary of his birth. The most recent full-scale biography is James L. Haley, *Sam Houston* (Norman: University of Oklahoma Press, 2002).

Little has been published to provide context on Houston's role as a Unionist in Texas politics from 1846 to 1861. Ernest Wallace, *Texas in Turmoil, 1849–1875* (Austin, TX: SteckVaughn, 1965), sketches major developments, and Earl W. Fornell, *The Galveston Era: The Texas Crescent on the Eve of Secession* (Austin: University of Texas Press, 1961), is helpful. Walter L. Buenger, *Secession and the Union in Texas* (Austin: University of Texas Press, 1984); James Marten, *Texas Divided: Loyalty and Dissent in the Lone Star State, 1856–1874* (Lexington: University Press of Kentucky, 1990); and Dale Baum, *The Shattering of Texas Unionism: Politics in the Lone Star State during the Civil War Era* (Baton Rouge: Louisiana State University Press, 1998), analyze the defeat of unionism and success of the secessionists. Two articles that focus on Houston during these years are Edward R. Maher Jr., "Sam Houston and Secession," *Southwestern Historical Quarterly* 55 (1952): 448–58; and Andrew F. Muir, "Sam Houston and the Civil War," *Texana* 6 (1968): 282–87.

10

David Emmons Johnston
A Soldier's Life in the Confederate Army

Carol Reardon

In 1861, at age sixteen, David Johnston joined the Confederate army. Filled with fervor for the cause, he expected a brief fight and ultimate victory. He was wrong on both counts. Four years later, when the last southern armies surrendered west of the Mississippi, an estimated 620,000—60 percent of them Union, 40 percent Confederate—would never return from the war. More Americans died of wounds and disease in the conflict than in all other U.S. wars combined, until Vietnam's 58,000 casualties tilted the balance. In the South almost one in five white males aged 13-43 had died. And, as in any conflict, each death meant not only the ending of a life but also the effect of that loss on families and friends at home.

Biographies tell the accounts of the generals and even some junior officers, but seldom are heard the words of those in the lower ranks, such as Johnston. Although he may have shaped his memories to fit a later audience on such matters as the importance of slavery as a reason for the war, his story still gives a detailed picture of the individual soldier's travails and triumphs. His simple words often spoke eloquently of the cost of the war, and about the hopes of those who fought. His fighting abilities, his loyalty, and his passion help explain why a bloody civil war between people and states, North and South, went on so long and cost the nation so much.

Carol Reardon is associate professor of history at Pennsylvania State University in University Park. Her books include *Soldiers and Scholars: The U.S. Army and the Uses of Military History, 1865–1920* (1990) and *Pickett's Charge in History and Memory* (1997).

David Emmons Johnston knew he would join the army. Only fifteen years old in the fall of 1860 when Abraham Lincoln was elected president of the United States, he understood that the results of that national canvass most likely meant war, and he fully intended to serve in defense of Virginia's best interests. But which course would Virginia follow?

Born in 1845, David Johnston was raised in Giles County in the southwestern part of the state, nearly three hundred miles from Richmond. According to the 1860 census, 6,816 people lived there, 6,038 of them white. Farming remained the backbone of the local economy. In their political leanings, the residents of Giles County split nearly evenly between Democrats and those holding old Whig sentiments, with a slight preponderance of the former. Nonetheless, most in Giles County counseled against any hasty move that might lead to secession and to war, even after South Carolina and six other Deep South states left the Union.

At school, David's classmates debated "Shall Virginia Secede from the Union?" Most argued against any such move, but young David felt differently. Influenced by the strong Democratic leanings of an uncle who had been "educated and trained in the State Rights school of politics," David argued fervently that Virginia must follow the trail blazed by South Carolina. "My youthful mind was inspired by the thought that I lived in the South, among a southern people in thought, feeling, and sentiment, that their interests were my interests, their assailants and aggressors were equally mine, their country my country—a land on which fell the rays of a southern sun, and that the dews which moistened the graves of my ancestors fell from a southern sky," he explained.[1] If the South called him to arms, he intended to answer with enthusiasm.

When news of the fall of Fort Sumter arrived in Giles County, David rushed to enlist. He and his friends expected a short war and doubted the North's willingness to fight. More to the point, "Enlisting men for war was something new," he explained, and "people are always ready to try something new." David believed that even a company of "old women with corn cutters" could drive "a host of Yankees away."[2] But since the term of service extended for only one year, the women did not need to answer the call just yet; 102 men stepped forward to fill the company's ranks by April 25, 1861.

Like most companies in the Confederate army, the unit in which David enlisted as a private contained great numbers of friends, schoolmates, and kinsmen. David's company included four men who all answered to the last name of French; three men each with the last names of Bane, Frazier, Johnston, Meadows, Minnich, Stafford, Thompson, and Young; and fourteen more family names were shared by at least two recruits. This arrangement assured every man that he need not worry if he fell sick or wounded, since a friend always would be nearby to help. Nobody yet considered the consequences if this same company of friends and family saw hard combat; they would learn that in time.

For now, picking a name for their company occupied their minds, and they called themselves the "Mountain Boomers." They also elected their officers, choosing James H. French as captain. Most of the men gathered at Pearisburg, the county seat, to begin daily squad drill. They also played pranks on their friends, convincing one easily flattered boy that he had been promoted to the imaginary rank of "fifth lieutenant," with the duty of carrying water to the horses and catching the fleas in the soldiers' beds.

When the Boomers received orders to report for duty, the citizens of Pearisburg held a solemn and impressive departure ceremony for them. The women already had sewn gray uniforms with brass buttons for the men, and now they presented the company with a flag they had made. A little boy presented a Bible. As the Boomers left for their rendezvous at Lynchburg, David saw over and over again the "fond and loving mother clinging to her baby boy, weeping, sobbing, praying the Father of all Mercies to protect and preserve the life of her darling child," while a father begged his son to "act the man, be brave, do his duty, refrain from bad habits and to shun all appearance of evil."[3]

David Johnston had dreams of high rank and martial glory, but he embraced his private's role with enthusiasm. Most of the young men, on their first train ride ever, stayed awake through the entire trip to Lynchburg and Camp Davis, their first post of instruction. David took an immediate dislike to the camp commander, Lieutenant Colonel Hairston, who seemed "better qualified to manage his farm down in Henry County than a green military force composed of Virginia gentlemen, unused as they were to restrictions on their personal liberties."[4] He also discovered quickly that soldiering did not meet all his expectations. David and his company stayed in rough wooden sheds instead of barracks. They learned to cook for themselves. They drew Springfield rifles, bayonets and scabbards, and cartridge boxes, but they were issued no ammunition for target practice. With no combat training to speak of, David and his company left on May 31 for Manassas Junction.

Soon after arriving there, the Mountain Boomers learned that they no longer served as an independent company. They had become Company D of the Twenty-fourth Virginia Regiment, commanded by Colonel Jubal A. Early, a crusty and profane West Point graduate and, more recently, a prominent Lynchburg lawyer. David found just how much he had to learn. During the day, in camps near Manassas Junction and nearby Occoquan, he and his comrades drilled constantly. He found guard duty at night far more frightening, however. His first time on post, he imagined that every noise was an enemy sneaking up on him. Because of a squabble between senior officers, David's company left

Colonel Early's Twenty-fourth Virginia Regiment in mid-June to become Company D, Seventh Virginia Regiment, commanded by Colonel James L. Kemper. David learned more about army organization, too. When combined with the First, Eleventh, Seventeenth, and Twenty-fourth Virginia Regiments, David's Seventh Virginia became part of Brigadier General James Longstreet's brigade. In mid-July, when Brigadier General Irvin McDowell's Union forces marched "on to Richmond," it fell to Longstreet's men, including the Seventh Virginia, to block them.

David's baptism by fire came on July 18, 1861, at a small crossing of Bull Run Creek called Blackburn's Ford. He saw General P. G. T. Beauregard, the Confederate commander, ride along his line and advise his new soldiers: "Keep cool, men, and fire low; shoot them in the legs." David noticed that his comrades did not always follow that sage advice; he saw one aim his rifle toward the sky and another aim straight at the ground. When Union artillery opened fire, they fell behind any shelter they could find. David watched Private George Knoll calmly eat bacon during the shelling. He saw Private John East double over with stomach pains from the excitement. When the fighting ended, seven men in the Seventh Virginia had been wounded, but none of David's friends was hurt. Still, the screams of the wounded made the night "hideous and weird."[5]

Three days later, on July 21, David heard firing to the north. The Battle of First Manassas had begun. After noon the Seventh Virginia rushed to the support of the threatened Confederate left flank. As they arrived, David heard a mounted Confederate shout "Glory! Glory! Glory!" and announce the capture of a Union battery. Deployed at the right place at the right time, the Seventh Virginia, along with two other regiments, advanced with enthusiasm. When ordered by a senior officer to hold their fire to avoid harming friendly troops in front of them, a captain who had a better view yelled back, "They may be your friends, but they are none of mine. Fire, men!!" The Southern volley sent the Union troops reeling, the Northern line collapsing so quickly that David claimed the "only reason seemingly the enemy had for running as he did was because he could not fly."[6] David and the Seventh Virginia enjoyed the sweet taste of victory, but they learned more about war's cost, too. The regiment had lost nine killed, including Private Joseph Bane, who had enlisted with the Mountain Boomers in April.

The fall and winter of 1861 were quiet ones for David and the Seventh Virginia while they lived in log huts near Centreville, not far from the Bull Run battlefield. The regiment occasionally ventured forward toward Washington and took a few shots at Union observation balloons, but it fought no more big battles for nearly ten months. Just the same, death visited the Boomers as five of David's friends died of disease that fall. The young private noticed that sickness felled many of the strongest men while the weaker ones stood the service well.

In the spring of 1862 the men of the Seventh Virginia—like most Confederate soldiers who had enlisted initially for one year—learned that the Confederate Congress had extended the term of service "for the war." The Boomers now had to sign new enlistment papers. A bounty payment and a thirty-day leave at home lured at least eighteen to reenlist on the spot, but David noted that four men deserted rather than reenlist. At the same time, with Colonel Kemper's promotion to brigadier general, the Seventh Virginia got a new commander, Waller Tazewell Patton, one of several members of that illustrious military family to command Virginia regiments in the Civil War.

Before Colonel Patton could complete his unit's reorganization, however, the Seventh Virginia evacuated the Centreville line on March 10. Union General George McClellan had moved a huge army to the peninsula bounded by the James and York Rivers that led straight to the Confederate capital at Richmond. Confederate General Joseph E. Johnston moved toward Yorktown to stop McClellan, and David and the Seventh Virginia arrived there on April 10. While they took the time to view the historic battleground of 1781, they also completed their regimental and company reorganization. The Mountain Boomers ousted James French as their captain and replaced him with Joel Blackard, one of their original lieutenants. David won his sergeant's stripes, his first promotion.

On May 4, General Johnston ordered the evacuation of Yorktown to pull back to more defensible ground near Richmond. To buy time for the army to withdraw safely, the Seventh Virginia participated in a vicious fight near Williamsburg on May 5. Facing New York and New Jersey troops in a tangle of fallen timber, David fired his rifle thirty-six times, the recoil nearly disabling his shoulder. In the fight the Boomers' Private William Stafford was killed and fourteen others, including David, were lightly wounded. Although he dismissed the severity of his injuries, David remained impressed by the twenty-three bullet holes in his regiment's flag, irrefutable evidence of a hard fight. Morale remained high. David recalled passing an old man along the way, to whom one of the boys yelled out, "Boys, here is old Father Abraham." The soldiers howled when the gentleman responded, "Young man, you are mistaken.

I am Saul, the son of Kish, searching for his father's asses, and I have found them."[7]

On May 31 and June 1 the Seventh Virginia went into battle again at Fair Oaks, only five miles outside the Confederate capital. David's most graphic memory of the fight centered on the weather; his regiment fought in a driving rainstorm. During that battle, General Robert E. Lee became the new commander of the Army of Northern Virginia. If the announcement made an impact on David, he did not mention it. He remained far more concerned by the growing realization that much hard fighting would be required to drive McClellan away from the gates of Richmond.

On June 25 signs of an approaching battle grew unmistakable. Both General Kemper and Colonel Patton "made soul-stirring speeches, telling us that the great battle of the revolutionary war was now to be fought, and if we were successful the Confederacy would be a free country; if beaten, the war must be prolonged for years."[8] David and his comrades stayed out of the opening fight at Mechanicsville on June 26, the first of the Seven Days battles. Their luck continued the next day at Gaines Mill, where the Seventh Virginia remained in reserve and watched fellow Virginians from Brigadier General George Pickett's brigade break through a seemingly impregnable Union line.

David and his comrades faced their toughest test on June 30 at Glendale. To intercept McClellan's army and cut it in two before it could reach its new base on the James River, Kemper's brigade, including the Seventh Virginia, led the attack. Officers yelled, "Forward! Forward!" The prospect of survival did not seem promising. As David recalled, "The enemy is posted in that timber across the field; before we move many yards he will open on us with shot and shell; this is perhaps my last day on earth."[9] He saw men near him blown to "bloody fragments" by the Union artillery. Wide gaps appeared in their ranks, but David's regiment helped to capture a Union artillery battery before falling back. The regiment lost fourteen men dead in that charge, including three Mountain Boomers and David's new company commander, Captain Blackard. After the final battles at Malvern Hill on July 1, McClellan withdrew to Harrison's Landing. Richmond was saved, but the marching and fighting had exhausted David. On July 8 he entered a Richmond hospital to be treated for fatigue and the consequences of his earlier wound.

He did not return until August 8 when he rejoined the Boomers as the Army of Northern Virginia headed north. The march was difficult for David because—like many of his comrades—he had no shoes. On August 28 as the Seventh Virginia cleared Thoroughfare Gap with General James Longstreet's wing of Lee's army, David heard gunfire ahead. The rest of the Confederate army under Stonewall Jackson had opened the Battle of Second Manassas against Union Major General John Pope. David and the Boomers marched to the sound of the guns. Late in the afternoon of August 30, Longstreet launched a crushing attack against Pope's left flank. After much hard fighting, David and his comrades cleared Chinn Ridge, close to where they had fought during the Battle of First Manassas in July 1861. The cost to the Seventh Virginia was high; its colonel, lieutenant colonel, major, adjutant, and sergeant major all fell wounded. Lieutenant Colonel Charles Floweree, only twenty-one years old, had fallen far to the front, yelling "Up to the fence, 7th regiment, and give them h—l!"[10] Sixteen Boomers—one-third of the regiment's entire loss—had fallen in this engagement, three of them sharing the name Wilburn.

After the battle, David refitted himself with shoes and trousers from a dead Union soldier. He soon discovered, however, that the trousers were infested with lice. "After more than fifty years," he wrote long after the war, "the thought of this wretched parasite makes my flesh itch."[11] On September 4, when the leading elements of General Lee's army began to cross the Potomac River into Maryland to begin his first march into Union territory, David recalled that thousands of men threw away their shoes as an excuse to fall out of ranks and stay in Virginia, but, he boasted, he made the trip with bare feet.

On September 14, the Seventh Virginia went into battle at South Mountain near Boonsboro in western Maryland to buy time for Lee's scattered army to concentrate against General McClellan once more. On that day, of the original 102 men who had joined the Mountain Boomers in April 1861, only twenty-four remained in the ranks. One of them, Sergeant Tapley Mays, had become the regimental color bearer, and he fell dead. David always considered Mays and three other Boomers who had marched so hard for so long, only to fall on those dark slopes, to be "iron soldiers equal to the emergency."[12] On September 17 at Sharpsburg (also called Antietam), only 117 men stood in the ranks of the Seventh Virginia—a far cry from the 1,000 under arms when initially organized—and the Boomers of Company D now counted only two officers and fifteen enlisted men. When Union forces threatened the Confederate right flank and the road that led to the Potomac fords, one of the regiment's captains yelled, "Men, we are to hold this position at all hazards. Not a man leave his place. If need be, we will die together in this road."[13] The Boomers all survived their stand.

David returned to Virginia with them, and over the next two months of relative calm, Lee reorganized his battered army yet again. David's company remained part of the Seventh Virginia of Kemper's brigade, which belonged to Major General George Pickett's Division of Lieutenant General James Longstreet's new First Corps in Lee's Army of Northern Virginia. More personally important to David, perhaps, was his promotion in November 1862 to the rank of regimental sergeant major, the senior noncommissioned officer in the Seventh Virginia, an honor that made him "as proud as anything that has come to him since."[14] The calm was broken by the battle of Fredericksburg on December 13. While wave upon wave of Northern soldiers unsuccessfully assaulted the Southern defenses on Marye's Heights, the Boomers remained in reserve with the rest of Pickett's division.

Mostly, David remembered the severe winter that followed. Snowball battles broke the routine, but David could not ignore the prevalence of homesickness that swept through the camp. Belief in their cause and their admiration for General Lee kept most of the Boomers in the ranks, but they drove out Private Dan East, who "never was in a battle, and never intended to be; yet Dan knew more about it than anyone who had gone through it, always turning up after the battle with a full haversack, good blanket, overcoat and shoes." Colonel Patton had even made him parade through the camp wearing a sign with "COWARD" printed on it.[15] Privates were not the only ones prone to lapses in good discipline. The Seventh Virginia's Lieutenant Colonel Floweree drank too much too often, was court-martialed in February for drunkenness on duty, and remained under arrest until midsummer.

In the early spring of 1863 the Boomers marched with two of Longstreet's divisions through Richmond and toward Petersburg, charged with obtaining supplies and pushing back Union threats in southern Virginia and northeastern North Carolina. Discipline remained loose. Private Gordon stole a hat, explaining that "I swapped a fellow—but he wasn't there!" Three Boomers deserted to the enemy. Drummer boy John Whitlock kept losing his drumsticks, and when he could not perform his duties at an important parade, Colonel Patton forced him to wear a "drum shirt"—a hollowed-out drum—as punishment.[16] These measures rarely tamed the high spirits of the men, however.

When David and his comrades rejoined the Army of Northern Virginia in May, too late to participate in the Battle of Chancellorsville, they learned that Stonewall Jackson had fallen mortally wounded. Nonetheless, in early June, Lee began his second advance into Union territory. Despite the appearance of high morale, not all was well in Lee's army. The Seventh Virginia lined up with the rest of Pickett's division to watch the execution of a deserter from the Eighteenth Virginia. This disconcerted some of David's friends, who argued now, as they had the previous fall, that they had enlisted to defend their homes, not invade the Union. But David did not share their doubts. Only a recent dream disquieted him, one in which he saw his left shoulder mangled by a cannon ball, leaving him lying helpless and alone on the field of battle. He could not get it out of his mind.

On July 2 the Boomers marched with the rest of Pickett's division nearly twenty-five miles to the outskirts of a small Pennsylvania town named Gettysburg. For nearly two days hard fighting had swirled over the ridges and through the woodlots north, west, and south of the town. They had approached the battlefield by a route that prevented them from seeing the worst of the carnage. Indeed, they heard they were winning. But David could not shake a sense of foreboding about what might happen on July 3.

Early that day, Pickett's division moved forward into the main Confederate battle line on Seminary Ridge. David's unit deployed near an orchard belonging to a man named Spangler. The day grew hotter and more humid as the hours passed. David paid special attention to the Boomers—now grown to twenty-eight as some sick and wounded returned to the ranks—and saw both Captain R. H. Bane and Lieutenant John Mullins prostrated by the heat. Anticipation of the coming battle seized others, including Colonel Patton, who believed he would die in this fight. Colonel Joseph Mayo of the Third Virginia, deployed next to David's regiment, noted the quiet in the ranks. He came over to Colonel Patton and commented that the upcoming advance "has brought about an awful seriousness with our fellows, Taz." "Yes," Colonel Patton replied, "and well they may be serious if they really know what is in store for them. I have been up yonder where [artilleryman James] Dearing is, and looked across at the Yankees."[17] But David tried hard not to think about it. As he recalled, "a soldier in the field rarely thought his time to die had exactly arrived—that is, it would be the other fellow's time—and well it was so."[18]

All silent contemplation ended about 1 P.M., when more than 135 Confederate cannon began to prepare the way for an infantry assault against the Union center. A similar number of Union cannon answered.

The rounds that overshot the Southern guns on the ridge above their position landed in the ranks of Pickett's division. David never forgot the horror. "Not again could the writer look upon such a sight. In any direction might be seen guns, swords, haversacks, heads, limbs, flesh and bone in confusion or dangling in the air or bounding on the earth." Only a few feet away from David, a cannonball "trounced a man, lifting him three feet from the earth, killing him but not striking him."[19] David saw four men lying nearby in Company E killed by the explosion of a single shell. Yet another shell decapitated two men in the nearby Third Virginia before it exploded and killed two more in the Seventh Virginia. A hot fragment of that same shell also struck David. As he had dreamed, it hit his left shoulder and then pressed downward, breaking three ribs and leaving a contusion on his left lung.

The wound so stunned David that he could not answer Pickett's call: "Up, men, and to your posts! Don't forget today that you are from old Virginia!" Colonel Patton gave David his canteen, since he knew that the first thing a wounded man wanted was water. As his comrades advanced, David could only yell a weak farewell. Sergeant Major David Johnston missed the attack that became famous as Pickett's Charge.

It was perhaps best that he did, for when the assault ended—in failure—the names of many of David's friends could be found on Lee's long casualty lists. Of the twenty-four Boomers who went into the attack—four had been wounded in the bombardment and did not make the charge—seventeen had fallen, with Privates David Akers, Daniel Bush, Jesse Barrett, and John P. Sublett among the killed. Corporal Jesse Young of the Boomers had carried the Seventh Virginia's battleflag, but he fell wounded near the stone wall that marked the Union line, and a soldier from the Eighty-second New York captured the prized banner.[20] Colonel Patton fell mortally wounded, dying of his injuries three weeks later. A captain commanded the small fragment of the Seventh Virginia that recrossed the Potomac to safety. As one of Pickett's men wrote later, "The sun that had risen so brightly upon our confident hopes, buoyant in anticipation of victory, set in sullen, angry sadness upon that field of carnage, where our bravest and best lay weltering in their gore and glory," adding "we never—no, never—recovered from that blow."[21] The Seventh Virginia left behind wounded Sergeant Major David Johnston as a prisoner of war.

The severity of David's wounds made it impossible to move him at first. He could not eat solid food, but frequently drank lemonade and diluted whiskey. He never forgot the kindness of an Ohio soldier who read to him from a Philadelphia newspaper. Finally, on July 20, Union army doctors sent him to a hospital near Philadelphia. The trip nearly killed him, but his spirit survived intact. In late August he and other Confederates wounded at Gettysburg were sent to City Point, near Petersburg, Virginia, to await their formal exchange. On November 1, David returned to his regiment.

David saw few familiar faces in the small fragment of the Seventh Virginia that survived Pickett's Charge. Requiring nearly complete reorganization after its disastrous losses, Pickett's division spent the fall and winter of 1863–1864 assigned to the defenses around Petersburg and northeastern North Carolina. David noticed that many preachers visited the camps, part of the general rebirth of religion in the army that winter. Rekindling their spirit was one thing, but rebuilding physical strength proved to be an even greater challenge. During that winter, David noted, the typical daily ration included a pint of unscreened meal, a quarter-pound of bacon, a coffee substitute of parched wheat or rye, and—when available—rice, turnips, or potatoes.

A brief flurry of activity in North Carolina brought David's regiment into action in January 1864, well before Lee's main body to the north began active campaigning. Near Goldsboro, Pickett's men captured thirty-five soldiers of the First and Second North Carolina Union Regiments. At least twenty-two of the prisoners had previously served in the Confederate army, so they were tried by court-martial and hanged for desertion. David did not witness the executions, but he wondered if it would dissuade more Confederate soldiers from leaving the ranks. Even David's own regiment no longer remained immune to desertion; one man from the Seventh Virginia described the death by firing squad of the condemned man, who was bound, blindfolded, and tied to a post: "Half the muskets only were loaded with ball cartridge, so that no one who fired knew who fired the fatal shots. The band played a death march, the chaplain spoke a few final words with the condemned, stepped aside, and at the command the fire was delivered. The unfortunate man was riddled by a half a dozen bullets; when the smoke cleared away he was hanging a helpless mass on the stake."[22]

While Lee's army first met U. S. Grant's forces fifty miles north of Richmond in May 1864, David and his comrades missed the bloody clashes at the Wilderness and Spotsylvania. Instead, they manned defenses around Petersburg and Richmond to fend off another Union army,

this one under General Benjamin Butler, that threatened the Confederate capital from the east. By the second week in May, Pickett's men
deployed against Butler at Drewry's Bluff, along the James River. Aggressive action had become "imperative," David recalled. Indeed, "to
become the assailants was a necessity, for if the enemy should maintain
his position then occupied in front of Drewry's Bluff (only seven miles
below Richmond) and General Grant continued his flank movement to
the James River until he formed a junction with General Butler, the fate
of Richmond . . . would have been decided."[23]

On May 16, in a dense fog, Pickett's 4,000 men advanced silently
across Kingsland Creek to move on the Union position. At the first
Union volley they fell to the ground for cover. But not wanting to lose
momentum, Colonel Floweree yelled to the Seventh Virginia, "Stand
up, men! Don't you see the balls are striking the ground at your feet,
and there is greater danger lying down than standing up?"[24] The men
rose, roared out a loud Rebel yell, and charged the Northern lines, not
stopping even to fire a single round.

The fighting did not last long. David had accompanied the Seventh
Virginia and one other regiment that swung around the flank and rear
of the Union position, quickly convincing the Northerners they had to
run or surrender. The firing had been so rapid that many soldiers forgot
to remove the ramrods from their rifles, and David noticed that the
breastworks and trees were full of the metal rods. Pickett's men captured one Union general, and a sergeant from the First Virginia gave
David a fine black felt hat taken from one of the captured Northern
officers. The entire Seventh Virginia came through the fight in splendid
condition, losing only two killed. But good fortune did not smile on
David's friends for long. On May 18, as they tried to move to a stronger
position close to the Howlett house near the James River, the First and
Seventh Virginia charged across an open field to take the most commanding ground. For eleven hours, "Every species of missile was hurled
against us from eleven gunboats, while we were unable to respond with
a single shot," a soldier in the First Virginia remembered.[25] In the exchange, Lieutenant John Mullins of the Boomers fell mortally wounded.

When Pickett's division rejoined Lee's main force for the brutal fight
at Cold Harbor in early June, David still stood in the ranks of the Seventh Virginia. Although his own unit saw little action there, David noted
that "during the war I never saw so many dead Union soldiers on any
field." The stench alone was "not to be endured long by the living."[26]

Once back with the Army of Northern Virginia, David noted its thinning ranks and observed the ever-growing strength of the enemy they faced. He recalled a comment made by a frustrated comrade after Pickett's Charge a year earlier: "Do we have to whip the world?" Now it seemed increasingly likely that there might be a grain of truth in the once-jocular rejoinder—a Federal officer shouting "Attention, World! By nations, right wheel, by states, fire!"[27] Grant continued sidling around Lee's army to the south, trying to find a way to crush it, take Richmond, and end the war. But Lee countered Grant's every effort. David was lightly wounded at Port Walthall Junction, during one attempt to stop Grant, and Pickett's entire division played a starring role at holding Grant's men back at Bermuda Hundred. Intending to hold down his own casualties by relying on a stout defense, Lee had not planned aggressive actions, but Pickett's men had attacked aggressively. Indeed, as Lee's own report noted, "We tried very hard to stop Pickett's men from capturing the breastworks of the enemy, but couldn't do it." David remained especially proud of his regiment's work that day, writing that the Seventh Virginia was "never ordered to take the enemy's line that it did not take it, never gave up or lost a position it was ordered to hold, and never left a position or battlefield unless ordered to do so."[28] Grant did not take Richmond in June 1864.

Indeed, by late June, both armies hunkered down for a long siege. Long lines of entrenchments began northeast of Richmond, stretched south to Petersburg, and curled south and west around that city to protect the rail and road network considered the entry into the back door of the Confederate capital. David, with the rest of Pickett's division, was posted not far from Richmond itself. Soldiering in the trenches alternated between boring and lethal. In no way did it seem to be ending the war. David recalled an Alabama soldier visiting the Virginians' camp to solicit one dollar from each enlisted man and five dollars from each officer to build "a machine to navigate the air, carry shells, and drop them on the Northern armies, and in their cities." David dismissed him as "a crank," only years later recognizing him as "a little ahead of his time."[29]

David heard about the fighting at the Crater near Petersburg on July 30, and he saw some of the fighting at Fort Harrison outside Richmond in late August, but the daily grind in the trenches wore on the weary men. Desertions rose. During the fall of 1864, David witnessed yet another execution of a deserter from the Seventh Virginia. The victim was just a boy, but he did not elicit much pity from David, who noted that "war is at best a horrible thing," but "discipline must be enforced."[30] Still, David grew increasingly aware that news of privations at home presented trying dilemmas for many good and dutiful soldiers. Nonetheless, he saw no reason to give up hope. Religion had become the bulwark of David's commitment, and he viewed Lee's entire force as a "truly Christian army." He had formalized his religious ties in September 1864, when he was baptized in a creek near Petersburg.

Despite the fact that it had been devastated by the war, David's home state still provided a great feast for Lee's entire army at Christmas in 1864. David took courage from his benefactors and hoped those at home would keep up their faith as well. As late as February 1865, he wrote: "There is nothing left us but to fight it out, the cry is for war— war to the knife. If the people at home will support the army and drive all the skulkers and absentees" into the ranks, he believed the Confederacy still could win.[31] Indeed, he believed for years that even during the winter of 1864–1865, "the great bulk of the army was ready to make almost any sacrifice required for independence and separate governments." But he admitted that not all shared his optimism. During the winter three of his fellow Boomers were sentenced to be shot for encouraging insubordination and mutiny. The end of the war saved their lives.

By late March 1865, David—along with Pickett's division—had moved from the outskirts of Richmond to the Confederate lines southwest of Petersburg. Union forces under General Phil Sheridan probed the Confederate lines near Dinwiddie Court House at a key crossroads called Five Forks and attacked on April 1. David remembered the Five Forks fight as one of the most fiercely contested battles of the war. He recalled Pickett behaving coolly and the glee club of the First Virginia stabilizing the line with a chorus of "Rally Round the Flag, Boys, Rally Once Again." Finally, however, with both flanks broken and Union cavalry probing toward their rear, David and his comrades broke and ran. He still carried his rifle but had not a single round of ammunition.

After a brief break for food on April 2—the first he had eaten in four days and the last he would be issued for eleven more—he began the march west toward Appomattox. About the fighting on April 4, 5, and 6, in constant contact with Union cavalry, David wrote that "if all our marchings, sufferings, hardships, privations, and sacrifices for all the preceding years of the war were summed up, shaken together, and pressed down, they would not equal those we were now undergoing on this tramp."[32] On April 6, at Saylers's Creek, after a hard fight, David was captured. Three days later, Lee surrendered. David did not witness the final days of the Army of Northern Virginia.

David's war had not ended, however. He marched back to Petersburg with his fellow prisoners to board transports for Point Lookout prison. They arrived shortly after the guards heard the news of the assassination of Abraham Lincoln. The guards warned the prisoners that any sign of exultation would be met with bullets, and David noticed that cannons had been turned to aim at the prison.

David remained in prison until June 28. Even though the war was over, men died from starvation and the bullets of guards. David's weight dropped from 165 to 127 pounds. When he had a chance to take the loyalty oath and leave for home, he took it. Traveling by steamer, train, and on foot, David reached home on July 5, 1865.

In the spring of 1861, 102 men had enlisted in the Mountain Boomers. Twenty recruits had joined over time, accounting for a total enlistment of 122 soldiers. Of those men, seventeen had been killed in action or died of wounds. Another fourteen had died of disease, meaning that one in every four never returned from the war. Twenty-nine men had been discharged for a variety of reasons that prevented them from carrying out their military duties. Six had transferred to other commands. Twenty-seven spent time as prisoners of the Yankees, some more than once. Eight were in the hospital when the war ended. Twelve had deserted. Only nine laid down their arms at Appomattox.

Who were these men, and how did they feel about their service in the Confederate Army? According to David, "I, in common with my fellow soldiers, repudiate as unsound and baseless any charge of rebellion or treason in the war. We had resorted to the revolutionary right to establish separate government vouchsafed to us in the Declaration of Independence. I did not fight to destroy the government of the United States, nor for the perpetuation of the institution of slavery, for which I cared nothing, but did fight for four years in my young manhood for a principle I knew to be right. Had such not been true, I would not have risked my life, my all," to be a Confederate soldier.[33]

Yet once the war ended, David—like most of his comrades—strove once more to become good citizens in the now-united nation. David Emmons Johnston became a writer and a lawyer. Interested in politics, he served as a member of the West Virginia state senate and the U.S. House of Representatives, and he sat as a circuit court judge. But his greatest success, he believed, was his family. He died at home in its warm embrace in 1917.

Notes

1. David E. Johnston, *The Story of a Confederate Boy in the Civil War* (Portland, OR: Glass and Prudhomme Company, 1914), 6.

2. Ibid., 27, 29.

3. Ibid., 41–42.

4. Ibid., 43.

5. Ibid., 64, 71.

6. Ibid., 74–75.

7. Ibid., 103.

8. Ibid., 109.

9. Ibid., 114.

10. Ibid., 129.

11. Ibid., 130.

12. Ibid., 143.

13. David F. Riggs, *7th Virginia Infantry* (Lynchburg, VA: H. E. Howard, 1982), 16.

14. Johnston, *The Story of a Confederate Boy*, 167.

15. Ibid., 174–75.

16. Ibid., 180–81, 186.

17. Quoted in Lee A. Wallace Jr., *3rd Virginia Infantry* (Lynchburg, VA: H. E. Howard, 1986), 36–37.

18. Johnston, *The Story of a Confederate Boy*, 204.

19. Ibid., 206, 207.

20. Riggs, *7th Virginia Infantry*, 26.

21. Walter Harrison, *Pickett's Men: A Fragment of War History* (New York: D. Van Nostrand, 1870), 101.

22. Charles T. Loehr, *The War History of the Old First Virginia Infantry Regiment, Army of Northern Virginia* (Richmond, VA: William Ellis Jones, 1884), 41.

23. Johnston, *The Story of a Confederate Boy*, 250.

24. Ibid., 252.

25. Loehr, *The War History of the Old First Virginia Infantry Regiment*, 49.

26. Johnston, *The Story of a Confederate Boy*, 265.

27. Ibid., 270.

28. Ibid., 271.

29. Ibid., 273.

30. Ibid., 278.

31. Ibid., 281, 283.

32. Ibid., 325.

33. Ibid., 347.

Suggested Readings

David Emmons Johnston's full story can be found in his personal military memoir entitled *The Story of a Confederate Boy in the Civil War* (Portland, OR: Glass and Prudhomme Company, 1914). See David F. Riggs, *7th Virginia Infantry* (Lynchburg, VA: H. E. Howard, 1982) for the history of David's regiment. The Seventh Virginia served in Major General George E. Pickett's division, and Walter Harrison's *Pickett's Men: A Fragment of War History* (New York: D. Van Nostrand, 1870) tells its story. Important modern accounts may be found in Carol Reardon, *Pickett's Charge in History and Memory* (Chapel Hill: University of North Carolina Press, 1997), and Lesley J. Gordon, *General George E. Pickett in Life and Legend* (Chapel Hill: University of North Carolina Press, 1998). Pickett's division served in General Robert E. Lee's Army of Northern Virginia, and J. Tracy Power's *Lee's Miserables: Life in the Army of Northern Virginia from the Wilderness to Appomattox* (Chapel Hill: University of North Carolina Press, 1998) ably narrates the travails faced by David Johnston and the other common soldiers in the ranks during the last year of the war. Other useful works on the common soldier who fought for the Confederacy are Bell I. Wiley, *The Life of Johnny Reb: Common Soldier of the Confederacy* (reprint ed., Baton Rouge: Louisiana State University Press, 1998), and James I. Robertson Jr., *Soldiers Blue and Gray* (paperback ed., Columbia: University of South Carolina Press, 1998).

11

Lucy Virginia French
"Out of the Bitterness of My Heart"

Connie L. Lester

War affects not just those fighting on the battlefield. Others fought at home for economic survival or even for their lives. For those who saw a family member march off to combat, the conflict brought them even more worry, doubt, and fear. Many of the men who left never returned, and their deaths left widows and orphans as further casualties of war. Some who did survive came back to their homes with severe wounds, both to their physical self and to their psyche. On the home front, with many men gone, some women took on new tasks; others began to look at their lives differently.

Lucy Virginia French was one of those women. Her diary entries reveal just some of the ways women saw the unfolding of the war. For her, the conflict shattered expectations—soldiers drank too much, for example. It changed her views from Unionist to Confederate nationalist. It loosened community and family bonds around her and intensified class conflict. It left behind serious economic problems for her family. And it made her a very different person than before Fort Sumter.

French's story is presented by Connie L. Lester, an assistant professor of history at Mississippi State University, and previously an associate editor of the *Tennessee Encyclopedia of History and Culture* (1998).

Through their actions during the emerging sectional crisis of the ante-bellum period, Tennesseans, like their neighbors in the other upper South states, expressed their belief that slavery and the rights of southern slaveholders could best be protected within the Union and the constitutional framework. Even as the national parties dissolved over the issue of slavery, Tennessee voters continued to operate within a two-party framework, thinking that their differences could be resolved through the political process without destroying the government. In the election of 1860 Tennessee voters cast their ballots for the "national" candidates, Stephen A. Douglas and John Bell. Bell carried the state,

This essay originally appeared in Steven E. Woodworth, ed., *The Human Tradition in the Civil War and Reconstruction* (Wilmington, DE: Scholarly Resources, 2000), 137–52.

and the combined votes for Douglas and Bell totaled more than 81,000, compared to the 65,000 garnered by John C. Breckinridge of the more extreme southern wing of the Democratic Party.

In the days following the election, as the lower South states seceded from the Union and organized the Confederate States of America, most Tennesseeans remained unpersuaded by the impassioned agitation for disunion. In January 1861 prosecessionist governor Isham G. Harris called an emergency session of the Tennessee General Assembly, in which he outlined the grievances suffered by the state as a result of "systematic, wanton, and long continued agitation of the slavery question."[1] He proposed a state convention, sanctioned by the state's electorate, to determine whether Tennessee should secede. On February 9, 1861, Tennesseeans rejected a state convention by a vote of 69,000 to 57,000. Although the electorate seemed willing to await further developments, Harris nevertheless continued his pro-Confederate campaign and began preparations for a provisional army in anticipation of secession.

The firing on Fort Sumter and Lincoln's call for volunteers to put down the rebellion changed the minds of most Tennesseeans and drew the state into the Confederacy. In a second referendum on June 8, 1861, voters demonstrated that they no longer expected protection in the Union, for they approved secession by a vote of 105,000 to 47,000. The vote also revealed significant divisions within the state. Voters in Middle Tennessee (25 percent slave) and West Tennessee (40 percent slave) overwhelmingly favored secession, with some counties even claiming unanimous support for disunion. But East Tennesseeans (15 percent slave) again rejected the action and threatened to secede from the state. The quick deployment of pro-Southern troops by Governor Harris prevented the eastern counties from carrying out their threat, but that portion of the state remained strongly Unionist throughout the war.

Tennessee's Civil War and Reconstruction history mirrored the divisions so evident across the South at the time of secession. The last state to join the Confederacy, it became the first to reenter the Union. In the interim, more major battles were fought on Tennessee soil than in any other state except Virginia, and some of these contests—Shiloh, Stone's River, Chattanooga, Franklin, and Nashville—were among the bloodiest of the war. Tennessee also sent more soldiers (approximately 186,000) to the Confederate armies than any other southern state. At the same time, however, it provided more Union troops than all the other southern states combined (31,000 soldiers, a pro-Union militia of 15,000 whites and 4,000 African Americans, and another 7,000 men who left the state to enlist).

The statewide divisions also resonated through local communities and within Tennessee families. Most men of fighting age in Middle and West Tennessee marched away in gray, but a few in virtually every county joined the Union forces. After secession, Unionists in Middle and West Tennessee either retreated to their farms and plantations to await the outcome or joined their neighbors in support of Confederate nationalism. Once Union occupation came, a number of pro-Unionists (most notably William Bowen Campbell) reemerged to take positions in the military government of the state. Finally, some areas of the state that were not dominated by either army erupted in lawlessness as "bushwhackers" and thieves fought in their own self-interest. Thus, to understand the war in Tennessee, we must study the many people whose views fell between those of the radical supporters of either the Union or the Confederacy. For these men and women, support for either cause was tempered by their experiences with loss—loss of friendships, loss of economic stability and social order, loss of a sense of well-being and health, and, for many, the loss of life itself.

One such person was Lucy Virginia French. The diary she kept from January 1862 to August 1865 offers a thoughtful and articulate presentation of the ambivalence that accompanied secession and war and the rise of Southern nationalism, as well as a poignant chronicle of the breakdown of the ties that supported antebellum southern life. The daughter of a wealthy Virginia family, French taught school in Memphis and achieved modest fame as a poet and writer before her 1853 marriage to Col. John Hopkins French of McMinnville, Tennessee. A wealthy breeder of fine horses, Colonel French was older than his wife and offered her a genteel future in Tennessee's antebellum society. Lucy French continued to write after the birth of her three children, a boy and two girls. In 1856, she published a book of poems, *Wind Whispers*, and a drama, *Iztalilxo*.

Throughout the war, French received visitors from the ranks of both armies who were anxious to meet the poet and author. Her residence, Forest Home, was located in Warren County on the eastern edge of Middle Tennessee and at the periphery of much of the fighting: she reported hearing the sounds of artillery during the battles of Stone's River, Franklin, and Nashville. Although seemingly isolated, she remained well informed about military and political activities through her contacts with many of the major participants. She begged visitors and friends to send her accounts of their own experiences, hoping to incorporate this eyewitness information into a history of the war. French never published a historical account, but her war diary provides a vivid description of the effect of military and political decisions on community and family life. Her access to information, astute powers of observation, and literary skills enabled her to write a compelling account of the changes produced by war and offer insight into the sources of Southern nationalism that survived the war and Reconstruction as the mythology of the Lost Cause.

Lucy Virginia French did not support secession. Like many Tennesseeans, she and her husband steadfastly upheld Unionism during the turbulent weeks following the election of Abraham Lincoln. Her efforts went beyond personal support as she marshaled southern and northern women to sign a peace memorial that was read to the U.S. Senate by Stephen Douglas and printed in the *Nashville Patriot*. On New Year's Eve 1860, French and her family and friends celebrated the coming year with a "Union party," and she recorded the year's end "with 'Union' on heart and lip."[2]

Although French soon embraced Southern nationalism, she never entirely rejected her earlier patriotism and repeatedly referred to that 1860 Union party as a touchstone of devotion to the United States. She first acknowledged and explained her conversion to Southern nationalism during a confrontation with a Union soldier who had asserted that "the South had brought this army with its consequent troubles upon herself." French countered by briefly tracing Tennessee's road to secession and declared that the state's citizens loved the Union until driven into exile and rebellion, adding, "Now here you are with your armies to drive her back again."[3] Like many Southerners, her resistance grew with the presence of Federal troops.

Nevertheless, her earlier Union patriotism resurfaced on several occasions. In July 1862, following Nathan Bedford Forrest's successful raid on nearby Murfreesboro, French recorded her first sight of captured Federal soldiers. A long procession of wagons and prisoners passed before her gate throughout the day and into the night, filling her with joy over the Confederate success. She admitted, however, that she shed tears at the sight of the "stars and stripes a *captive banner*." She confessed, "I felt badly to see it thus . . . it was the old flag I had loved so long."[4] She expressed her anger and bitterness at the "trouble this vile thing 'Secession' had brought upon us" and proclaimed, "I was sincere then [as a Unionist] and I am sincere still but oh how changed in sentiment." A proud Unionist initially, she was "glad I am not now,—though I am not a *secessionist* now nor ever will be."[5]

French's support for the Confederacy intensified as the result of personal encounters with Union soldiers rather than through her identification with secession and antebellum southern radicalism. Initially, Union officers followed a policy of conciliation, hoping to produce a change of heart in the presumably misguided civilian population. The failure of that policy led to a more aggressive and less tolerant approach in which all Southern sympathizers were labeled "secesh." As part of the antebellum elite, French expected a degree of deference that Union soldiers were unwilling to give her. She was filled with resentment and bitterness by their lack of respect for her family, their property, and their obvious position in the community; the material losses that resulted from troop movements and confiscations or thefts; the arrest of friends; and her perception of American troops as "miserable wretches . . . brutal looking . . . so impertinent . . . and so insufferable in every way." At war's end, she declared, "I don't think I should be half so Southern if it were not for the stupid troops." She went on to explain that whenever she managed to achieve a feeling of goodwill toward the North, the sight of "these blue things" filled her with rebellion. "How I do hate them!" she wrote, "and how I want to let 'em know it to the full."[6] The transformation of French's loyalties followed the disintegration of communal, familial, and personal ties that called into question political authority, the efficacy of the law, and the limits of human morality.

Throughout the war, French maintained a strong sense of skepticism, if not cynicism, toward political and military leaders on both sides of the conflict. A political foe of the secessionist governor, Isham Harris, she condemned his flight to Memphis in anticipation of the February 1862 fall of Nashville as a disgrace, the result of his "inefficiency and cowardice." She also joined many others in criticizing Confederate general Braxton Bragg following the Battle of Murfreesboro in January 1863, repeating the views of her neighbors that Bragg had chosen a poor position. She blamed the Confederate loss on his failure to renew the fight the following day, a delay that allowed the Federal troops to reorganize. In the wake of Bragg's losses at Stone's River and his subsequent retreat, French believed, incorrectly, that the Army of Tennessee remained in the state only at the insistence of the soldiers themselves, who "swore to his face that they [would] not leave their homes to the invaders."[7] Such overt rebellion within the ranks boded ill for the army and the fortunes of the South. In French's view, it was an unsettling example of what she came to perceive as an unexpected consequence of war—the rise in the power of "the masses."

As the Army of Tennessee retreated from Stone's River and established winter quarters, French was offered a closer view of Confederate officers at numerous social events in her community. During the Christmas celebration in Murfreesboro the previous December, thirty-seven-year-old Gen. John Hunt Morgan, the dashing cavalry commander, married twenty-one-year-old Mattie Ready in a ceremony unexcelled for military pomp. In late January 1863 the newlyweds took up residence in McMinnville, and the women of the town attempted to make the couple feel welcome with dinners, balls, and benefit concerts, despite criticism by some who felt displays of gaiety were inappropriate during wartime.

French declared her disappointment with the results of the first event, a benefit concert for the Confederate wounded. On this occasion officers filled the house, but their determination that "everybody near them should know that they were Cols." and their loud talk "about my regiment and my regiment and my regiment until they thought everybody near them should know of their *officership*" disgusted her. Squeezed "jam up" between the men, she was aware that they passed "coarse remarks upon the girls and wish[ed] the bore would stop and the ball commence so that they could get brandy." She soon became "sick with the fumes of their breath—disgusted with their conversation—and indignant at their ingratitude." The officers followed up their earlier rude behavior with an evening of flirting, displaying elegant manners designed to impress the very women they had mocked. Although French conceded that "it always hurts me to find people worse than I imagine them to be," she continued to expect an elegance of manners in Southern officers that the realities of war undermined.[8] In particular, she took exception to the heavy drinking she noted among both officers and their men.

French found Morgan's officers and men generally of suspect character. When Bragg sent reinforcements in early March, she described them as "rough looking troops" and believed they were intoxicated. Although she held Gen. Joseph Wheeler's cavalry in higher esteem, she admitted later that month that his staff was "very drunk" when they left to investigate Federal troop movements. In addition to drunkenness, Morgan was upbraided by both French and the *Chattanooga Rebel* for acts of arson, thefts, and unreasonable confiscations committed by his cavalry in the nearby Sequatchie Valley. As area farmers viewed the destruction the troops wrought, they declared they would be just as happy under Yankee occupation, a view French did not endorse.⁹

Lucy French held an even dimmer view of Northern leaders. Her criticisms of Yankee behavior revealed a distinct class consciousness not found in her judgments of Southern officers, as she routinely described the "plebian [sic]" activities and manners of Union officers and public officials. On several occasions Federal officers dined at the French home or stayed overnight—often at the insistence of the family, who viewed their official presence as a guarantee against theft and vandalism by enlisted men. French made no effort to hide her disdain for the officers whose attempts to "put on the courtesy and easy dignity of Southern gentlemen" fit them like "a stiff suit of new clothes to a 10 year old boy." She described one Union general and his wife as "people in the middle walks of life—clever enough in their way" but clearly inferior in class to General Morgan and his wife.¹⁰

French saved her most vitriolic comments for Andrew Johnson, the onetime tailor from East Tennessee who had served before the war as governor, congressman, and U.S. senator and who now, by virtue of Lincoln's appointment, was military governor of the state. In the view of most Tennessee Confederates, the appointment of the East Tennessee Unionist unleashed a period of tyranny and gave him free rein to attack his political enemies among the state's "aristocracy." Johnson replaced elected Southern sympathizers with loyal Union appointees and controlled Nashville newspapers by closing opposing presses. French reported his well-known alcoholic excesses and gleefully expressed the view that Johnson "made an ass of himself."¹¹

On Johnson's election to the vice presidency, she vented her hatred toward the "Tennessee Tailor." Calling Johnson's inaugural speech "the climax of absurdity and plebianism [sic]," she accused him of confirming nothing but his own low birth. She accepted his "shoddy" performance as appropriate to the people over whom he ruled. With the death of Lincoln and Johnson's elevation to the presidency, French accused him of carrying out his "leveling" war on the aristocrats with a vigor that threatened impoverishment. Although popular mythology supported her assessment of Federal control, recent scholarship suggests that Tennessee's upper class, though reduced in wealth, remained firmly in control of the political and economic future of the state.

If the war did not displace the antebellum power brokers, it did undermine the bonds of community and family. It took men away from their homes and families, leaving women to manage farms, plantations, slaves, and households. In this regard, French proved an exception, for "Darlin' " (her name for Colonel French) remained at home throughout the war. Although she rejoiced that he was too old for military service, she was often separated from the colonel by business and the circumstances of war. Thus, like other Southern women, French faced potentially dangerous situations alone or with only her minor children and her female household slaves for support, and she increasingly viewed herself as a planner and the mainstay of the family's future. Indeed, with her husband's blessing, she moved to Beersheba Springs in the spring of 1863 to be alone and work on her writing, hoping to sell a manuscript and replenish the family's diminishing fortune.

French's experience and that of other women across the South altered the social perceptions of gender in important ways. Although few of these women emerged from the war as suffragists, their actions in defense of home and in support of Southern nationalism gained the respect of Confederate men and even a grudging admiration from Union soldiers. In the postwar period these same women took a leading role in perpetuating the myth of the Lost Cause—a potent reminder of their own part in the war.

Female support for the war drew public attention almost immediately. Soon after the fall of Nashville in 1862, French added a clipping from the *Knoxville Register* to her diary. In it the paper's editor praised the "Spirit of the Ladies" of Nashville, who reportedly refused to renew acquaintances with old friends who had joined the Union army. The editor predicted such defiance would "nerve [men's] arms in the hour of battle" and bring victory to the Southern cause.[12]

Within months, French also stood defiantly against Union soldiers, initially attacking them for what she perceived as the invasion of an otherwise peaceable land. As the cost of war escalated, she planted herself in the doorway of her home to prevent marauding soldiers from entering to steal her possessions and vandalize her property, and on several occasions during particularly chaotic times, she stood guard with a loaded gun through the night. Like other Southerners, she buried the family's silver and other valuables, moved beloved pieces of furniture to the more secure homes of friends, and kept her jewelry in pouches sewn to the hoops of her skirts.

A year after clipping the editorial praising Nashville's women, however, French recorded a very different view of the city's females. She labeled the occupied capital a city "full of bad women" who lived in hotels and private homes pretending to be the wives of Union officers.

In addition, she said, the town harbored "female spies and detectives" who reportedly entrapped honest Southern men by appealing to their charitable nature and rewarding their generosity with arrest for supporting the Southern cause.[13]

In French's view the most inexcusable example of the flaunting of public morality occurred in 1864 during her stay at Beersheba. One April afternoon the resort was visited by a mounted party of thirty Union soldiers accompanied by five McMinnville women. The unchaperoned group stayed overnight and returned home by horseback the next day. "What in the name of common sense and common decency" could the mothers of the young women have thought? French wondered. She knew the women sensed the condemnation of their "improper" behavior, but no one dared criticize their conduct. French took further offense when the young ladies later paid a social call at Forest Home as if unaware of her disapproval. Fearing future retaliation, French again kept her silence.[14]

The breakdown of sexual mores paralleled a general fraying of community and familial ties. The tensions associated with life so near the major battlefields, the disruptions that accompanied massive troop movements and periodic skirmishes, the loss of material possessions, the inability to plan for the future, the overall decline in health, the separations from loved ones, and the deaths of friends and family combined to create a sense of hopelessness, exhaustion, and lethargy. Many found it difficult to carry out routine daily tasks, and petty annoyances and minor character flaws assumed greater importance under the stresses of war. Suspicion and jealousy increasingly controlled the actions of men and women of otherwise generous and caring natures.

French initially worried that the war would isolate her from newspapers, books, and correspondence with friends and family. In the early days of the war, she fretted over these inconveniences, but she soon found ways to route letters to both Northern and Southern friends—communicating by mail became much slower but was not impossible. Likewise, she obtained both Northern and Southern newspapers but despaired of reading the truth in either. She noted the early effects of the Federal blockade—"calicoes, domestics, linseys, etc. are at ruinous prices"—but cheerfully anticipated that her own family would "make out" until the blockade was lifted. French reported that life went on as usual and ended her entry with the assurance that "we are well and quite social and happy among ourselves."[15]

In time, however, her cheeriness gave way to the pressing concerns of life in a war zone. By the end of the conflict, she confessed to an "insurmountable weariness" and bitterness of the heart. Although she believed she had always "tried to do my duty," she said she had lost "until there is little now left to lose." She further confessed, "I do feel so much discouraged—so weary—so worn out with hoping and working, and all to no purpose." The events that brought French to such feelings of despair tore at every facet of Southern life.[16]

With the collapse of the Tennessee state government in February 1862, courts closed and county governments were suspended. Churches soon stopped holding regular services, and schools ended classes, leaving many children without access to education for extended periods. French, a former teacher, taught her children at home and kept up their religious education with Bible lessons and prayers. Yet even that proved impossible at times. In the fall of 1864, for example, French promised to "have the children commence with their lessons again," admitting "they have done no studying now for some time." Even when schools opened, as they did briefly during the Confederate occupation of McMinnville in 1863 and again after the war, parents worried about exposing the children to the presence of soldiers as they traveled to and from school.[17]

As the institutions of community life disintegrated, people became more cautious and watchful in their behavior and less confident of associations that had sustained them in the past. Soon after the war began, French observed that "there are informers among us who keep [the Federals] thoroughly posted." As a result, a "perfect reign of terror" had been imposed by the occupying army, and French feared that she might soon have to burn her journal to keep it from falling into the wrong hands and incriminating her. During such "feverish times," with the "community split to pieces," she concluded that "the best place for a quiet woman" was at home.[18]

The war also affected the health of men and women caught in the path of armies, for the stress of living near a battle zone and dealing with competing armies produced a weariness and a decline in overall well-being. In her diary, French recorded an endless succession of medical complaints as her health steadily worsened, and her chronic migraine headaches grew more intense until she found little relief even in repeated doses of laudanum and brandy. For days at a time, she was unable to leave her bed to write, teach her children, or supervise the household. Consultations with physicians produced the expected diagnosis—"nervous excitement" brought about by the war—but no prognosis for recovery.

The communicable diseases that accompanied the armies posed a more serious threat. Early in the war, French and her children received smallpox vaccinations as a deterrent to that dreaded disease, but in August 1863 she reported "a great deal of sickness in McM[innville]," where "scarlet fever" and "flu" had reached epidemic proportions. The presence of so much illness caused the town to "smell to Heaven" with a "nauseous scent" detectable for more than a mile outside the city limits. Not surprisingly the health of the family's slaves suffered to a greater degree, and two of the five slaves named in French's diary died during the course of the war.[19]

In addition to illness, French and her fellow Tennesseeans faced food shortages as armies foraged and confiscated meats and vegetables intended for home consumption. On more than one occasion, she wondered how her family would survive the winter: "Our place shows what it is to live near the track of an army," she wrote in 1862. "Fences, gates, etc. are no more, cornfields bare or trodden under foot—livestock, all or nearly all disappeared—gardens and flowers withered and gone." In addition to the pillaging and confiscations, lawless men of "neither or both armies" roamed the countryside, robbing and burning. Reports of house fires in nearby White and Van Buren Counties filled French with concern about the safety of her own home and family. But she stoically declared, "I should not be surprised at any time [to] have our house burned over our heads, and if it were to happen, I think I could bear it resolutely."[20]

The most shocking examples of lawlessness and the breakdown in social restraints occurred in Beersheba during the summer of 1863 as Union and Confederate armies moved toward Chattanooga, briefly leaving the area without any form of authority. The mountain gulphs around Beersheba and nearby Altamont provided sanctuary to bands of "lawless desperadoes"—men who used the cover of war to attack and rob their neighbors. The few males remaining in Beersheba slept with shotguns and revolvers close at hand, and the tiny community posted a guard to warn against attacks. The bands of outlaws had threatened John Armfield, the resort founder and owner of the hotel, and French reported periodic robberies on unoccupied outlying cottages. Generally the thieves helped themselves to blankets, bedding, china, and clothing but little of significant value. After expressing some concerns for her safety soon after her arrival, French declared that she slept through the nocturnal raids.

By mid-July, Bragg and the Army of Tennessee were in another "advance backward," and the mountains were full of deserters. To add to the concerns of the Beersheba residents, news of the fall of Vicksburg arrived on July 19, and soon afterward the men of the community, including Armfield and Colonel French, were called to McMinnville to take the oath of allegiance to the United States. French predicted that their community would be "abandoned to fate." Within a week, her prediction proved correct as Beersheba came under attack not by the renegades and desperadoes but by the poor mountaineers. The attackers focused on sacking the cottages and hotel, reminding French of the Reign of Terror and the mob of Paris. Although they never physically harmed the residents, "the masses had it all their own way on this memorable day—the aristocrats went down for nonce, and Democracy—Jacobinism—and Radicalism in the meanest form reigned triumphant!" The scene she described in detail bore a striking resemblance to other examples of class warfare.[21]

"Gaunt, ill-looking men and slatternly, rough barefooted women" hauled out furniture, matting, and carpets, French wrote of the scene, and "the women [were] as full of avaricious thirst as the ruffianly men." Successful plunderers sat on their piles of loot and glared defiance at all who approached their treasures; one old woman even "*crooned a hymn*" as she guarded her booty. A younger woman carried an armful of dresses from a cottage, dropped them at a fence corner, and tried them on with the help of an "overgrown boy." Another woman ran from the cottage of Episcopal bishop James Otey with her arms full of "very profound theological [books and] pamphlets of Church proceedings," declaring her intention to encourage her children to read.[22]

French's detailed description illustrates several characteristics of wartime Tennessee. For example, it reveals how areas under the control of neither army were at greater risk from the unlawful acts of deserters, renegades, and common thieves. The lack of institutional controls also exposed the class antagonisms that had long simmered between the wealthy "aristocrats" and the poorer subsistence farmers. French clearly interpreted the sacking of Beersheba in class terms and understood the ramifications of the event. She saw the act as a repudiation of the paternalistic endeavors of Armfield, a man who had worked to "build up" the mountain people. She also recognized the "demoralizing effect" the event had on slaves who witnessed the thefts and revelry, and she worried "what its effect would be upon an army; if allowed to revel in the license which has marked the proceedings this day."[23]

The armies never succumbed to the loss of discipline that French feared, but their activities were more costly in terms of the destruction of material possessions. Bettie Ridley Blackmore told French that Fair Mont, the Stone's River home of a family friend, had been burned, and she asserted that within a four-week period in early 1863, "17 [cotton] Gins and several dwelling houses had been burned by the Federals in a circle of seven miles." But though arson accounted for much of the destruction of the Tennessee countryside, confiscations also took a toll. By the end of the war, Colonel French had lost all his fine horses but one, a gray mare that remained at Beersheba. Most had been confiscated, but some younger ones had escaped, and they ran wild in the surrounding meadows and woods, useless to everyone. French reported that "all the horses and mules in the country have 'gone up'—scarcely a farmer that has one left." Such losses could not be easily recouped, and they compounded the difficulties of sustaining area families. In a period when human and animal muscle still provided the energy for most work, the loss of mules and horses, combined with the loss of shelter, left many Tennesseeans destitute.[24]

Arsonists spared Forest Home, but the house needed numerous repairs, and French quickly grew impatient with her husband "Col. Knockaround," who seemed more intent on daily excursions to town to learn the latest war news than providing for the comfort of his family. The colonel's lethargy brought an unusual outburst from French, reflecting the tensions that war placed on marriages. "I often wonder what men are made for!" she wrote. "To keep up the species I suppose—which is the only thing they are 'always ready' and never slow about doing! For my part I am quite wearied and worn out with their general no-accountability—and wish they were all put into the army, where they could kill each other off—the less of them the better!" Although she admitted that the accumulated bitterness of "years of hardship, privation, and sorrow" had provoked her outburst, she nevertheless continued to question her husband's willingness and ability to fulfill his role as protector and provider, believing him to have become a spinner of grand schemes rather than a doer of necessary work.[25]

Perhaps her doubts stemmed from her renewed correspondence with family members living in West Tennessee, for letters from her sister, Lide, depicted a life of travel and pleasure now lost to French. Lide confided, with no apparent recognition of her sister's circumstances, that she and her husband had survived the war with their wealth intact. French attributed this good fortune to the Memphis couple's cotton speculation. She knew her brother-in-law, Henry French, was guilty of that illegal practice—and had even been arrested for it by the Confederates. Arrest did not end his speculative ventures, though, and he, too, ended the war with few losses. Beyond that, everyone at Beersheba had heard the story of Adelicia Acklen and her cotton deals. The determined widow of slave trader Isaac Franklin and subsequently the wife of Joseph Acklen, Adelicia had moved her cotton, with the help of both Confederate and Union soldiers, to New Orleans, where it had run the blockade; at the end of the war, Acklen was one of the wealthiest women in the South. Such examples of "success" moved French to "very bitter thoughts." She herself had been dutiful, but those who had been "mean and inconsistent, nay even wrong [were] successful in life."

By war's end, Lucy French was weary, hopeless, and desperate. Her despondency might have led her to reject Southern nationalism, but she, like many other Tennesseans, ultimately blamed the North for her difficulties. Certainly material losses and bitter experience with Union soldiers encouraged a continuing adherence to everything Southern. But French's diary offers a more compelling explanation for Southern nationalism and the Lost Cause ethic that succeeded it: a powerful sense of obligation to the soldiers who had fought and gained nothing and a belief that their sacrifice could only be validated through remembrance and public honor.[26]

French's diary contains several descriptions of the experiences of ordinary soldiers in the Army of Tennessee. Her most poignant entry centered on the Battle of Stone's River, perhaps the event that truly shaped her Southern nationalism. At daylight on December 31, 1862, French wrote, she first heard the sound of "very heavy cannonading" from the direction of Murfreesboro. Dozens of local men hurried to the site of the battle, some forty miles to the northwest, and "everything in the shape of a soldier went" as well. A "continuous roar of artillery" filled the morning hours, leaving French nervous and edgy, concerned for the outcome of the battle and the possibility that she and her family would need to flee to safe sanctuary farther south. In the afternoon the sounds of battle tapered off, and that night, word arrived of a Southern victory. French received the news gratefully but with an awareness that even as she celebrated, men were suffering and dying. She vowed to join other "noble Southern women" and "do everything in my power" for the wounded, some of whom would surely be brought to McMinnville. Having made her promise, French turned her attention to mundane household matters (specifically, the purchase of new furniture) before finally offering a brief reflection on the deaths of several acquaintances in earlier skirmishes and battles. On that New Year's Eve in 1862, French's worries seemed superficial and without personal connection to the conflict beyond a concern for her personal safety.[27]

On the following evening, she learned of the death of Capt. D. C. "Cap" Spurlock, a family friend. Hurrying to the home of his parents to offer condolences on the death of a second son (the first died at Perryville), French was filled with grief as she viewed the bloodied body of her friend. In the heat of the battle on the north side of the railroad near the Cowan house, Spurlock had been leading a charge when a bullet entered "just below his left nostril and passed through his head stopping just below the skin." The battle continued over his body throughout the afternoon, with his men returning under cover of darkness to retrieve the corpse. Earlier in the day, Spurlock had visited with his mother and father, who made the trip to Murfreesboro to bring him Christmas gifts. The distraught parents brought their son's body home in the very wagon that hours before had conveyed the Yuletide joy.[28]

French described a painful scene—the frantic mother, the "still silent agony of the aged father," and a young friend, Sophia Searcy, who "stood for hours beside the coffin, weeping." She wondered if Searcy remembered her earlier defiant words, when she had proclaimed, "Let the war come—we are ready." But then French questioned, "Were any of us ready to part with 'Cap'?"[29]

The distant sound of renewed cannonading accompanied the minister's prayers and the "voices tremulous with tears raised [in] hymns around the soldier's coffin. All the way to the graveyard—and while we laid him down to his last rest—and as we returned—it came rolling up from the northwest—a fitting requiem for the gallant dead." The earlier victory had turned to defeat, and French began to understand the true cost of war. For her, the retreat of the Army of Tennessee from its position on Stone's River called into question the value of Cap's sacrifice and demanded some form of validation.[30]

As the war ended and soldiers returned to their families, French reflected on the future of the South and the men who had fought the war. By 1865 their army was a poorly led body of hungry, ragged men, but, she believed, "their constancy deserved a better fate." As she thought about those who died and "slept among strangers in unknown graves on dreary battlefields," she asked, "For what? Did God permit this war? Shall we ever find out why it was allowed?" Such questions emerged in private throughout the defeated South, but public discussions of the war reflected a different view, one that French expressed when she asserted, "We are just as proud of [the returning soldiers] as if they had been successful—for they deserved it!"[31]

After1865, pride in the war records of friends and family became the validation for the sacrifices so many made, and sanctification of the Confederate experience was the mortar used to rebuild the white community into a semblance of harmony—with the aristocracy once more in control and the lower classes bound to them in a brotherhood of sacrifice and loss. Unfortunately for the future of the South, it was not a community built on joyful expectation but one that emerged, in French's words, "out of the bitterness of [the] heart."[32]

Notes

1. Robert H. White, ed., *Messages of the Governors of Tennessee, 1857–1869*, 12 vols. (Nashville: Tennessee Historical Commission, 1959), 5:355.

2. Diary of L. Virginia French, December 31, 1860, Tennessee State Library and Archives, Nashville, Tennessee.

3. Ibid., June 12, 1862.

4. Ibid., July 12, 1862.

5. Ibid., June 12, 1862, and January 19, 1863.

6. Ibid., August 20, 1862, and May 14, 1865.

7. Ibid., February 22, 1862, and January 11, 1863.

8. Ibid., February 8, 1863.

9. Ibid., March 10, March 22, and February 8, 1863; *Chattanooga Rebel*, January 31, 1863.

10. Diary of L. Virginia French, April 16 and September 20, 1863.

11. Ibid., September 14, 1862.

12. Ibid., April 2, 1862.

13. Ibid., January 13, 1863.

14. Ibid., April 17, 1863.

15. Ibid., January 5, 1862.

16. Ibid., August 20, 1865.

17. Ibid., September 25, 1864.

18. Ibid., June 29, 1862.

19. Ibid., August 16, 1863.

20. Ibid., September 3, 1862, and July 7, 1864.

21. Ibid., July 12, July 19, and July 26, 1863.

22. Ibid., July 26, 1863.

23. Ibid.

24. Sarah Ridley Trimble, ed., "Behind the Lines in Middle Tennessee, 1863–1865: The Journal of Bettie Ridley Blackmore," *Tennessee Historical Quarterly* 12 (1953): 49; Diary of L. Virginia French, November 6, 1864.

25. Diary of L. Virginia French, September 25, 1864.

26. Ibid., June 1, 1865.

27. Ibid., January 1, 1863.
28. Ibid., January 4, 1863.
29. Ibid.
30. Ibid.
31. Ibid., May 10 and May 14, 1865.
32. Ibid., August 20, 1865.

Suggested Readings

Lucy Virginia French has no biography, but on the general topic of women in the Confederacy, see Catherine Clinton and Nina Silber, eds., *Divided Houses: Gender and the Civil War* (New York: Oxford University Press, 1992); and George C. Rable, *Civil Wars: Women and the Crisis of Southern Nationalism* (Urbana: University of Illinois Press, 1989).

12

Robert Smalls
"I Stand Here the Equal of Any Man"

Richard Zuczek

Black slaves meant money and labor for the white South. The "peculiar institution" also represented a system of control by one racial group over another. Few whites in the South could envision a world without slavery coming to pass in their lifetime. However, the Civil War soon threatened that outlook and eventually caused the end of the slave system.

As historian Steven Woodworth noted, "The slaves themselves were not always mere passive observers of the events around them; some took an active part in helping to gain their freedom and that of their race. . . . Many more slaves took the opportunity offered by a passing blue-coated column to get away from their plantations, 'stealing themselves,' as the saying went, and reducing the domain of slavery that much more with each departure. For more than one hundred thousand black men, taking an active part in gaining their freedom meant enlisting in the Union army, in which many of them saw action before the war was over."

One of those who fled slavery and helped the Union war effort was Robert Smalls. Once the conflict ended, he became a strong and active leader in his native state, eventually serving in Congress. His accomplishments show how talent, once unfettered from the restrictive bonds of slavery, could burst out under freedom. Smalls's later life also demonstrates how blacks found new limits being imposed on them as the years passed. Other fights still remained to be fought.

Richard Zuczek, author of *State of Rebellion: Reconstruction in South Carolina* (1997), is an associate professor in the Department of Humanities at the U.S. Coast Guard Academy in New London, Connecticut.

The Civil War settled many of the political, economic, and constitutional issues that had plagued Americans, but it also created others. Controversies about slavery were replaced by questions concerning the status of 3.5 million freedpeople. The black experience during the Civil War and Reconstruction defies generalizations. Although most

This essay originally appeared in Steven E. Woodworth, ed., *The Human Tradition in the Civil War and Reconstruction* (Wilmington, DE: Scholarly Resources, 2000), 199–211.

blacks, North and South, became Republicans, rarely was their allegiance to party blind. Even the term "black" itself is inadequate in this context, for there were freeborn blacks, former slaves, northern-born blacks who went South after the war, and both mulattoes and pure-bloods. But despite their countless differences, one goal unified them all: the desire for *equality* and the same rights and opportunities enjoyed by white Americans. This is the story of a man who won his own freedom and went on to fight for his people, demonstrating for an entire nation the potential and capacity of all black Americans.

Robert Smalls was born into slavery in 1839 in Beaufort, South Carolina.[1] He was not a full-blood African but a mulatto; his mother was Lydia, a slave, and his father—or so it is believed—was John McKee, her white owner and a Beaufort planter. This mix was more common than many whites wanted to admit. Robert served as a house slave and personal valet for McKee's son Henry, but his mother wanted him to understand fully the harshness of slavery. So when Robert was not tending horses or accompanying the McKees hunting, Lydia would take him to the jail to watch slaves being whipped or send him to the fields to help other slaves toil.[2]

In 1851, after the death of John McKee, Henry sold the Beaufort property and moved to a plantation outside Charleston, where he began hiring Robert out. For some time, Smalls worked as a waiter and then a lamplighter, with his earnings going to Henry McKee, his new owner. Before long, Henry found Smalls work around the Charleston waterfront. He unloaded ships before landing a position repairing sails and fixing rigging.[3]

By about 1857, Smalls's future—perhaps his destiny—began to take shape. First, his harbor work expanded to include sailing, and soon he was operating boats with notable skill. Also, he convinced McKee to allow him to hire himself out, and pay McKee a flat fifteen dollars per month. Smalls kept any money in excess of that. He needed the extra cash, for he had just married Hannah Jones and had offered to pay her owner seven dollars a month for her freedom. Their relationship became more complicated in 1858 with the birth of their daughter, Elizabeth Lydia. Hannah's (and therefore also the daughter's) owner, Samuel Kinginan, agreed to release both mother and child from slavery for a flat fee of eight hundred dollars. Despite overwhelming odds, Smalls's opportunism and intelligence marked him as a man destined for success: by 1861, he had accumulated seven hundred dollars for the "purchase" of his wife and daughter.[4]

After the Civil War broke out in 1861, Robert's sailing abilities did not escape notice in the Confederacy, and he found service as pilot of the *Planter*, transporting supplies and munitions between Charleston's harbor forts. On May 12, 1862, Smalls's courage and cunning were put to the test. Along with eight other black crewmen, he had decided to escape from slavery and the Confederacy by sailing the *Planter* out of Charleston harbor and up to the blockading U.S. fleet. The plan was crafted carefully: Smalls chose a night when the white officers were ashore, learned the whistle signals needed to pass the forts, and prepared a white sheet for surrendering to Federal vessels. Nonetheless, the risk was great because capture meant death; the men had decided to blow up the ship if they were stopped "since they knew they would have no mercy."[5] There was also no guarantee the Federal ships would not open fire as Robert and his crew approached. But the operation proceeded flawlessly, and the *Planter* slipped out of the harbor, picked up Smalls's wife, daughter, and several other women and children, and sailed past Fort Johnson. With the Confederate and state colors flying, the proper signal given, and Smalls walking the deck in the captain's clothes (taken from the officer's stateroom), the ship glided out of Confederate waters.[6] By the morning of May 13 the *Planter* proceeded past Fort Sumter, heading toward the Federal fleet. A crewman replaced the flags with a white sheet of surrender, and the USS *Onward* took possession of the *Planter*'s crew and cargo.[7]

The U.S. Navy and government were nearly as jubilant as the refugees, for they gained a ship, several cannon, and a man with an intimate knowledge of the Charleston harbor defenses and waters—Robert Smalls. In return, Smalls not only gained freedom for himself and his family— and a fifteen-hundred-dollar bounty for the ship—he also became a national hero. Missionary groups and even the U.S. Army were soon using Smalls as a spokesman for the famous Sea Island experiment on South Carolina's coast. In Philadelphia in 1864, when the hero was evicted from a city streetcar, an uproar resulted that led to the integration of the city's public transportation system. Smalls was even made a delegate to the National Union Convention in 1864, but he could not attend.

Most of his first three years after the escape to freedom were spent around the South Carolina coast, piloting vessels (including, at times, the *Planter*) and operating ships in attacks on Confederate forts. Several naval officers commented on his courage under fire, and it appears that by December 1863 he had been promoted to captain (although bureaucratic errors complicated his attempt to get a pension after the war). If that history is correct, then Smalls was the highest-ranking South Carolina black in the Civil War.[8]

At war's end, however, it did not seem likely that other southern blacks were to share in Smalls's triumphs. After the Confederacy collapsed in the spring of 1865, Andrew Johnson, who became president following the death of Lincoln, began his policy of presidential reconstruction. Slavery was abolished under the new Thirteenth Amendment, but Johnson placed former Confederates in power in southern states, and they established "black codes" that severely restricted freedpeoples' rights. Blacks could not sue in court, for example, or hold any job besides farming without a license. They also could not own firearms, vote, or hold office. Consequently, Smalls was again caught between worlds, just as he had been before and during the war.

When many blacks were forced to work under former masters, Smalls was insulated by being an employee of the Federal military. He held special status and lived fairly well, continuing to operate his transport into 1866 and accumulating a fair amount of savings in the process. He apparently spent some of his money on private tutors; barely literate (he may have learned some reading skills in the North and in the military), he was intent on improving his education. With the decommissioning of the *Planter* in late 1866, Smalls returned to Beaufort, where he opened a store (using the bounty money awarded earlier) and moved into a house he had bought at a government auction—the very house he was born in, which had belonged to John McKee. It was fitting that Smalls should possess his master's home, and his fame, connections, and experience would lead him into other formerly white areas as well.[9]

What those areas might be became evident soon enough. The obstinacy of the southern states—which had passed black codes, rejected the Fourteenth Amendment, and ignored violence against the freedpeople—drove Congress to embark on a new reconstruction program. Determined to protect blacks in the South and expand the Republican Party there, Radical Republicans in Congress passed the Military Reconstruction Acts in 1867. In South Carolina and nine other former Confederate states (Tennessee had already been readmitted to the Union), the U.S. Army supervised the voting registration of black men and the holding of state conventions that would create new state constitutions. Then another election would select a new governor and a new legislature to replace the governments President Johnson had established.

Through the summer and fall of 1867, South Carolina's black population prepared for the November election of delegates to the state convention. One candidate from Beaufort was Robert Smalls, who established his own Beaufort Republican Club. The November vote resulted in a Republican landslide, since Democrats—mostly native whites—boycotted the election. Blacks held 76 of the 124 seats, and Smalls was one of 5 blacks in the 7-man Beaufort contingent. So began a political career that would last, including appointments, until 1913.

Smalls did not stand out at the state constitutional convention of 1868, although a witness called him one of the "more distinguished" delegates.[10] He was a member of the Committee on Finance—quite an honor for a former slave—but his chief interest was education, and he supported a sweeping provision that included compulsory school attendance. Once the constitution was completed, he returned to Beaufort to stand for election again, this time for state representative in the new South Carolina government.

With the new black Republicans outnumbering white Democrats, the election of 1868 resulted in a predominantly Republican general assembly, which (unlike that of any other southern state) had a majority of blacks in the lower house. Among these was Robert Smalls, who had already begun to consolidate his power in Beaufort County. His election was no surprise: Despite his slave background, he was rapidly becoming a man of means through his postwar business and continued purchases of federally confiscated properties. Most important, he was a slave turned hero in an overwhelmingly black district, and, as one observer put it, "The voters of Beaufort had less confidence in white people than in Negroes."[11] He spent the next seven years in the South Carolina General Assembly, first as Beaufort representative (1868–1870) and then as state senator (1870–1875). Smalls so dominated local politics that one newspaper called him "the King of Beaufort County."[12]

In the legislature, Smalls divided his attention along several lines: direct help for his local constituency, general support and protection for his race's newfound rights, and self-preservation, both in terms of election success and financial status. His experience illustrated the difficulties of Reconstruction, including the problems facing the freedmen, the challenges facing the new government, and the temptations facing the new politicians.

Eager to help his constituents get back on their feet, Smalls tried to improve the economic condition of the Beaufort area. As a representative, he demanded the U.S. government release confiscated property in his district, property that could be put to good use. Knowing access to transportation would benefit the local economy, he supported the state-assisted building of a railroad connection from the Port Royal–Beaufort area to the Charleston and Savannah Railroad line. Other measures he pressed for included a special levy to rebuild the county courthouse and jail and a bill granting a monopoly to two companies that mined phosphates from the state's rivers. (These companies employed hundreds of blacks and provided supplemental income for farmers in the low country.) Understanding political rights as well as economic needs, the fledgling politician advocated the use of Federal soldiers to protect black voters, for during the election of 1868 the Ku Klux Klan had terrorized, attacked, and murdered white and black Republicans.[13]

White violence was only one problem the Republican Party faced. Another dilemma came from within and dominated the headlines after Smalls moved to the state senate in 1870. Republican Reconstruction governments became legendary for their scandals, and South Carolina's was the worst. The inexperience of the politicians, the greed of some adventurers, and the demands and challenges of the period came together to foster an environment ripe for corruption. Facing a ruined economy, the legislature plunged into dubious schemes involving mining, railroad development, bond sales, and land investments in an effort to raise cash and bring in external investment. Most of these ventures failed due to economic conditions, poor strategy, or internal fraud.[14]

Despite the pervasive nature of government malfeasance—legislators, cabinet members, and even the governors were involved—Robert Smalls stood apart. In fact, his drive for fiscal responsibility alienated some fellow Republicans even as it impressed white Democrats. He supported cutting judges' and attorneys' salaries, opposed per diem accounts for legislative travel, disbanded investigative committees that had ceased functioning, suggested reduced pay for short "special sessions" of the legislature, and called for investigations of the phosphate companies when their payments were in arrears. Playing on his wartime exploits, Smalls told an audience in 1871 that he intended to "guide the ship of state . . . past the rocks, torpedoes and hostile guns of ignorance, immorality and dishonesty."[15]

Typically, Smalls based his stance on practical reasons as well as moral ones. Corruption divided the party and damaged its reputation in the North. Further, although a loyal party member and true to his race, Smalls understood the need to cultivate connections to Carolina's whites, even Democratic ones. One example of this was his assistance to his former owner's family. Legend has it that he opened his home to his former master's widow and allowed her the use of his horses and carriage.[16] One English traveler found Smalls "not unpopular among the white people. He behaved well toward his former master's family and assisted them." This traveler, Sir George Campbell, also commented on the state of racial affairs in Smalls's district, where "black rule has been most complete and lasted longest." Whites complained of this "black paradise," but Campbell was surprised to find "exactly the contrary. At no place that I have seen are the relations of the two races better and more peaceable . . . white girls go about as freely and pleasantly as if no black had ever been in power."[17]

Robert Smalls could not, however, escape the taint of Republican dishonesty. One Democratic complaint revolved around his position in the "black militia." By the early 1870s, Smalls was a general in the state militia, which was largely black because whites refused to serve with blacks. As a general, Smalls received an extra paycheck and further patronage power, and he could appoint men to certain positions under him. Whites bridled at this whole system, but the only official charge of misconduct came by way of his role on the state senate's Committee on Printing, to which he was appointed after his reelection in 1872; even so, evidence indicates that the charges were unfounded and politically motivated. As for Small's followers in Beaufort, Sir George Campbell observed that Robert "seems to have their unlimited confidence."[18]

This confidence carried him from the state legislature to the national one, and in 1874 he was elected to the U.S. House of Representatives for the first of five terms. In December 1875 he arrived in Washington accompanied by his daughter, Elizabeth Lydia, who served as his private secretary. Even though he faced a Democratic House— the first in eighteen years—the freshman dived head first into his new role. As always, the needs of his constituents were not far from his mind. The Port Royal naval station received added appropriations for improvements, he sponsored a bill for the relief of his former master's family, and he fought, albeit unsuccessfully, for racially integrated army units.[19]

The central issue of his first term, however, was the ending of Reconstruction. The program was in its twilight when he went to Washington, for northern interest had declined and southern Democratic violence had intensified. State after state in the old Confederacy returned to Democratic control, and the legal and political rights blacks had struggled for were swept away. Nowhere was this more evident than in

South Carolina, the last southern state held by the Republican Party. The 1876 campaign between the Republican incumbent, Daniel H. Chamberlain, and the Democratic challenger, former Confederate general Wade Hampton, was marred by rampant violence and fraud. Democratic "gun clubs" terrorized black and white Republicans in an effort to overcome a black majority. One incident that attracted national attention was the murder of a number of black militiamen in the town of Hamburg in early July. Using the assault as evidence, Smalls made an impassioned plea in Congress for the retention of Federal troops in his state. Samuel Cox, a Democrat from New York, challenged the reliability of Smalls's sources and even asked who vouched for Smalls. "A majority of 13,000," Robert replied, to the cheers of fellow Republicans. He even defended South Carolina Republicans; when Cox complained of their corruption, Smalls turned the tables and remarked upon the infamous abuses of New York's Boss Tweed ring. Seasoned politicians found an able rival in this former slave, described by one contemporary as "excellent in repartee."[20]

His wit could not help his state through the election, though, so Smalls ventured back and took an active role in campaigning. Although up for reelection himself, he spent most of his time speaking on behalf of incumbent Daniel Chamberlain. In 1876, Smalls took his life in his hands on the stump, and at least two rallies in Edgefield County had the governor and congressmen fleeing for their lives.[21] Smalls described how Democrats planned to win the election by "the killing of colored men; making threats of personal violence . . . riding armed through the country, by day and night; by firing into the houses of Republicans; by breaking up Republican mass-meetings."[22]

The election of 1876 ended Reconstruction in South Carolina and in the nation. Violence and fraud brought Democrats back to power and so complicated the 1876 presidential election that many historians maintain a deal occurred, the so-called compromise of 1877. According to the terms of the alleged compromise, Republicans traded the South for the presidency: Republican Rutherford B. Hayes was chosen president by special commission and agreed to cease interfering in southern affairs. In other words, Federal soldiers and marshals would no longer supervise elections or protect voters in the South.[23] Economic power, especially land ownership, had long been in white hands, and now political power would reside there as well. In an address to Congress, Smalls criticized whites for "securing by fraud and murder what could not be obtained by honorable means" and thereby forcing blacks "into a condition of political dependence upon the former slaveholders." Understanding how the legacy of terror would reflect on the South, he predicted that "the blood of innocent freedmen, shed by Southern Democrats would in the future prove one of the dark spots upon the fair name of the American Republic."[24]

An immediate result of the Democratic victory in South Carolina was an attack on one of Reconstruction's remaining symbols—Robert Smalls. Even though Democrats seized the legislature and the governorship, Smalls continued to dominate coastal politics and had won reelection to Congress. With his constituency still loyal, Democrats needed another way to remove him from political affairs. When the new government began investigating prominent Republican politicians, hoping to discredit the party and convict its members of corruption committed earlier, one of the chief targets was Smalls, whom Democrats charged with accepting a bribe for awarding a printing contract in 1872 while on the state's printing committee. The Democrats' goal was simple: to threaten Smalls with trial in a Democratic-controlled court to convince him to resign his seat and avoid conviction. Robert remembered a conversation he had held with the chair of the investigating committee, who told him that "these men have the court, they have got the jury, and an indictment is a conviction."[25] One newspaper editor even offered that "if you will vacate your office we will pay you $10,000 for your two years' salary." Smalls replied that if Democrats could "get the people who elected me to pass resolutions requiring me to resign, then you can have the office without a penny." Otherwise, he declared, "I would suffer myself to go to the Penitentiary and rot before I would resign an office I was elected to."[26] Knowing his people needed a voice in Congress, Robert, displaying his usual fortitude, refused to buckle under pressure.

As predicted, the trials, held in late 1877, resulted in convictions for several leading state Republicans, including Smalls. Evidence in his case was flimsy, and his sole accuser had been convicted of stealing hundreds of thousands of dollars before fleeing the state; he returned and was pardoned in exchange for turning state's witness. Even the state attorney general and lieutenant governor admitted that the charges could not stand up to legal scrutiny.[27] But Congress refused to let the state ruling interfere with the "privilege of a sitting member of Congress," and so Smalls retained his seat. He went about his business for the rest of his term, and the petitions he presented included one for upkeep of the Port Royal naval base and another in favor of women's suffrage.[28]

When Smalls ran again in 1878, the Democrats focused on destroying him directly; according to Laura Towne, a teacher on the Sea Islands, Governor Hampton said "there was but one man he thought ought to be out of the way, and that was Robert Smalls."[29] Robert's speaking engagements drew hundreds of armed whites, who harassed him and the listeners. He was shot at, chased, and even hunted like an animal. Towne said that if Smalls was elected, "I do not think his life would be worth a button."[30] In the end, he was not elected, and he attributed his defeat, according to Sir George Campbell, "entirely to fraud and intimidation."[31] Evidently, Republican voters did also, for Laura Towne noted that "the people are greatly grieved about it, and are not reconciled to the result."[32]

With Smalls out of office, Carolina Democrats had the opportunity to wiggle out of another jam. In a new deal with the Federal government, state authorities freed themselves from more residue of Reconstruction. State Democrats agreed to drop charges against Republicans, and, in exchange, the Justice Department would not prosecute Democrats accused of voting violations in the 1876 election. In 1879 the new governor, William D. Simpson, pardoned Robert Smalls and several other Republicans, but none of those suspected of atrocities in the 1876 campaign was ever brought to trial.[33]

Robert Smalls prepared to return to Congress. His decision demonstrated courage and conviction, for Reconstruction had ended and the struggle for black rights was unpopular, even within his own party. With southern whites manipulating elections, each year saw fewer and fewer blacks in the state and federal governments. In addition, the nation's attention had moved on from the divisive subjects of black rights and Civil War. With each session, Smalls became more anachronistic, a leftover from an earlier struggle. As the nation looked to industrialization, economic expansion, and a final confrontation with Native Americans in the West, Smalls watched helplessly as disfranchisement, racial violence, and segregation reduced blacks to a situation little better than slavery.

Undaunted, he ran and was reelected to Congress in 1880 and again in 1884. His actions were meager but sincere as he stood fast for the people and issues that had always driven him. He opposed a bill allowing railroad companies to provide "separate" accommodations for blacks and whites, and he presented an amendment to another bill, calling for equal access to "eating-houses" and similar establishments in the District of Columbia. He sponsored a number of relief bills for constituents, requested funds for naval facilities in his district, and won a pay raise for black servants at the United States Naval Academy. He introduced a pension bill for Maria Hunter, widow of David Hunter, an "abolitionist" general who, without authority, emancipated slaves and enlisted black soldiers. Smalls called Hunter one of "freedom's pioneers," a man whose actions were "so far advanced" that Lincoln invalidated them. Blacks would not forget "the Moses who led us out of the land of bondage," he said. Allowing his frustration with racial relations to get the better of him, Smalls warned the president, Democrat Grover Cleveland, that a veto of the pension would expose "the hypocrisy of the assurances for the colored man by striking a blow at the nation's brave defenders and the colored man's best friend." Maria Hunter received her pension.[34]

Like the race he represented, Smalls's time on the national stage was at an end. In 1886 he lost his last campaign for Congress in a close race with former Confederate colonel William Elliott.[35] Before Smalls left Washington, he laid the groundwork for his new career as a collector of customs at the port of Beaufort. Robert's national fame, state service, and many Civil War connections prompted Republican president Benjamin Harrison to nominate him to that post, and the Senate confirmed him in 1890. Such positions were patronage assignments handed out to party men as rewards; Smalls held the post, with one four-year exception, until 1913.

His last great public appearance in defense of his race came in 1895 during the state's constitutional convention. White Carolinians, led by Governor Benjamin "Pitchfork Ben" Tillman, decided to revamp the state's constitution to disfranchise blacks legally. The Fifteenth Amendment, ratified in 1870, prohibited voting discrimination based on race, so whites planned to make land ownership, poll taxes, literacy, and a knowledge of the U.S. Constitution requirements for suffrage. Since blacks trailed far behind whites in educational level and economic circumstances, these qualifications would effectively eliminate much of the black vote.

Outnumbered at the convention 154 to 6, Smalls and his black colleagues knew opposition was futile. Yet in his last public role as defender of American constitutional guarantees, Smalls was at his best. One observer called his arguments "masterpieces of impregnable logic, consecutive reasoning, biting sarcasm. . . . His arguments were simply unanswerable, and the keenness of his wit [showed whites] that the negro's capacity for intelligence, courage, and manhood was not inferior to the bluest blood in the old Palmetto State."[36] When Benjamin Tillman dared him to explain why blacks deserved to vote, Smalls countered, "My race needs no special defense, for the past history of them in this country proves them to be the equal of any people anywhere. All they need is an equal chance in the battle of life." When Tillman turned his attack on Smalls, Robert replied, "I stand here the equal of any man. I started out in the war with the Confederates; they threatened to punish me and I left them. I went to the Union army. I fought in seventeen battles to make glorious and perpetuate the flag that some of you trampled under your feet [and] no act of yours can in any way blur the record that I have made at home and abroad."[37]

Smalls's principles and logic were no match for the force of numbers and the power of racism. The new state constitution, with its stringent qualifications for voting, became law in December 1895. When Robert refused to sign the finished product, the assembly presented a resolution denying travel reimbursement to him; in response, a witness reported, "Smalls said he would rather walk home than sign the instrument."[38] Nonetheless, most South Carolina blacks ceased to play a role in state politics. When legal segregation—the Jim Crow laws—appeared in the state in 1898, the two races became more separate than ever before.

In his final years, Smalls was frustrated and depressed, for he was helpless to change the racist political, social, and economic structure that was now in place in South Carolina. He continued as a customs collector until 1913, when he was removed by the Democratic Wilson administration. By then his health had deteriorated, his political career had ended, and he was a widower twice over; his first wife, Hannah, died in 1883, and his second, Annie Elizabeth Wigg, passed away in 1895.[39] Once out of office, his drive seemed to dissipate, and his rheumatism, diabetes, and lingering ailments from wartime malaria became intolerable. He died in Beaufort on February 23, 1915.

Two years earlier, writing to black leader Booker T. Washington, Smalls expressed the hope that "I have succeeded to so manage affairs that when I leave . . . I will do so with credit to myself, my family, and my Race."[40] Although he was discussing the collectorship, his statement was an eloquent comment on his life. He was, indeed, the equal of any man—and perhaps a great deal more.

Notes

1. Before the war, he was apparently called "Robert Small," but during the war, "Smalls" became the accepted usage. Edward A. Miller Jr., *Gullah Statesman: Robert Smalls from Slavery to Congress, 1839–1915* (Columbia: University of South Carolina Press, 1995), 7.

2. Okon Edet Uya, *From Slavery to Public Service: Robert Smalls, 1839–1915* (New York: Oxford University Press, 1971), 3–4.

3. Ibid., 5–6.

4. Miller, *Gullah Statesman*, 8–9; Uya, *From Slavery to Public Service*, 7.

5. Elizabeth Ware Pearson, ed., *Letters from Port Royal, 1862–1868* (New York: Arno Press and the New York Times, 1969), 47.

6. Joel Williamson, *After Slavery: The Negro in South Carolina during Reconstruction, 1861–1877* (Chapel Hill: University of North Carolina Press, 1965), 7.

7. Miller, *Gullah Statesman*, 1–3.

8. Ibid., 18–24; Uya, *From Slavery to Public Service*, 20–23, 26–27.

9. Uya, *From Slavery to Public Service*, 36–37.

10. Miller, *Gullah Statesman*, 49.

11. Ibid., 66.

12. Uya, *From Slavery to Public Service*, 60.

13. Miller, *Gullah Statesman*, 54–55, 58; Uya, *From Slavery to Public Service*, 64–65, 70, 72–73.

14. The most comprehensive treatment of the Republican scandals is found in the Democrats' investigations, which, although heavy on political verbiage, contain a great deal of useful testimony. See General Assembly of the State of South Carolina, *Report of the Joint Investigating Committee on Public Frauds and Election of the Hon. J. J. Patterson to the United States Senate Made to the General Assembly of the State of South Carolina, at the Regular Session of 1877–1878* (Columbia, SC: Calvo and Patton, 1878).

15. Uya, *From Slavery to Public Service*, 70–76; *Beaufort County Republican*, January 4, 1872, quoted in Miller, *Gullah Statesman*, 64.

16. George Tindall Brown, *South Carolina Negroes, 1877–1900* (Columbia: University of South Carolina Press, 1952), 56; Miller, *Gullah Statesman*, 127; Uya, *From Slavery to Public Service*, 59.

17. Sir George Campbell, MP, *White and Black: The Outcome of a Visit to the United States, or "A Bird's-Eye View of the United States," Being the Substance of a Series of Addresses Delivered in Scotland in February, 1879* (New York: R. Worthington, 1879), 176–77, 332.

18. Ibid., 345.

19. *Congressional Record*, 44th Cong., 1st sess., 442, 1484, 3272–75, 3457–68, 3757, 4161.

20. *Congressional Record*, 44th Cong., 1st sess., 4641–43; Miller, *Gullah Statesman*, 102.

21. Miller, *Gullah Statesman*, 103; Uya, *From Slavery to Public Service*, 100–102.

22. *Congressional Record*, 44th Cong., 2d sess., appendix, 125.

23. For accounts of this "compromise," see C. Vann Woodward, *Reunion and Reaction: The Compromise of 1877 and the End of Reconstruction* (Boston: Little, Brown,

1951); Allan Peskin, "Was There a Compromise of 1877?" *Journal of American History* 60 (1973): 63–75; and Vincent P. DeSantis, "Rutherford B. Hayes and the Removal of the Troops and the End of Reconstruction," in *Region, Race, and Reconstruction: Essays in Honor of C. Vann Woodward,* ed. J. Morgan Kousser and James M. McPherson (New York: Oxford University Press, 1982), 417–50.

24. *Congressional Record,* 44th Cong., 2d sess., appendix, 123.

25. Miller, *Gullah Statesman,* 115; Uya, *From Slavery to Public Service,* 85.

26. Miller, *Gullah Statesman,* 115–19; Uya, *From Slavery to Public Service,* 85.

27. Uya, *From Slavery to Public Service,* 83; Williamson, *After Slavery,* 414–15.

28. *Congressional Record,* 45th Cong., 2d sess., 323, 372, 1805, 2706, 4034.

29. Rupert Sargent Holland, ed., *Letters and Diary of Laura M. Towne, Written from the Sea Islands of South Carolina, 1862–1884* (Cambridge, MA: The Riverside Press, 1912; reprint ed., New York: Negro Universities Press, 1969), 289–91.

30. Holland, *Letters and Diary,* 291.

31. Campbell, *White and Black,* 341.

32. Holland, *Letters and Diary,* 292–93.

33. Miller, *Gullah Statesman,* 130.

34. Ibid., 155–56; *Congressional Record,* 48th Cong., 2d sess., 316, 2057; *Congressional Record,* 49th Cong., 1st sess., appendix, 319–20.

35. Miller, *Gullah Statesman,* 158–70.

36. Uya, *From Slavery to Public Service,* 148.

37. *Journal of the Constitutional Convention of South Carolina Begun to Be Holden at Columbia, S.C., on Tuesday, the Tenth Day of September Anno Domini Eighteen Hundred and Ninety-Five* (Columbia, SC: Charles A. Calvo Jr., 1895), 474–76.

38. Miller, *Gullah Statesman,* 214.

39. Ibid., 191–213.

40. Robert Smalls to Booker T. Washington, April 22, 1913, Washington Papers, Library of Congress, Washington, DC, quoted in Miller, *Gullah Statesman,* 244.

Suggested Readings

For more on Robert Smalls's home state in this period, see Joel Williamson, *After Slavery: The Negro in South Carolina during Reconstruction, 1861–1877* (Chapel Hill: University of North Carolina Press, 1965); and George Tindall Brown, *South Carolina Negroes, 1877–1900* (Columbia: University of South Carolina Press, 1952). Consult also two biographies: Edward A. Miller Jr., *Gullah Statesman: Robert Smalls from Slavery to Congress, 1839–1915* (Columbia: University of South Carolina Press, 1995); and Okon Edet Uya, *From Slavery to Public Service: Robert Smalls, 1839–1915* (New York: Oxford University Press, 1971).

Index

Oconee River, 51
Ocumulgee River, 51
O'Kelly, Elizabeth Meeks, 65
O'Kelly, James: early life of, 65;
  religious conversion of, 65; and
  schism in church, 65–76; on slavery,
  66, 73; writings of, 72–72
O'Kelly, William, 65
Oklahoma, 11, 140, 156
Olmsted, Frederick Law: early life of,
  121; books by, 121, 123, 126; views
  on slavery of, 121–22, 124, 129–32;
  travel accounts of, 122–32; descrip-
  tion of Appalachia by, 129–30; later
  career of, 119–20, 132
Olmsted, John Hull, 121, 126–27
Opata Indians, 15
Opothle Yoholo, 55–56
Otey, James, 198

Pamela (Richardson), 26, 28
Patton, Waller Tazewell, 173–74, 176–
  78
Pecos River, 14
Penasco River, 14
Pensacola Bay, 9
Petersburg (VA), 124, 179
Pharoah (slave), 91
Pickett, George, 174, 176–82
Pima Indians, 15
Pinckney, Charles, 24, 30–31, 33–37
Pinckney, Charles Cotesworth, 35–41
Pinckney, Eliza Lucas: early life of, 22–
  25; correspondence of, 22, 24–28,
  37–40; family background of, 23–24;
  in England, 22–23, 35–37; and
  slavery, 24, 31–33; as amateur
  lawyer, 29; as agricultural experi-
  menter, 29–32, 38, 41; marriage of,
  33–37; children of, 35–42; economic
  hardship of, 40–41; and republican
  motherhood, 39–42; later life of, 41–
  42
Pinckney, Elizabeth, 24, 27, 33–34
Pinckney George, 35
Pinckney, Harriott. *See* Horry, Harriott
  Pinckney
Pinckney, Thomas, 22, 35–41
Pole Cat Springs law, 54–55
Politics: in antebellum South, 110,
  144, 146, 158–64, 170, 187; role of
  women in, 106, 111. *See also by party*

Polk, James K., 106–7
Ponce de León, Juan, 4
Pope, John, 175
Porter, William T., 141
Presbyterian Church, 144
Preston, James Patton, 102
Preston, Margaret Wickliffe: early life
  of, 102; education of, 102; family
  connections of, 102–3, 106; marriage
  of, 102, 107–11; and honor, 103–6,
  110–11; children of, 107, 110–11
Preston, William, 102–3, 105, 107–11
Prosser, Ann, 83
Prosser, Thomas Henry, Jr., 83–85, 93
Prosser, Thomas Henry, Sr., 82, 84
Pueblo Indians, 14, 18

Raymond, Henry, 122, 125–26
Reconstruction, 208–13
Red River, 126, 154, 157
Religion: in colonial America, 33, 35,
  37–38; in Early National Period, 64–
  76; and antebellum South, 144,
  146–47; and Civil War, 179, 182,
  196; fundamentalism in, 64
Reply to an Apology (Snethen), 73
Republican Methodist Church, 71, 74
Republican motherhood, 39–42
Republican Party, 90, 144, 162, 206,
  208–16
Republic of Texas. *See* Texas
Restoration Movement, 64–65, 74–75
Richmond (VA), 82–94, 123, 173–74,
  179, 181
Richmond Virginia Argus, 90
Rind, James, 92
Rio Grande River, 2, 14–15
Rogers, Tiana, 156
Runnels, Hardin R., 160–61
Rusk, Thomas J., 160

Sabine River, 126
Sampson, William D., 214
Sanitary Commission, 119–20
Sayler's Creek, battle of, 182
Scott, John, 89
Scott, Winfield, 110
Searcy, Sophia, 201
Second Manassas (Bull Run), battle of,
  175
Second North Carolina Regiment, 179
Selden, Miles, 92–93

Wirt, William, 93
Women: in colonial America, 22–41; in Early National Period, 40–41; in antebellum South, 99–111, 125, 148–49; in Civil War, 189–202; and marriage, 34–37, 101–2, 106–11; role in public life of, 101–6, 108, 110–11; and honor, 103–6

Woolfolk, Ben, 93
Wyatt-Brown, Bertram, 109

York River, 173
Young, Jesse, 178
Young, William, 89, 91

Zuni Indians, 18

Volumes in the Human Tradition in America series:

Ian K. Steele and Nancy L. Rhoden, eds., *The Human Tradition in Colonial America* (1999). Cloth ISBN 0-8420-2697-5
Paper ISBN 0-8420-2700-9

Nancy L. Rhoden and Ian K. Steele, eds., *The Human Tradition in the American Revolution* (2000). Cloth ISBN 0-8420-2747-5
Paper ISBN 0-8420-2748-3

Ballard C. Campbell, ed., *The Human Tradition in the Gilded Age and Progressive Era* (2000). Cloth ISBN 0-8420-2734-3
Paper ISBN 0-8420-2735-1

Steven E. Woodworth, ed., *The Human Tradition in the Civil War and Reconstruction* (2000). Cloth ISBN 0-8420-2726-2
Paper ISBN 0-8420-2727-0

David L. Anderson, ed., *The Human Tradition in the Vietnam Era* (2000). Cloth ISBN 0-8420-2762-9   Paper ISBN 0-8420-2763-7

Kriste Lindenmeyer, ed., *Ordinary Women, Extraordinary Lives: Women in American History* (2000). Cloth ISBN 0-8420-2752-1
Paper ISBN 0-8420-2754-8

Michael A. Morrison, ed., *The Human Tradition in Antebellum America* (2000). Cloth ISBN 0-8420-2834-X   Paper ISBN 0-8420-2835-8

Malcolm Muir Jr., ed., *The Human Tradition in the World War II Era* (2001). Cloth ISBN 0-8420-2785-8   Paper ISBN 0-8420-2786-6

Ty Cashion and Jesús F. de la Teja, eds., *The Human Tradition in Texas* (2001). Cloth ISBN 0-8420-2905-2   Paper ISBN 0-8420-2906-0

Benson Tong and Regan A. Lutz, eds., *The Human Tradition in the American West* (2002). Cloth ISBN 0-8420-2860-9
Paper ISBN 0-8420-2861-7

Charles W. Calhoun, ed., *The Human Tradition in America from the Colonial Era through Reconstruction* (2002). Cloth ISBN 0-8420-5030-2   Paper ISBN 0-8420-5031-0

Donald W. Whisenhunt, ed., *The Human Tradition in America between the Wars, 1920–1945* (2002). Cloth ISBN 0-8420-5011-6
Paper ISBN 0-8420-5012-4

Roger Biles, ed., *The Human Tradition in Urban America* (2002).
Cloth ISBN 0-8420-2992-3   Paper ISBN 0-8420-2993-1

Clark Davis and David Igler, eds., *The Human Tradition in California* (2002). Cloth ISBN 0-8420-5026-4
Paper ISBN 0-8420-5027-2

James C. Klotter, ed., *The Human Tradition in the Old South* (2003). Cloth ISBN 0-8420-2977-X   Paper ISBN 0-8420-2978-8

Nina Mjagkij, ed., *Portraits of African American Life since 1865* (2003). Cloth ISBN 0-8420-2966-4   Paper ISBN 0-8420-2967-2

Charles W. Calhoun, ed., *The Human Tradition in America: 1865 to the Present* (2003). Cloth ISBN 0-8420-5128-7 Paper ISBN 0-8420-5129-5

David L. Anderson, ed., *The Human Tradition in America since 1945* (2003). Cloth ISBN 0-8420-2942-7 Paper ISBN 0-8420-2943-5

Eric Arnesen, ed., *The Human Tradition in American Labor History* (2003). Cloth ISBN 0-8420-2986-9 Paper ISBN 0-8420-2987-7